WHAT WERE THEY
THINKING?

WHAT WERE THEY
THINKING?

THE 100 DUMBEST EVENTS IN
TELEVISION HISTORY

DAVID HOFSTEDE

FOREWORD BY TOM BERGERON

Back Stage Books
An imprint of Watson-Guptill Publications, New York

Senior Editor: Mark Glubke
Cover Design: Eric Olson
Interior Design: Michelle Thompson
Production Manager: Ellen Greene

First published in 2004 by Back Stage Books, an imprint of
Watson-Guptill Publications, a division of VNU Business Media, Inc.,
770 Broadway, New York, NY 10003
www.wgpub.com.com

Library of Congress Control Number: 2004108938

ISBN: 0-8230-8441-8

Photos of *Breakfast Time, Life with Lucy, The Lone Ranger, Wonder Woman, Quark,*
and *Lost in Space* courtesy of the author. All other photos: Photofest.

Manufactured in the United States of America

First printing 2004

1 2 3 4 5 6 7 8 9 / 11 10 09 08 07 06 05 04

CONTENTS

ACKNOWLEDGMENTS

The author wishes to express his appreciation and gratitude to the following people who shared their thoughts and memories of the moments remembered in this book: Kevin J. Anderson, Danny Antonucci, Catherine Bach, Tom Bergeron, Steve Bryant, Timothy Burke, Craig Byrne, Jack Condon, Brian Forster, Mark Glubke, Mark Guerra, Larry Hagman, Ron Harper, Laurie Hibberd, Rick Hurst, Dr. Tim Kasser, David L. Lander, June Lockhart, Ron Maestri, The Museum of Television & Radio, Thomas O'Neil, Walter Padron, Jim Parish, Herbie J. Pilato, James Quinn, R.D. Reynolds, Lori Saunders, Robert E. Schnakenberg, John Schneider, Sherwood Schwartz, Kathryn Leigh Scott, Aneesh Sehgal, Rhonda Shear, Ron Simon, Blake Snyder, Professor Robert Thompson, Marie Wallace.

Special thanks to Dwayne McDuffie for his observations on the final episode of *St. Elsewhere*, reprinted here by permission.

FOREWORD

Normally, the goal of a book's foreword is to entice you to continue reading. This is usually accomplished by gushing about the book's contents, its author, and/or its timeliness and value. I thought I might try a different approach.

STOP READING THIS BOOK NOW! PUT IT DOWN AND BACK AWAY! I'M NOT KIDDING! IT'LL TURN YOUR BRAIN INTO PUDDING!

Are you still reading? Fine. Be that way. Just don't say I didn't warn you.

Here's the thing: how would you feel if some opportunistic writer dug through your dirty laundry and published the 100 dumbest events in your life? Maybe late one night, delirious with insomnia, you phoned QVC and ordered the Poopin' Moose (#89). Or, concerned that God would kill Oral Roberts if he didn't reach his fundraising target (#13), you mailed in a check along with a cheery note. Worse still, maybe you belonged to the *Pink Lady and Jeff* Fan Club (#33). Trust me; you don't want this stuff getting out. I sure don't want to be reminded of #23, let me tell you.

So please, in the interest of basic human compassion, don't sit howling at the unbelievably stupid programming missteps recounted here. These people have suffered enough (with the exception of the executives responsible for #23).

Profiting from the stupid behavior of others is downright indefensible!

Sincerely,
Tom Bergeron

Tom Bergeron is the Emmy-winning host of *Hollywood Squares*, *America's Funniest Home Videos* and *The Miss America Pageant*, and former cohost of the legendary but short-lived *Breakfast Time*.

INTRODUCTION

Everybody makes mistakes. But when television makes them they are witnessed by millions of people and captured forever on videotape, to be watched and wondered at for generations to come.

What Were They Thinking? The 100 Dumbest Events in Television History ranks the most memorable of these mishaps in a countdown format, beginning with #100 and proceeding all the way to the single most indelibly awful television moment. Organizing the material in this manner invites readers to debate whether *Cop Rock* was a bigger fiasco than *The New Monkees,* or whether the presentation of Elvis Presley from the waist up on *The Ed Sullivan Show* was a sillier bit of censorship than the coverage of Barbara Eden's belly button on *I Dream of Jeannie.* Your list may vary, but that's part of the fun.

I hear you—just what we need, another book on bad TV, right? Well, yes and no. I've read the others, as well as such reference works as David Bianculli's *Dictionary of Teleliteracy.* What bothered me is that I like many of the shows these books dismiss. Bianculli berates three of my all-time favorites: *The Brady Bunch, The Dukes of Hazzard,* and *Scooby-Doo.* He tells me these shows insult my intelligence, but they don't. Maybe that means I'm not that smart.

So let's be clear from the outset–this is not a book for intellectual highbrows who dismiss television as prosaic, except for the occasional HBO series or the movies presented by Hallmark Hall of Fame. That's not me; in fact, I've always suspected the Hallmark folks of running the same movie over and over under different titles. Either that or they're all set on the same farm.

In this book all types of TV shows are respected, from *Gilligan's Island* to *Battle of the Network Stars,* but there's a line that must not be crossed. I will proudly proclaim my affection for *The Dukes of Hazzard,* but when CBS replaces Bo and Luke with two lookalike cousins, figuring the audience at home won't know the difference, that's when television goes too far.

What Were They Thinking? also differs from its predecessors in its inclusion of every genre of television programming, because moments of stupidity are equally abundant outside of prime time. Entries are devoted to news, sports, soaps, cartoons, even the shopping channels. Also note that the word "event" in the title doesn't suggest that prestige played any role in the selections or the rankings. You'll find moments that were witnessed by millions, and some that went virtually unnoticed. There are chapters devoted to a single occurrence, and others covering a series that ran for years. The only common denominator is they all happened on television, to the eternal shame of those responsible for their broadcast.

Choices and rankings were determined by me; there were no polls taken, no scientific formulas devised, no industry analysts consulted. I believe you'll find everything you'd expect in a list devoted to this topic, and hopefully a few intriguing surprises. I freely confess that when presented with this opportunity, I could not resist the chance to grind a personal axe or two.

I was an only child who grew up in front of the television and into an observer of popular culture. I've written other books on the small screen and articles for a variety of magazines, and I've even been responsible for one humble contribution to the medium, when one of my books was adapted into a made-for-TV movie. But these are all subjective credentials, and I'm satisfied to let the following list establish my qualifications for this unique assignment. No doubt some of you know as much about TV as I do, but I got there first and I got the job. That's life.

Dumb things happen on TV every day. The challenge wasn't to find a hundred examples but to narrow the field from several thousand contenders. Twice I thought my work was done, only to have yet another infamous event demand a rewrite (thanks a lot, Janet Jackson). A few or your favorites probably didn't make the cut, but I am always interested in opposing viewpoints. Let me know what you think.

David
DumbTVMan@AOL.com

100

THE PERILS OF PROFESSOR PRICE

The Price is Right
CBS, 1977

Most Americans have never lived in a world without *The Price is Right*. After a 1956–1965 run with Bill Cullen as host, the durable game show returned in 1972 with a new format and a new host in Bob Barker. More than three decades later, coffee and the morning paper just wouldn't be the same without Showcase Showdowns, yodeling mountain climbers and Hole in One or Two.

A true TV landmark, *The Price is Right* has survived everything from quiz show scandals to sexual harassment lawsuits. It flourished when there were dozens of game shows in the 1970s and 1980s, and only increased its audience when *Card Sharks* and *Sale of the Century* were replaced by the likes of Ricki Lake and Montel Williams. *While Who Wants to Be a Millionaire?* and *The Weakest Link* debuted in prime time amidst much fanfare, only to fizzle out a year or two later, *The Price is Right* rolls on.

Through it all, it's amazing how little about the series has changed, outside of the Barkers Beauty lineup, Bob's hair color, and the suggested retail price of Mercury Cougars and Turtle Wax.

There were just five pricing games back in 1972, including Bonus Game and Clock Game, which still made appearances 30 years later. Gradually the rotation grew to more than 70, including such fan favorites as Plinko and Hole in One. In an effort to keep the show fresh producers introduce a couple of new games every season. Some last, some don't.

Among the more celebrated misfires was Walk of Fame, which offered autographs of the models as consolation prizes; wonder what Holly Hallstrom's signature fetches on eBay? The short-lived Shower Game prompted mass salivation among male viewers until they found out it wasn't busty prize pointer Dian Parkinson going into the shower.

In On the Nose, contestants could win a car by completing a sports-related challenge, such as throwing a football, hitting a tennis ball or shooting a basketball. When retired housewives from Waukesha proved unable to fire a tight spiral, the game quickly wound up on the scrap heap. On the Nose created several embarrassing moments, but it's not the worst game ever played on *The Price is Right*. That dubious distinction belongs to Professor Price, which appeared only twice before disappearing deep into the CBS vault of bad ideas.

Most people don't remember it. Some believe they must have hallucinated the memory, because the game was so bizarre. But Professor Price is no urban legend, as its only two contestants can attest.

After winning their way on stage, these unfortunate players followed Bob back to a platform upon which sat a hideous green desk with a clashing pink top. Bookshelves, a blackboard, a clock, and an owl perched atop a Grecian bust rounded out the set. Seated behind the desk was Professor Price, an animatronic puppet garbed in a dark suit and tie with a bald pate, bushy eyebrows, and mustache and round spectacles.

With a car on the line, the contestant might naturally expect to guess the price of the car, or to predict prices on other items to win the game. Instead, the objective was to find the numbers in the price of the car by answering general knowledge questions, such as "How many goals makes a hat trick in hockey?", "How many ounces are there in a half pint?", or "How many face cards in each suit of a standard deck of playing cards?"

For each correct answer, a number in the price of the car was revealed. Three wrong answers and the game was over. If five questions were needed to reveal the four numbers in the price, the contestant still had to solve one last brainteaser to win.

Every other game in *Price is Right* history was based on knowledge of prices, whether it was items up for bids to get on stage, grocery items in various games, or grand prizes like cars and trips. But here was a game that had nothing to do with the suggested retail cost of anything, which made as much sense as going on *Jeopardy* and having to win a dance contest.

Certainly the concept was a mistake, but that alone doesn't account for the game's infamous reputation. One had to see Professor Price in action to fully appreciate its absurdity. The Price puppet, controlled by a stagehand crouched under the desk, would keep track of right and wrong answers with its fingers. When the contestant answered a question correctly, the puppet's right arm would shoot up, Dr. Strangelove-like, with one finger extended into the air. Though it wasn't his middle digit (he only had four on each hand), for a moment it looked as if the Professor had performed an obscene gesture.

If the contestant won, all hell broke loose on the Professor Price platform. The hands on the clock spun out of control, the owl furiously flapped his wings, and the Professor's head would shake and his arms would flail as if he was having a seizure. And so, after flipping off contestants and frightening small children watching at home, Professor Price was retired, though for a while he could still be spotted in reruns when GSN aired *The Price is Right*. If it happens again, have the TiVo ready.

99
AMERICAN MOVIE CLASSICS GOES COMMERCIAL

AMERICAN MOVIE CLASSICS
October 2002

A moment of silence, please, to honor the memory of a once-great cable network. For much of its 20-year existence, American Movie Classics (AMC) was for lovers of great cinema what Nick at Nite was to fans of great TV—a safe, reliable haven where a viewer could switch over any time and find something worth watching. The movies weren't just aired, they were introduced as something of value by hosts who enriched the viewing experience, and then they were screened the way movies were meant to be watched—complete, uncut, and without commercial interruption.

Its presence in the channel lineup was particularly welcome because, until the arrival of AMC and Turner Classic Movies, watching films on television sucked. It just flat-out sucked. Most of us still do it anyway, because during a channel search we see a familiar moment from a beloved flick and can't resist staying for a while. But then the commercials kick in, usually every fifteen minutes, and take up residence for what seems like days. Ninety-minute movies are aired in two-hour time slots, and cutaways are made no matter what is happening on screen. During its perpetual airings of *Grease*, TNT contemptuously breaks for a visit with Jared from Subway right in the middle of a John Travolta-Olivia Newton-John dance number. Would it kill them to wait for a Jeff Conaway scene?

So we treasured American Movie Classics, and its dedication to the great motion pictures of the past. "It's more than nostalgia. It's a chance to see black-and-white films which may have slipped through the cracks. It's wall-to-wall movies with no commercials, no aggressive graphics, no pushy sound, no sensory MTV overload, no time frame," raved the *New York Times*. "There's a sedate pace, a pseudo-PBS quality about AMC. It's the *Masterpiece Theater* of movies."

But all that has changed now, as American Movie Classics has devolved into just plain old AMC and, like the fast food chain KFC, refers to itself exclusively by acronym to shroud the content of its product. The word "Classics" no longer applies, as you could watch AMC for days and never see one. The schedule used to boast Charlie Chaplin and Buster Keaton festivals, and films such as Katharine Hepburn's debut in *A Bill of Divorcement*, and the rarely-screened Frank Capra feature *The Bitter Tea of General Yen*. Now, AMC is home to *Halloween IV*, *RoboCop*, *Mary Reilly*, *Saturn 3*, and marathons devoted to the cinematic *oeuvre* of Elvis Presley. Thankfully, host Bob Dorian retired before having to expound on the subtle nuances in *Harum Scarum* and *Clambake*.

Gone are the uncut presentations, especially on films rated 'PG' or 'R', which includes practically every movie made since 1970. Features are edited for language, violence and nudity, as well as simply to fill a time slot, and are shown in pan-and-scan as opposed to letterbox. The network that once educated its viewers on the necessity of preserving vintage films now can't be bothered to preserve the proper screen ratio on *Raiders of the Lost Ark*.

Gone also are the commercial-free broadcasts. After testing the waters by running ads between movies, AMC now airs commercials throughout its films. Ten minutes of every hour are turned over to sponsors, roughly the same formula in place at USA, TNT, and other cable nets. "We've gotten some feedback from some of our viewers who are disappointed," admits AMC General Manager Noreen O'Loughlin. "But these are movies that people are used to seeing on television, with commercial interruption."

All this was done, according to AMC, to attract a younger audience, because heaven knows there just aren't enough cable networks devoted to the 18–34 demographic. So it's goodbye to Bob Dorian and Nick Clooney, who were, like, 60 or something, and hello to rotating celebrities introducing films, including such noted cinephiles as Carmen Electra.

AMC also features more original programming now, but not of the caliber of its earlier film documentaries, and the charming series *Remember WENN*. The network that once billed itself as "the movie fan's best friend" proudly presented *Monsters Wanted*, an animated comedy series about monsters living in Hollywood, and *The Wrong Coast*, a stop-motion program in which movies are recast to answer such questions as "What if Woody Allen were Spiderman?" or "What if Britney Spears choreographed *Braveheart*?" And in its "DVD TV" block, movies are aired with behind-the-scenes trivia rolling across the screen like CNN's news ticker. It's only a matter of time before they yank the exclusive rights to *Beastmaster* away from TBS, and pepper the screen with fun facts about Marc Singer and Tanya Roberts.

The principles that once defined American Movie Classics no longer exist, but AMC eventually heard the outcry of its most loyal viewers and created a digital, commercial-free outlet, AMC's Hollywood Classics, to air the films that the network once took such pride in presenting. Thanks, but I'll stick with Turner Classic Movies, · which has picked up AMC's standard and its lost viewers, and still knows the difference between airing *The Bandwagon*, and jumping on it.

98
BRATS IN THE BUFFYVERSE

Buffy the Vampire Slayer
WB/UPN, September 26, 2000–May 20, 2003

Angel
WB, November 19, 2001–May 7, 2004

There are many reasons why *Buffy the Vampire Slayer* (BTVS) and *Angel* are two of television's most brilliant jewels, and most of them have their origins in the contributions of creator Joss Whedon. The son of a talented television writer, Whedon knew the conventions of the medium well enough to tweak it in ways previously undiscovered, resulting in a new and delightful hybrid of horror, comedy, and soap opera.

So it's all the more shocking that a writer so astute, with such an instinctive command of what works and what doesn't, would twice fall into one of TV's original crap traps—the introduction of a snot-nosed brat into a group of characters that have far more interesting things to do than look after one. Surely he was aware of the previous examples, from *All in the Family* to *Mad about You* to *The Godzilla Power Hour*. Perhaps Whedon didn't worry because his new kids in town were not babies, though from their behavior it was sometimes hard to tell the difference.

Dawn Summers (Michelle Trachtenberg) was part of the master plan for BTVS long before she debuted in the first episode of season four, "Buffy vs. Dracula". Whedon knows every corner of his fictional universe and does not alter his canvas casually. Turns out Buffy's late-arriving little sister was more than just a whiny irritant; she was also "the Key," a vessel created by monks to contain a mystical energy capable of destroying an evil demigod named Glory. That story arc spans the entirety of the fifth season, but along the way Dawn's "Key" status takes a backseat to her status as pain in the butt.

In "The Real Me," she complains about always being left behind by the Slayer and her friends, and must be rescued by Buffy when, through her own stupidity, she is nearly killed by the ditzy blond vampire Harmony (Mercedes McNab). Dawn turns to kleptomania to get attention, and when that doesn't work she conjures up a spell to lock everyone in the house in "Older and Far Away." "How else can I get anybody to spend any time with me?" she moans.

On the eve of apocalypse in the season finale, "The Gift," it is suggested that Dawn can save the world with the energy within her, though the action would claim her life. Had she done so and the character perished, Buffy's little sis might be remembered more fondly. Instead, it is Buffy who makes the ultimate sacrifice, resulting in her death, resurrection and season-long bad mood in the series' downbeat sixth year, cited as the nadir for BTVS by most fans.

Excuses abound for viewers' animosity toward Dawn; Joss wanted us to hate her, so we'd empathize with her alienation both as an awkward teenager and a mystical being in human form; the character was originally envisioned as much younger, but the scripts were never changed after the role went to 15-year-old Trachtenberg; Joss was busy with *Firefly* and turned over the reins on BTVS to producer Marti Noxon, and the series became a moody, despondent melodrama without his lighter touch.

Few blamed Trachtenberg for her character's flaws, and rightly so. She's a talented young actress. But Dawn's intrusion into the beloved group dynamic of the Scooby Gang was a distraction that turned the series away from its strengths. The character grew up some in the show's final two seasons, and became less troublesome for it, but by then she served no real purpose. Though BTVS released several classic episodes in its final years, its 144-episode run will forever be divided into pre-Dawn and post-Dawn eras.

The *Buffy* spinoff *Angel* struggled with a similar dilemma after a one-night tryst between Angel and vampire Darla (Julie Benz) resulted in the birth of a son. Despite his undead heritage Connor (Vincent Kartheiser) was not a vampire, which was regrettable since someone would surely have staked him soon after his first appearance in the third season episode "The Price."

Where Dawn was merely annoying, Connor invoked the urge to throw large objects at the television screen. Granted, the kid had issues; abducted as a baby by

5

one of his father's enemies and raised in a hell dimension, he returned to earth a few weeks later as a teenager with an understandably bad attitude. But that doesn't excuse his poor decision-making in too many episodes which jeopardized the fate of Angel Investigations, not to mention his frequent attempts to kill his father at the slightest provocation.

Space does not permit a complete retrospect of Connor's idiocy, but among the high points: he chained Angel inside a crate and dropped him to the bottom of the ocean for three months; after being forgiven, he betrayed his friends to the demon Jasmine, ignoring the pleas of his mother; after Jasmine's death, he took an innocent family hostage in a sporting goods store, vowing to kill them unless Daddy showed up.

But his most unforgivable sin was hooking up with Cordelia (Charisma Carpenter), just as she was about to begin a romance with Angel. Again, there were extenuating circumstances, as Cordy was possessed at the time. Still, when you diaper a guy one week and date him the next, it's bound to make viewers a little queasy. The Cordelia affair, resulting in a Cordelia pregnancy, grossed out more viewers than every hideous demon to spring from Whedon's fertile imagination. Negative reaction on the show's various online bulletin boards and newsgroups was as close to unanimity as possible among such a large and diverse following.

Kartheiser, like Michelle Trachtenberg, just played what he was told, and he never had a chance given the aggressive stupidity of the character. Thankfully, through some mystical mojo, Connor's memories of Angel and his past were replaced with memories of growing up with a loving family, and the character made his final regular appearance in the season four finale, "Home."

The extent of Connor's damage was limited to one regrettable season. In fact, when Kartheiser returned for the fifth season show "Origin", he played the character as a normal, well-adjusted young man and was not only tolerable but downright likable. An appearance in the inevitable reunion movie is not out of the question, but if there's any chance of Connor getting his daddy-hating memory back, I hope Whedon will just leave well enough alone.

97
LEAKY FAWCETT

The Late Show With David Letterman
CBS, JUNE 6, 1997

If Farrah Fawcett can take anything positive away from the press coverage given her bizarre 1997 appearance on *The Late Show*, it's that the attention was inspired as much by compassion as derision. People don't care when people they dislike appear foolish.

Farrah's interview evoked much laughter but there was also concern, as a generation of males hoped the girl with whom they once fell in love was going to be okay.

For those who are too young or were too stoned to remember the 70s, Farrah Fawcett-Majors became the most prominent sex symbol since Marilyn Monroe after just one season on *Charlie's Angels*. A famous poster sold eight million copies, and her image graced t-shirts, dolls, beanbag chairs, towels, pillows, rugs, and beer mugs. One entrepreneur offered her $5 million to bottle water from her kitchen. Her face became so ubiquitous on the pop culture landscape that the June 10, 1977 issue of *New Times* magazine actually ran as its cover headlline: "Absolutely nothing in this issue about Farrah Fawcett-Majors."

She endured countless interviews when the Farrah phenomenon was at its height (and "endured" is the right word judging by her demeanor during the questioning), but didn't speak to the press often after that, perhaps still shellshocked from coping with a level of adulation very few celebrities have experienced. The Letterman appearance was her first, and was booked to promote her appearance in *Playboy* and her erotic pay-per-view special *All of Me*.

The segment began with an appropriately off-kilter moment. After Letterman's introduction, as Paul Shaffer's band launched into the *Charlie's Angels* theme, Farrah didn't appear. Instead, we saw her arm, then leg, then backside, the rest of her still off-camera engaged in some sort of animated discussion. She would later explain that her assistant had tried to stop her from walking out with a lipstick still in her hand.

Finally she trotted on stage, in a slinky black dress, her blond curls shorter than the cascading mane immortalized on the red swimsuit poster. "You've never been on the show before," says Letterman after an exchange of greetings. "Why haven't I been?" she responded, while pretending she had been a guest before, and that Dave had forgotten. "I don't know," says Dave, "That's what I was asking you." To which Farrah dissolved into laughter, amidst a symphony of nervous tics. "Are you all right?" Letterman asked. "Don't I seem all right?" said a still-giggling Farrah. All of this happened in the first 60 seconds.

Responding to a question about the reactions she gets from people on the street, Farrah managed a moment of coherence, though all the while she fiddled with her bracelet, rubbed her hands together and rocked back and forth in her chair. But in the midst of a story about a fan encounter in Central Park she stopped, apparently lost for the next word. "There's ... there's ... oh, I'm so sorry," she lamented as nervous audience laughter first becomes audible. Dave tried to get her back on track, as she fretted and struggled until finally uttering the word she couldn't remember, "embankment", with the awed solemnity of Madame Curie discovering radium. "Somebody over there thinks this is hysterical," Farrah says, acknowledging the undercurrent of laughs.

A question about her 50th birthday produced more disjointed ramblings. Talking as much to the band as to Letterman, Farrah appeared serious one moment, confused the next. And by the time the questioning turned to her pay-per-view show, even Farrah's occasional complete sentences drew guffaws from the crowd. Letterman found comic gold in descriptions of Farrah painting with her butt, though his smile is strained as if unsure what his guest is going to do next.

The most infamous moment in the interview occurred as Farrah attempted to tell the story of her son's reaction to her *Playboy* appearance. She was distracted, mid-sentence, by the New York City skyline backdrop behind Letterman's desk. "Wow," she muttered, apparently fascinated, before jumping back into her response. The audience roared with laughter. Dave, now looking a little frightened, could only respond with a "wow" of his own. "I really thought I was looking out the window," she explained, surprised once again by the crowd reaction. At this point, a stupefied stage manager tripped and fell, prompting another audience outburst. A relieved Letterman went to commercial with Farrah saying, "Wait, I want to finish my story!"

The break sadly did nothing for Farrah's composure, as the final segment of the interview unfolded much like the first. Her attempts at conversation became even more strained. "Because, you know, the thing is, I, first of all, it's my..." she stuttered as the interview drew to a close. Dave lobbed one last softball question about the pay-per-view; "Is it an hour long?", to which Farrah replied, "It's, ah, 58 minutes."

"As a pubescent boy in Missouri, gazing at the Poster, I never, ever could have imagined that one day, the sight of Farrah Fawcett would evoke protective feelings in me" wrote *Mirabella*'s Steve Friedman in a post-*Letterman* article. A spokesman for *Playboy*, whose products Farrah was there to promote, admitted "No question about it, she was very, very distracted."

The fallout from the interview was swift and severe—"Farrah Drug Agony" was the headline of one tabloid—but Fawcett denied that the spot had gone badly. "God forbid I should have fun," she said of the appearance on *The Howard Stern Show*. "Were you high?" Stern asked. "I guess I should have been," she said. The drug accusations were unfair when her behavior could also be explained by exhaustion or illness. In the months prior to her Letterman appearance, Farrah had separated from longtime companion Ryan O'Neal, and had been accused by a former acquaintance of stealing $72,000 worth of clothes from the home of a mutual friend.

"She was just tired beyond belief," said Farrah's manager, Marjorie Ashley, who forced her client into taking a vacation. "That's what I had to decide. I don't know what else to call it."

96
STAR BORES

Quark
NBC, February 24–April 14, 1978

The idea behind *Quark* ... well, 'idea' may be too strong a word; let's say the intent of *Quark* was to send up *Star Wars*, a film that opened a year earlier and became a pop culture phenomenon. The *Star Wars* faithful still number in the millions and rarely has a fictional galaxy and its cast of characters become so prominent and so beloved. But whatever greatness was achieved by George Lucas's series of cinematic sci-fi adventures, let us not forget they must also be held accountable for inspiring several disastrous knock-offs and more dreadful fan fiction than any films in history.

At least *Quark* didn't cloak its intent, unlike *Battlestar: Galactica*, which also debuted in 1978 but would never acknowledge its lineage (What is this "Star Wars" you speak of?" creator Glen Larson would ask, while Lucas lawyers filed injunctions). But *Quark* borrowed elements from other sci-fi franchises as well. The character of Ficus (Richard Kelton), a plant in human form, was obviously inspired by *Star Trek's* Mr. Spock; the central console on Perma One looks exactly like the one in the TARDIS on *Doctor Who*; in the first pilot Adam Quark (Richard Benjamin) mentions being attacked by intelligent vegetables, a reference to a famous *Lost in Space* episode.

There's a fine line between parody and rip-off, and maybe when all is said and done it doesn't really matter as long as the result is entertaining. So if it's not fair to criticize *Quark* for stealing from every sci-fi property except *Pigs in Space*, the sitcom must be held accountable for not doing anything interesting with the material.

That Buck Henry had a hand in the original concept is hard to believe. When the sardonic writer spoofed the James Bond genre, the result was *Get Smart*, a certified television classic. It doesn't seem possible that when Henry turned his sights toward sci-fi, *Quark* was the best he could do. Though his name appears as a cocreator, he did not write any of the scripts, an indication that perhaps his best ideas were never used.

Set in the year 2222, the series opens on a garbage scow from United Galaxy Sanitation commanded by Adam Quark, bland straight man to a bizarre crew. Second in command is Gene/Jean (Tim Thomerson), who has a full set of male and female chromosomes, and alternates between a masculine and feminine personality; the aforementioned Ficus, the science officer, speaks in a soft monotone and acts superior to his human crewmates. The ship's sexy navigators are cloned sisters Betty I and Betty II, played by Cyb and Tricia Barnstable, twin blonds in hot pants who might have gone somewhere in show business if the Landers sisters hadn't already been discovered. Otto Palindrome (Conrad Janis) is the fussy ship's architect. Rounding out the crew is Andy (Bobby Porter), a malfunctioning, manic-depressive robot that grates on his shipmate's nerves (viewers could sympathize).

Quark receives orders from space station Perma One to abandon his usual collection route for a special mission from 'The Head' (Alan Cailou), an oversized, disembodied cranium. For reasons never adequately explained, the commander of a garbage ship is ordered to seek out and destroy the Gorgon doomsday vessel, a mission that may decide the fate of the galaxy. The Gorgons, black-garbed villains in Darth Vader helmets, are after 'The Source,' a powerful weapon entrusted to Quark. In the first episode, 'May the Source Be with You,' Adam Quark defeats the Death Star-like Gorgon ship, though the Source, rusty from 500 years out of action, proves to be no help at all. The series would subsequently send up other sci-fi shows in later episodes.

"The Good, the Bad and the Ficus" takes its inspiration from the "Mirror, Mirror" episode of *Star Trek*, in which Quark's crew meets their evil doppelgangers in a parallel universe. And "All the Emperor's Quasi-Norms" recalls *Flash Gordon* with its Ming-like villain, Zorgon the Malevolent (Ross Martin). Joan Van Ark plays Ficus love interest Princess Libido, and may send me a nasty letter for reminding anyone about that.

The quirky cast of Quark: *Tim Thomerson (left), Richard Benjamin, Richard Kelton, Tricia & Cyb Barnstable.*

Quark was one of NBC's most highly-touted series, and was considered a surefire hit. The network even distributed humorous fake press releases featuring "interviews" with the characters, conducted by a Woodward S. Bernstein (get it?). The show replaced *Sanford Arms*, the *Sanford and Son* spinoff that was the only weak link in NBC's Friday night lineup of *Chico and the Man, The Rockford Files*, and *Quincy*.

Inexplicably, the show received several excellent reviews, but this was one instance where the public knew better and stayed away in droves. *Quark's* knockoff characters proved no match for Lynda Carter as *Wonder Woman* on CBS or *Donny and Marie* on ABC. Despite heavy network promotion, *Quark* finished dead last in the ratings and was canceled after a half-dozen episodes.

And yet, *Quark* still claims a small group of devoted fans, though not enough (thank

The Lone Ranger (Clayton Moore) waits his turn to save the day during the great cowboy stampede of 1958.

heaven) to prompt a revival. But there are web pages devoted to the intrepid garbage scow, and I can only conclude that for these fans *Quark* is what *The Secrets of Isis* is to me—a short-lived, obviously cheesy creation that I can't help loving. I can respect their passion, even if it's not shared.

95
SADDLE UP

Thirty Westerns Ride the TV Trail
ABC, CBS, NBC, 1958–1959

In the summer of 2000, the reality TV show *Survivor* captured the public's attention, mostly because it was provocative and unique, but also because it was summer and there wasn't anything else on. By August, when the castaways made their final visit to Tribal Council, the show had become a phenomenon, with Richard Hatch's victory celebrated at Survivor parties across the country and proclaimed in front page news stories the next morning.

In television, imitation is the sincerest form of avarice. Over the next few years the networks launched countless variations, including *Big Brother* (*Survivor* indoors!), *Temptation Island* (*Survivor* with sex!), *The Bachelor* (*Survivor* with marriage!), and *I'm a Celebrity, Get Me Out of Here!* (*Survivor* with people who still think they're celebrities!).

Reality TV is the current manifestation of television's herd mentality, a philosophy that proudly boasts "If they like it, give 'em ten more of the same." It's easier than thinking up an original idea, and it sells well to advertisers, who have even less imagination than network programming executives.

Somehow it's fitting that the first time TV indulged its herd mentality, there were actual cattle involved. Westerns had been a part of television from the medium's earliest days, with *The Lone Ranger* debuting in 1949 and *The Gene Autry Show* following one year later. But as the 50s progressed and networks noticed the high ratings for horse operas, they began adding more of them to their nightly offerings. By 1958, television was home to more cowboys than Dodge City. Any proposed series with horses or saloons or six-shooters found a spot on the schedule, and if ABC could figure out a way to put spurs on Donna Reed, she'd have been riding a dusty trail alongside Wyatt Earp and Yancy Derringer. When the craze peaked in the 1958 and 1959 seasons, the range was so crowded that Paladin, Lucas McCain, and Bat Masterson had to call ahead to reserve Main Street for their showdowns.

To be fair, many of the golden-age Westerns were well-crafted programs that still hold up today. We view the 50s now as a less cynical time, and imagine that networks back then figured if they were going to jump on the Western chuck wagon, they might as well put some thought into it first. Maybe that's true, maybe not. But with 30 shows on three channels, the perception that America's first couch potatoes would watch anything with cowboys is inescapable.

On Sunday nights, ABC presented the classic *Maverick*, followed by *The Lawman*, an unimaginative show starring John Russell as Marshal Dan Troop, and *Colt .45*, which somehow ran three years without an appearance by Billy Dee Williams. In 1959 they added a fourth series, *The Rebel*, best-remembered now for its theme song performed by Johnny Cash. NBC countered with *Northwest Passage*, Buddy Ebsen's first foray into series television, and the following year with *Riverboat*, starring Darren McGavin and Burt Reynolds.

Monday saw *The Texan* on CBS, with Rory Calhoun as fast-drawing Big Bill Longley, and on NBC the pairing of *Restless Gun*, the story of a loner in the Civil War Southwest played by John Payne, with the popular anthology series *Tales of Wells Fargo*.

Tuesday nights on ABC were must-see TV for Western fans, starting with *Cheyenne* and *Sugarfoot* alternating in the 7:30 time slot, followed by Hugh O'Brian in *The Life and Legend of Wyatt Earp*, one of the more unique Westerns of its day in that it dramatized the life story of the historical lawman of Tombstone through its six year run, culminating with the legendary Gunfight at the OK Corral. *Wyatt Earp* was followed by *The Rifleman*, another enduring staple of the era, starring Chuck Connors and his rapid-fire Winchester. NBC countered with *The Californians*, which nobody remembers, but the net had better luck in 1959 with *Laramie*.

Wagon Train, with Ward Bond playing Captain Stubing to a different array of stagecoach passengers every week, anchored NBC's Wednesday night schedule. *Bat Masterson* aired later that night, with the suave Gene Barry as the famed gambler/lawman, but *Wichita Town* with Joel McCrea didn't find an audience. The series was based on the film *Wichita*, in which McCrea played Wyatt Earp. Since that role was already taken on TV, his character name was changed to Mike Dunbar, but everyone knew what they were up to and stayed with Hugh O'Brian.

Zorro, which was kind of a Western, followed *Leave it to Beaver* on ABC's Thursday night lineup, which also included the more traditional horse operas *The Real McCoys* and *Rough Riders*, only one of which anyone still recalls. CBS trotted out *Yancy Derringer*, *Dick Powell's Zane Grey Theatre*, and *Johnny Ringo*, the first television series created by Aaron Spelling. NBC countered rather feebly with *Jefferson Drum*, about a newspaper editor turned gunfighter, and *Law of the Plainsman*.

Friday night brought out the lamest Westerns on the three network schedules. ABC shot blanks with *Man from Blackhawk*, about a gun-toting insurance investigator, and *Black Saddle*, featuring an outlaw turned lawyer (what's the difference?). NBC debuted *Buckskin*, set in a Montana boardinghouse where nothing much happened, while CBS offered up *Trackdown*, a Robert Culp vehicle about a famed Texas Ranger. The debut of *Rawhide* on CBS in 1959 restored some luster to the evening's fare, while introducing viewers to an actor named Clint Eastwood.

Gunsmoke and *Bonanza*, the two most enduring Westerns in television history, both aired on Saturday nights in 1959 (*Bonanza* debuted that year, while *Gunsmoke* premiered in 1955) and were still going strong a decade later. Joining Marshal Dillon and Miss Kitty on CBS were *Wanted: Dead or Alive* with Steve McQueen and *Have Gun, Will Travel*. Just prior to his days on the Ponderosa, Dan Blocker appeared in the short-lived NBC oater *Cimarron City*. The network had one other notable failure that season in *The Deputy*, starring Henry Fonda as an Arizona marshal tutoring a young deputy who'd rather talk than fight.

Add to all of the above reruns of *The Lone Ranger* and *The Cisco Kid*, which ran at different times throughout the country, and you've got one heapin' helpin' of head 'em up and move 'em out moments. As a result, once most of these series left the network schedule in the early 1960s, and *Gunsmoke* and *Bonanza* finally ran out of steam in the 70s, the genre was so burned out that only a handful of attempts have been launched ever since. We can only hope the same fate awaits reality TV.

94
WIFE VS. SECRETARY

Three's A Crowd
Syndicated, September 1979

There's naughty, and then there's nasty. "Naughty" worked for game show impresario Chuck Barris in *The Dating Game* and *The Newlywed Game*, but when he indulged his nastier demons, in *Three's A Crowd* and *The $1.98 Beauty Show*, the audience turned away. At least that's what happened 20 years ago. Today, in the current era of cruelty-fueled series like *Joe Millionaire* and *Are You Hot?*, Barris's failures no longer seem misguided, just ahead of their time.

"Who knows a man better, his wife or his secretary?" was the simple premise of this appalling game show hosted by smarmy Jim Peck, he of the worst white man's afro in television. Of course, the answers weren't derived from harmless questions like "What's your favorite color?" With a lascivious wink to the audience Peck grilled the four male contestants with such suggestive queries as "What's the main reason your secretary goes braless?" and "How much would one night with your secretary be worth to you?"

The implication, for those who need a house to fall on them, is that these swingin' dudes have either engaged in a little after-hours rumpy-pumpy with the hired help, or they've fantasized about it. It's a scenario of sophisticated swingers straight out of *Playboy after Dark*, though the average *Three's A Crowd* contestant looked like the night manager at a lumberyard.

After four questions, the secretaries were brought on stage to offer their answers, receiving one point for every match. This was the first minefield for our intrepid bosses, who may have held back a few details about that 'business trip' to Bermuda, knowing their wives were backstage. The secretaries, out for prize money, happily filled in the missing information.

Next, the wives appeared and the bosses, sweating profusely, turned the same shade as the show's garish red set. The color was an appropriate design choice, as the guys were snugly seated between a suspicious wife and a blabbermouth secretary, and felt they had slid into the first circle of hell.

Once again the same questions were asked, an awkward detail as the audience has already heard them twice, but necessary to compare the answers. Peck had the secretaries repeat their responses to the wives, who relished the opportunity to set the record straight about why her husband answered yes to "Do you know your secretary's bra size?" Murderous stares, heated exchanges, and sometimes full-out slap fights ensued, as *Three's A Crowd* offered the chance to watch a marriage dissolve on camera years before *Jerry Springer*. The secretaries usually won, but the prize money was just $1000 split four ways. The wives cashed in much bigger at the divorce.

Three's A Crowd almost never made it to air. Barris couldn't find any takers when he first pitched the idea in 1967, and didn't try again for a decade. His persistence finally resulted in a syndication deal in 1977, but it wasn't long before protests began from womens groups. In Detroit, a complaint from the United Auto Workers women's committee resulted in the series being taken off the air on the local affiliate.

"The questions are vile," said Chuck Barris's secretary, Ruthie Goldberg, when Barris asked her why the show was in trouble. According to Barris's book *The Game Show King*, Goldberg explained that "They create reactions between the wives and secretaries that are absolutely virulent."

"But if we didn't ask those kinds of questions, Ruthie, the show would be bland," Barris protested. "What kind of trouble can *Three's A Crowd* get us into, Ruthie?" he asked. He soon found out. The National Organization for Women turned up the heat, and further public backlash forced the show's cancellation in 1978, after just 105 episodes. The outcry was so severe that three other Barris series were dropped as well. The producer spent the next year in seclusion, rarely leaving his Malibu home. That's Hollywood justice—create a show that exposes workplace affairs and destroys marriages, get sentenced to 12 months in a beach house.

93
THE BAD OLD DAYS

The Dick Van Dyke Show
CBS, APRIL 4, 1962

One of the few situation comedies to approach perfection, *The Dick Van Dyke Show* brought a level of wit and sophistication to television that has rarely been equaled. It's a series for which a summary of the premise and characters can safely be skipped, as anyone who would read (or better yet, buy) a book about television must already be acquainted with Rob and Laura Petrie, Buddy and Sally, and *The Alan Brady Show*.

This is the series that set the gold standard for workplace comedies, while building equally memorable episodes on the homefront with a new spin on the husband-wife and parent-child stories that were already well-trodden sitcom territory in 1961. The Emmy Awards tossed 15 statues their way, and *The Dick Van Dyke Show* left the air before suffering any loss in quality or enthusiasm, and progressed from first-run to syndication to TV Land, where it still puts most contemporary sitcoms to shame.

So what is this much-beloved series doing here? Even the greats stumble occasionally, and sometimes lapses become more conspicuous when surrounded by excellence. *The Dick Van Dyke Show* didn't miss often in 158 episodes, but "The Bad Old Days" still resonates as a shockingly ill-conceived concept. "That was the worst one we ever did," Van Dyke lamented.

The episode, written by Norm Liebmann and Ed Haas (not surprisingly, their only contribution to the show) aired late in the series' first season, by which time *The Dick Van Dyke Show* had already served up several standout shows, among them "My Blonde-Haired Brunette," featuring Mary Tyler Moore's first classic TV moment; "Sally Is a Girl," a superb showcase for Rose Marie; "The Curious Thing about Women," a hilarious treatise of feminine curiosity; and "Where Did I Come From?," the series' best flashback episode.

We're in the Alan Brady Show writers' office as "The Bad Old Days" opens, with Rob (Van Dyke), Buddy (Morey Amsterdam), and Sally (Rose Marie) discussing a sketch set at the beginning of the 20th century. Rob throws out a line about a husband carrying packages, which Buddy rejects as unrealistic, because back then "a man ruled with an iron hand." Package-carrying, he says, was a chore for the wife, who "knew her place."

Displaying a misogynistic streak that is never revisited in future episodes, Buddy longs for the good old days, when a woman fetched her man's pipe and slippers and worked like a slave to take care of children and hearth. Rob argues that things are better in the present, when husbands and wives share the workload and the responsibility for the household. Buddy remains stubbornly unconvinced: "I still think that was a great time to live."

That night, back in New Rochelle, Rob finds himself setting the table for dinner while Laura (Mary Tyler Moore) fixes the toaster, and he begins to appreciate Buddy's theory about the decline of the American male. After being asked to tackle several emasculating tasks, he takes a stand and tells Laura his housework days are through. An argument begins at dinner and carries over into the bedroom, as Laura wonders what happened to her thoughtful, considerate husband.

The couple drift off to sleep while watching an old silent movie. What follows is a six-minute, silent-movie style dream sequence in which Rob imagines himself back in the early 1900s. He sees Laura slaving over a washboard, while their son Richie

(Larry Mathews) gathers firewood after a hard day at the factory. "Mrs. Petrie, I'm home!" Rob announces, every inch the domineering master of his house. He enjoys a cigar, taking time between puffs to bark orders at his wife: "Get my dinner!" "Do those dishes!" "Scrub those floors!" After watching the woman he loves suffer and starve, he finally comprehends that the dream is really a nightmare, and wakes up to realize the error of his ways.

Though the entire episode misses the mark, it's the dream sequence that stands out as the worst moment in the series. The plight of Laura and Richie is not exaggerated enough to be amusing; an imperious Rob shouting cruel taunts at his wife and child, apparently on the verge of physical violence at any moment, is straight out of Dickensian melodrama. The sets, costumes, and other production requirements dictated that the scene be shot separately from the rest of the episode, which spared the cast the indignity of having to perform it in front of the studio audience. "We shot it during the day. I don't know what the hell we were doing," Van Dyke told Vince Waldron in *The Official Dick Van Dyke Show Book*. "It didn't work, and we all knew it. But by that time we were too far in to stop!"

One of the series' greatest strengths is its contemporary portrayal of a successful middle-class American family. The Petries' lifestyle would not seem antiquated today, though more than 40 years have passed. Rob's desire to live in a less enlightened age contradicts everything we had learned about his character, and it's incomprehensible that one speech from Buddy would turn him into Ralph Kramden. With "The Bad Old Days," the modern family takes a step backward, though fortunately everyone comes to their senses before the closing credits.

92

THE EVER-CHANGING ALDRICH FAMILY

The Aldrich Family
NBC, OCTOBER 2, 1949–MAY 29, 1953

Cast substitutions on television are never easy, and rarely meet with viewer satisfaction. But such changes are a regular occurrence on daytime soaps, and even the most successful prime time series have occasionally replaced actors in prominent roles; among the most familiar examples are Dick Sargent taking over for Dick York as Darrin on *Bewitched*, Donna Reed replacing Barbara Bel Geddes as Miss Ellie for one season on *Dallas*, and Emma Samms replacing Pamela Sue Martin as Fallon on *Dynasty* .

The new actor inevitably faces an uphill battle for acceptance, but when there is no other alternative most viewers will go along with the change if it means keeping a good show around awhile longer. That said, some series abuse the privilege; *Petticoat Junction* comes to mind, with its revolving door of Billie Jos and Bobbie Jos. But no series endured more turnover among its stars than *The Aldrich Family*.

The character of perennial teenager Henry Aldrich was as well-known to audiences in the 1940s and 50s as Ross and Rachel are today. He first appeared in the play *What A Life* by Clifford Goldsmith, which was adapted into a 1939 film starring Jackie Cooper as young Henry. Ten more films followed throughout the 1940s, with Jimmy Lydon replacing Cooper for the final nine entries.

The Aldrich clan was also a hit on radio, and became one of the first situation comedies to make the jump from radio to television. The series debuted in 1949 and ran four tumultuous years. In every incarnation, Henry Aldrich was a not too bright kid who lived on Elm Street in the Norman Rockwell-esque town of Centerville. The stories always opened the same way, with Henry's mother calling "Hennnnreeeeee! Henry Aldrich!" followed by Henry's "Coming, Mother!" Not the most riveting catchphrase ever conceived, but then "Up your nose with a rubber hose" hasn't aged well either.

When the series premiered on NBC, Robert Casey played Henry, Lois Wilson played Mrs. Aldrich, and House Jameson played Henry's father, Sam. Charita Bauer played Henry's sister, Mary. Only Jameson would remain for the series' full run. In four years, five actors appeared as Henry, opposite three different mothers and three different sisters; Henry's best friend, Homer Brown, would also be played by three different actors. As a result, *The Aldrich Family* practically had an all new cast every year.

For the record, Richard Tyler followed Robert Casey as Henry, who was then succeeded by Henry Girard, Kenneth Nelson, and Bobby Ellis. After Lois Wilson, Mrs. Aldrich was played by Nancy Carroll and Barbara Robbins; Mary was played by Mary Malone and then June Dayton following the departure of Charita Bauer. Jackie Kelk, Robert Barry, and Jackie Grimes appeared as Homer Brown.

None of these actors went on to particularly significant careers, with one exception; Charita Bauer, the original Mary Aldrich, joined the cast of *The Guiding Light* in 1952 as Bertha Miller, a role she would play for the next 32 years. It's also interesting that one of *The Aldrich Family*'s recurring bit players was Paul Newman.

Though it's fun to scoff at a show that inexplicably couldn't keep a family together longer than one season, there was one other casting change on *The Aldrich Family* that wasn't so amusing. Actress Jean Muir, a veteran of 'B' movies throughout the 1930s and 40s, was hired to replace Lois Wilson as Henry's mother. But during the infamous Joseph McCarthy senate hearings, Muir was accused of being a communist sympathizer in a newsletter called *Red Channels*. General Foods, the show's sponsor, forced the cancellation of the show's first episode of 1950, and demanded that the network fire Muir, who was never given an opportunity to answer her accusers.

The blacklisted actress later appeared before a Congressional committee to refute the charges, but by then her career had been irreparably damaged. Muir suffered from emotional problems and alcoholism for the remainder of the decade, but returned to Broadway and television in the 1960s. She would later receive a star on the Hollywood Walk of Fame, and spent more than 20 years as a drama teacher at Stephens College. She died in 1996 at age 85.

91
THE UNKINDEST CUTS

USA Up All Night
USA NETWORK, 1989–1998

When cable TV first became available, it offered the prospect of a broader range of programming, sports coverage from beyond one's local and regional market, and a new era in broadcast journalism. But adolescent boys like myself (at the time), summed up our hopes for cable in one tantalizing word—nudity. Finally, we'd get to see the scenes we couldn't see on regular TV, and in the movies we weren't old enough to get into yet.

We all know how that turned out. The pay cable channels have indeed run uncut films and featured a variety of adult-oriented programming, but our parents wouldn't spring for those, so we were stuck with the basic cable networks that adopted the same policies as their broadcast counterparts.

One of the first shows to shatter our lusty illusions was *USA Up All Night,* which focused on just the sort of exploitation flicks we couldn't wait to see: *The Bikini Car Wash Company, Revenge of the Teenage Vixens from Outer Space, Prison A-Go-Go,* and *Legend of the Roller Blade Seven.* But just when they got to the good stuff, snip! Cut to the next scene, where all the girls had their tops on again. Bereft of nudity, these Z-grade flicks offered only awful writing and dreadful performances by actors who still hadn't left their day jobs at In-N-Out Burger. And yet, somehow the USA Network got away with this bait-and-switch for nine years.

The first *Up All Night* shows were hosted by comedian Caroline Schlitt, but the series is best remembered now for later hosts Gilbert Gottfried and Rhonda Shear—she took Fridays, he took Saturdays. Why anyone still watched Gilbert's installment after they figured out the deal with the movies is anyone's guess—at least Shear tried to compensate for the deleted scenes by vamping it up in the lowest cut frocks imaginable. In fact, that's how she got the job.

"They decided they wanted more sex appeal," she explained. "They interviewed a couple of hundred women. I wore a red low cut dress and blew dry my hair during the audition. Every other gal was wearing a newscaster suit."

Shear described her role as "Every male's fantasy. A blond that was obtainable, vulnerable, seemingly dimwitted, but smart as a fox. The joke was always on me and I knew it. The fans' favorite shows were the ones from 1991–1994—Playmates, lingerie, B-movie queens, and tons of cleavage. I have fans that taped every show and edited out the movies."

Even the former host admits the films were "terrible." "Mutant zombies, girls in prison, monsters, ninjas, we had them every Friday night." There was *Class of Nuke 'Em High*, about radioactive waste infecting a New Jersey high school; and *A Polish Vampire in Burbank*, directed by Mark Pirro and starring Pirro as "Dupah," which will amuse those who speak Yiddish. The film was shot on 8mm with such poor post-production that you can hear Pirro's stomach growl. Shear's choice as the worst *Up All Night* feature was *Hot Summer in Barefoot County*, a Southern-fried blend of *Billy Jack* and *The Dukes of Hazzard* featuring a dozen large-breasted hillbilly babes.

And every time one of the Daisy Duke wannabes tried to justify the movie's 'R' rating, those diabolic USA censors went to work. "[Viewers] hoped they would see something but never would. It was titillating but not nasty. That was the way we hosted the show, and that was the way the films were presented," said Shear, who interviewed everyone from Barbara Walters to Marilyn Chambers from her heart-shaped pink bed. "We did give them lots of t & a with me and my guests—that kept them glued to their seats. That was my role, to keep them watching these awful films. And we did."

Against all odds, the mix of sanitized sex films and bloodless horror movies lasted for more than 400 shows, an achievement as baffling as it is begrudgingly impressive. Late-night cable showings of cheesy movies don't win Peabody Awards, but by all the measuring sticks that matter in television—ratings, longevity, viewer loyalty—*USA Up All Night* was a success. For a series that consistently dashed the hopes of so many young men, it didn't have any business working that well. But if we couldn't see Jewel Shepard naked in *Hollywood Hot Tubs*, at least we still had Rhonda. "You could count on the show to be there after a long week at work, or a bad date, or in the middle of exams. We weren't brain surgery, but we were fun and colorful, and dependable. I had eight wonderful years with the show. And I brought a lot of young guys through puberty."

90
BEHOLD THE POWER OF CHEESE

Bad Ronald
ABC, OCTOBER 23, 1974

In the pre-cable era, television's three major networks churned out hundreds of made-for-TV movies, the majority of which were pretty dreadful. For every *Brian's Song, Something about Amelia*, or *The Autobiography of Miss Jane Pittman*, there were a dozen low-rent thrillers, disease-of-the-week weepers, and 'ripped from the headlines' dramatizations of news events. Most were broadcast once and promptly forgotten but a few linger on in the memory, though not always for the right reasons.

A movie called *Bad Ronald* has gained a cult reputation as an unsettling suburban gothic that gave nightmares to a generation of kids in 1974. But what terrifies at age nine can look like processed cheese 30 years later, and such is the case with *Bad Ronald*. And yet the film has more fans than ever now, who revel in its offbeat story, laughable technical credits, and over-earnest cast of TV Land bit players.

The story begins at a birthday party for Ronald Wilby (Scott Jacoby), a shy, bespectacled high school senior, attended only by himself and his overprotective mother (Kim Hunter). Ronald blows out his candles then scampers off to the home of Laurie Matthews, the girl of his dreams. But Laurie thinks Ronald's a big geek, and so do the other guests at her pool party, who ignore or belittle him until he heads back home. On the way, he runs into Laurie's snotty little sister Carol. "You're weird, Ronald," she says, "And so is your mother." Outraged, he pushes the little girl, who falls backwards, hits her head on a rock, and dies.

Ronald runs home to tell mother what happened, and how he "found a shovel … and buried her." "You could spend the rest of your life with degenerates in jail!" she cries, in the first of many quotable lines. She decides to hide her son until the investigation is over. Fortunately, Ronald got a toolbox for his birthday, which they put to good use. Working through the night, they plaster and wallpaper over a doorway to a bathroom, into which Ronald slides through a trap door behind the pantry. For weeks, Ronald remains concealed in his hiding spot, while the police investigation proceeds.

The plan succeeds until Ronald's mother dies during surgery at the hospital. Her last words had been "Close the door, and don't open until I return." Being a good son, Ronald does as he is told. He overhears the fate of his mother from a real estate agent, showing the house to new buyers. Still afraid to leave his room, Ronald pulls out his toolbox again and drills peepholes in many of the rooms, and just in time, too, because the house is purchased by a couple with three cute teenage daughters. Bad Ronald is now Happy Ronald.

But months of isolation have

Ronald, take off that silly plastic nose and glasses. What? Oh, sorry.

taken their toll on his sanity. Ronald wiles away the lonely hours drawing on the walls of his sanctuary. In true geek fashion he creates the fictional world of Atranta, and envisions himself as its leader, Prince Norbert, fugitive from the Land of the Tyrants. Having taken a liking to the youngest daughter, Babs, he decides that she shall be his princess.

Complications ensue when a nosy neighbor spots Ronald during one of his rare forays outside the hiding spot. She conveniently dies of a heart attack on the front steps, leaving Ronald with another body to bury. Meanwhile, one of the older sisters starts dating Duane, the brother of Ronald's first victim, and he tells the family about the twisted boy who used to live there. "This house ... is evil," says a frightened Babs.

The family may be slow, but when they hear strange noises from behind the walls, and discover food missing from the fridge, they realize that something is amiss. Nobody mentions the flushing sounds they must have heard at all hours, and the funky odor that probably pervaded the pantry, given that Ronald hadn't changed his shirt since his first night of seclusion.

But their concern doesn't stop them from leaving jumpy Babs home alone one weekend. Now, Ronald sees his chance to win the princess. He abducts the screaming girl and accosts a visiting Duane, but the boy fights back and in their struggle, they burst through the wall of Ronald's hidden bathroom, and into the arms of the police. Babbling incoherently, Bad Ronald is taken to jail.

Writer Andrew Peter Marin handles the bizarre scenario with not a trace of humor, which makes the result even more fun to goof on. And for those who first saw Bad Ronald on a bootleg video—it's not the condition of your tape, the movie was actually that poorly lit and murky in its first run as well.

Scott Jacoby inspires neither fear nor sympathy with his wooden performance. He may be the most boring crazed killer ever introduced. Fortunately, viewers can play spot the B-lister with appearances from John Fiedler, sisters Lisa and Cindy Eilbacher, Aneta Corsaut (*The Andy Griffith Show*), and Ted Eccles (*Dr. Shrinker*). It's something to do during several long stretches when Ronald is more bored than bad.

89
THE POOPIN' MOOSE

QVC
1997–1998

Hard to believe, but it's been more than 25 years since the first electronic retailer, the Home Shopping Network, opened for business. Back in 1977, the merchandise was limited to factory overruns, discontinued store items, and other stuff that didn't sell anywhere else. The reputation HSN acquired in those days, as a clearing house for cubic zirconia and flower-print muumuus, still haunts all the shopping channels, though it's now possible to buy brand name electronics, housewares, quality jewelry, and clothing from top fashion designers.

"Our biggest seller for awhile in our first year was a hard hat that held two cans of beer, with straws on each side," recalls Steve Bryant, a host with QVC for more than 15 years. "They couldn't keep them in stock for the longest time. Those were the humble origins of televised shopping."

Founded in 1986, the QVC network has emerged as a first class electronic retailer, though some may object on principle to the word "class" being used in association with the topic. Broadcasting live 24 hours a day, 364 days a year (they take Christmas off) from a $100 million studio in West Chester, Pennsylvania, the "Q" ships over 50 million packages annually, ringing up more than $1.5 billion in total sales.

Most viewers are customers, but there are thousands of people who actually watch QVC for entertainment, or background noise while dozing off at night, or for other reasons that do not require a credit card. Many of the hosts have a loyal fan base that a sitcom star would envy; favorites include Bryant, who proudly boasts of "having aged several network executives well beyond their years" with his on-air antics; Kathy Levine, whose defection from QVC to HSN was the equivalent of the Boston Red Sox trading Babe Ruth to the Yankees, and drop-dead gorgeous QVC babe Lisa Robertson, a former Miss Tennessee whose smile could make any guy switch off the Super Bowl to watch her explain the finer points of marcasite jewelry.

But even Bryant's wit and Lisa's bountiful charms met their match in 1997, when QVC proudly introduced the infamous Poopin' Moose. Handcrafted from the Poplar Company of Alaska, this once seen-never forgotten novelty gift turned up in several of the network's themed programs, where it reduced the usually unflappable hosts to stuttering and giggle fits.

The item was a piece of wood, sanded but unfinished, in the shape of a moose. Across the back was a small rectangular opening; once the covering was removed, the moose could be filled with candy ("oval and round shapes work best" we were told). Brown M&M candies were the favored demonstration treat. And when one lifted the moose's hinged head, candy would exit the moose, 2–3 pieces at a time, through a hole in its rear end.

"I believe it was discovered during a QVC 50/50 tour, where we traveled by bus to 50 states, and found the best products from each state. The vendor was selling them at county fairs before QVC," Bryant said.

The average product presentation runs anywhere from 5–7 minutes, which offered ample opportunity for the moose to discharge its contents several times. Valiant attempts were made to convince viewers that the item would make a perfect gift for a teacher, a business associate, or that special someone: "I love you, honey, and to show how much I care here's a moose that craps Milk Duds." No statistics exist on how many relationships have ended as a result.

"I was delighted to see it," Bryant admits. "It was handcrafted, it provided jobs for people in Alaska, and it pooped M&Ms. How cool is that?" The best QVC hosts, those with a sense of humor and a measure of job security, inevitably went off the script. Now departed host Patricia Bastia uttered the immortal line "What better way to dispense your candy than through the butt of a moose?" Steve Bryant asked "I wonder if you could stuff a Hershey bar up there and pretend it has diarrhea." "The memos came hard and fast after that," he remembers.

"The phone calls from viewers were colorful, to say the least," says host-turned stand-up comic Ron Maestri. "I asked one, 'What do you like about the Poopin' Moose?' Does it remind you of anyone? Which end?"

During one of Bryant's segments, the moose was loaded with peanut M&Ms, which promptly got stuck. "I do believe the little bugger is constipated," he said as he shoved a finger up the moose's rear end. "The cameraman followed my hand as it went up there, a most unattractive shot, and then I leaned over and said to the moose, 'What do you mean, a little to the right and wiggle?' I think that was my last presentation—every now and then they took a product away from me," he said, laughing.

What may be most amazing is that the moose was a hit. During one segment Bryant moved 30,000 of them in ten minutes. As for the Poplar Company of Alaska, they sold enough to inspire the creation of a full line of incontinent wildlife, including a bear, a duck and a horse. Poplar went out of business in 2003, which may have saved QVC hosts from describing the wonders of the upchucking chicken or the whizzing water buffalo.

88
LAVERNE AND … SQUIGGY?

Laverne & Shirley
ABC, September 28, 1982–May 10, 1983

The eighth and final season of *Laverne & Shirley* brought a couple of changes to the popular ABC series: there was no more Shirley, and for several episodes there was no Laverne. Other than that, it was business as usual.

The one-time top-rated spinoff from *Happy Days* was already on the downside of its successful run, and a change in location from Milwaukee to Los Angeles in search of fresh story ideas only hastened its march toward obsolescence. But stars Penny Marshall and Cindy Williams could still create moments of slapstick lunacy that recalled the glory days of Lucy and Ethel, and that held enough viewers for the eighth season renewal.

Unfortunately, things began to unravel almost immediately when Williams announced that she and husband Bill Hudson (of the almost famous Hudson Brothers) were having a baby. "They were going to write Shirley pregnant, and have a baby at the end of the season, and that would be a wonderful thing," recalled costar

David L. Lander (Squiggy). "But her husband began putting tremendous demands on the show. He said 'I don't want her to be on her feet longer than three hours a day' so they came up with the idea that Shirley would stay in bed to make sure that she wouldn't hurt the baby, and then Cindy said 'Well, that's no good, what am I supposed to do?'"

With time running out, producers couldn't decide how to approach the issue. "They never did settle on how to do it, and finally it was Bill Hudson who said I'm taking her out of here, and I'm suing Paramount for $20 million. And Cindy was so much in love she went along," Lander said. The suit was eventually settled for a three-pilot deal for Williams in which Hudson would produce all the shows. None of the three shows would ever make it to air.

The new season stumbled out of the gate with Shirley on her way to the altar, but not with longtime boyfriend Carmine Ragusa. "I think people would have accepted (their wedding), because he was a familiar face," Lander said. Cindy Williams suggested bringing in an A-list movie actor to play Shirley's betrothed—names such as Al Pacino and Robert De Niro were mentioned—but instead they hired an extra to play a soldier suffering from a rash, wrapped him in bandages like a mummy, and had Shirley marry him in the hospital. "The guy had no lines. He thought it was his big break, playing the husband of Shirley Feeney, but we never saw him," said Lander.

The producers held out hope that Williams might return at some point during the 1982–1983 season, but by the fifth show they reduced Shirley's role to that of a phone call at the beginning, which Williams did not participate in. "Penny got very upset. They thought 'Well, we'll just call it *Laverne*' and she said 'No, no, they'll think I pushed her out to get my own show!'", Lander recalls.

For obvious reasons, Williams' absence left a void that could not be filled, and after seven seasons no one felt much enthusiasm for finding a way to resurrect the concept. Lander and his onscreen partner Michael McKean (Lenny) signed for just 11 shows, most of which McKean missed while filming *This is Spinal Tap*. Penny Marshall gamely made the best of episodes such as "The Playboy Show," in which she trains to be a bunny in a Playboy Club, and "The Gymnast," in which Laverne becomes convinced that a former boyfriend is trying to kill her. But without her partner in comedy, the magic was missing.

"The Monastery Show" recalled better days. Laverne is upset with her love life and decides to sort things out at a monastery. Teamed with guest star Louise Lasser, Marshall once again has a funny lady to play against and the result was a rare bright spot in a sad season.

"Penny wanted to take a vacation every so often, and when she went away it would be a Lenny & Squiggy show," said Lander. There was one show in which I played Squiggy's sister, which was great for me, and there was another when Squiggy was a dead ringer for a Russian ballet dancer who had defected, so I played both roles. But it had nothing to do with *Laverne & Shirley*."

The series that once brought ABC its highest ratings was reduced to serving as a launching pad for potential new pilots. Carmine was sent to Broadway, where the network hoped his pursuit of showbiz stardom might spin off into a show; in "Rock-n-Roll Show" Charles Fleischer played the head of a struggling rock band. "It was a strange year," Lander recalls.

Not every television show can exit gracefully, but it's always sad when a series limps toward cancellation, having been abandoned by half of its cast and most of its audience. "None of us wanted to do the show any more," Lander said. "We felt it had run the gamut." No one thinks about legacy at the time, but 20 years later the evidence of *Laverne & Shirley's* sad departure still haunts the series in syndication.

87
SATURDAY MORNING SPACE RACE

Josie and the Pussycats in Outer Space
CBS, SEPTEMBER 9–DECEMBER 30, 1972

Partridge Family 2200 AD
CBS, NOVEMBER 30, 1974–MARCH 8, 1975

Yogi's Space Race
NBC, SEPTEMBER 9, 1978–MARCH 3, 1979

Gilligan's Planet
CBS, SEPTEMBER 18, 1982–SEPTEMBER 3, 1983

The 1970s saw no shortage of strange entertainment phenomena, but one of the most peculiar evolved on Saturday mornings, where the practice of launching familiar characters into outer space was perceived as the solution for reviving a fading franchise. Thankfully, that trend never made it into prime time, or we might have been subjected to *Kojak in Outer Space* and *Barnaby Jones-Galactic Ranger.*

First to blast off were Josie and the Pussycats, following a successful two-year run of earthbound adventures. One of Hanna-Barbera's better *Scooby-Doo* clones, the series revolved around the fortunes of Josie, Valerie, and Melody, a female power trio, Josie's hunky boyfriend Alan; Alex, the band's bumbling, cowardly manager, and Alexandra, Alex's spiteful sister, who was always trying to steal Alan from "that dumb redhead" Josie.

The music of the Pussycats holds up better than the cartoons, thanks to the performances of Motown recording artist Patrice Holloway and Cheryl Ladd, who provided Melody's singing voice. Still believing the Pussycats could chart a hit as big as the Archies' "Sugar Sugar," Hanna-Barbera revived the concept for a third season, this time as *Josie and the Pussycats in Outer Space.*

After another catchy theme song ("Josie's on a rocket ride/Pussycats, are by her side") the band and their supporting cast are invited to play at the launch of a new spaceship, but when Alexandra tries to shove Josie out of a photo-op, everyone ends up tumbling into the ship's open hatch. Alexandra pulls the wrong lever and before you can say "Houston, we have a problem" the gang blast off into 16 new adventures. Fans of the first series will enjoy spending more quality time with the band in episodes such as "The Four-Eyed Dragon of Cygnon," "The Forward Backward People of Xarook," and "Warrior Women of Amazonia." The rest need not apply.

And if the Pussycats need an opening act, the Partridge Family followed them into space in November 1974 in the very odd series *Partridge Family 2200 AD*. The concept had its origins in Joe Barbera's desire to update *The Jetsons* with a new show focusing on Judy, now a reporter, and high school student Elroy. CBS suggested keeping the futuristic teens bit, but using the Partridges instead. It must have sounded like a better idea at the time. Shirley Jones and David Cassidy passed on the chance to reprise their Partridge characters, but Danny Bonaduce (Danny), Brian Forster (Chris), and Suzanne Crough (Tracy) all returned. Susan Dey (Laurie) also came back, but left after the second episode after she was cast in a film. A robot dog named Orbit rounded out the cast.

As with the original *Partridge Family* series, many of the stories revolved around Danny, but the cartoon finally gave Chris and Tracy a reason to be there besides their drum and tambourine performance in the concert scenes. "Since it was a cartoon for

The Partridge Family 2200 AD. *While the band posed for publicity stills, Reuben Kincaid was arrested for harassing Judy Jetson.*

26

kids I guess they gave the kids more to do," recalls Forster. "Plus David wasn't there, so that probably helped our cause. When I saw them again recently, I thought 'My God, I actually have a character!' I realized that my acting was better on the cartoon than it was on the original show."

No new songs were recorded, which would have been difficult without David Cassidy's participation, and it's just as well as the series only lasted 16 episodes.

Next into orbit was *Yogi's Space Race*, a series incorporating several sci-fi segments starring most of Hanna-Barbera's benchwarmers, including Scare Bear, Quack-Up, and Captain Snerdly. Recurring features such as *The Buford Files* and *Galaxy Goof-Ups* served as filler between episodes of Yogi and his friends going on races through the cosmos, sort of an intergalactic version of *Laff-A-Lympics*. Yogi's companions are the heroes Captain Good and his sidekick, Clean Cat, but there's danger afoot when the duo are also revealed to be the villainous Phantom Phink and Sinister Sludge. None of it made much sense, and Yogi happily returned to Jellystone Park after one strange season.

Finally, after three years on *Gilligan's Island*, TV's seven favorite castaways found themselves in yet another predicament in *Gilligan's Planet*, a sequel of sorts to the 1974 animated series *The New Adventures of Gilligan*. The trouble begins when the Professor assembles a rocketship out of island debris (yes, I know, the same stuff he couldn't use to build a boat), and everyone is launched into the cosmos. The castaways crash on an uncharted planet, where they encounter all manner of strange creatures. Most were hostile, but an alien named Bumper is adopted by Gilligan and joins the group.

The original cast all returned to voice their characters with the exception of Tina Louise (Ginger). The budget must have been tight, because Dawn Wells wound up playing Ginger as well as Mary Ann. Viewing the series now it sounds as if she had fun exaggerating Ginger's breathy sexuality, before shifting back into her more familiar, wholesome alter ego.

The Saturday morning space race ended in the 1980s, when cartoons became 30-minute advertisements for tie-in merchandise (*Transformers*, *He-Man*, *Thundercats*, *Smurfs*). Compared to that profit-motivated development in children's programming, the attempts to resuscitate familiar characters with a sci-fi format don't seem nearly as uncreative as they did at the time.

86

ELVIS IS READY FOR HIS CLOSE-UP

The Ed Sullivan Show
CBS, SEPTEMBER 9, 1956

"When legend becomes fact, print the legend," said director John Ford, a credo he unapologetically followed in several classic Westerns, when the historical facts of America's Wild West heritage sometimes turned out to be rather dull.

It's a sentiment suited to modern legend as well, as evidenced by the conjecture surrounding Elvis Presley's first appearance on *The Ed Sullivan Show*. What has been reported down through the decades is a mix of fact and myth, yet the truth is available to anyone within driving distance of a video store. Besides being a touchstone in Presley's rise to superstardom, what is remembered about his Sullivan appearance is the apprehension over Elvis's sexually-charged gyrations, that resulted in his performance being filmed only from the waist up. But that's only partially true, and the now famous story turns out to be much ado about very little. It is listed here not for the performance itself but for the CBS network's concern over what might happen to America as a result. Random acts of pelvis-shaking, perhaps.

Sullivan's first response to a proposed Presley booking was that he "wouldn't touch him with a ten-foot pole." But Colonel Tom Parker was determined to get his client on the air, and approached old friend Jackie Gleason, who produced the variety program *Stage Show*. Gleason liked Elvis and knew he'd be a huge ratings draw. "This guy is Brando with a guitar," he said. "If he can make any kind of noise at all, let's sign him up."

Despite the objection of CBS censors, Elvis performed "Shake, Rattle and Roll" on the January 28, 1956 edition of *Stage Show*, complete with his trademark swivels and thrusts. Gleason was so impressed that he had Elvis perform an encore, and booked him for five more appearances. Then in April 1956, Elvis performed "Blue Suede Shoes" and two other songs on *The Milton Berle Show*, again with no broadcast restrictions. The fact that he had twice been shot in full-frame prior to the Sullivan show diminishes the gravity attached to that memorable bit of censorship.

Next, Elvis appeared on *The Steve Allen Show*, though here he was goaded into wearing a top hat and tails and singing "Hound Dog" to a similarly garbed mutt. Allen was a brilliant wit and TV personality, but he had a blind spot when it came to rock'n'roll, and only booked the singer to win a ratings edge against *The Ed Sullivan Show*. "Elvis is a flash in the pan," Allen said. "He won't last a year."

By this time, Sullivan had no choice but to book the 21-year-old phenom, and called the Colonel to set up three appearances, for which Presley was paid $50,000. After watching clips of Elvis's earlier TV performances, Sullivan was convinced that Presley had stuffed the crotch of his pants, and that his leg movements were meant to focus attention on the space between. He told show producer Marlo Lewis to take whatever precautions were necessary to avoid offending the network or the audience.

Though Sullivan and Presley have been linked at this moment in rock history, Sullivan didn't even appear on the show the night Elvis made his debut, having been injured in a car accident. Actor Charles Laughton served as guest host in New York, and Presley appeared from Hollywood. Marlo Lewis was dispatched to the West coast to direct the segment.

Garbed in a flashy checked sport coat, Elvis took the stage, and appeared nervous as he addressed the audience before launching into "Don't Be Cruel." "This is probably the greatest honor I've had in my life," he said, as the camera moved in to frame a shot just above his belt buckle. There the camera remained, though Elvis's right hand fell out of frame every time he strummed his guitar. A second camera, to Presley's right, offered an even tighter shot; a third, left of the artist, also cut off the singer at his waist, and picked up The Jordanaires over his shoulder.

When something is hidden, it only makes people more curious to see it. Viewers at home could only wonder why the audience was shrieking between verses, and what else was happening while Elvis's shoulders bounced to the beat of the music. If we believe the story, that's all that happened that night, but Elvis actually returned for a second number, "Ready Teddy," and here he was shot full-frame. Most of the long shots were from the side, so the drum kit partially obscured his figure, but the viewers at home still saw plenty of the pelvic thrusts that really drove them insane.

Sullivan nervously awaited the public and network response, but when the episode became the most watched show in the history of television, his concerns evaporated. Critics continued to denounce Presley as obscene—the *New York Times* also described him as having a "tin ear" and "no discernible singing ability." But after two more appearances on *The Ed Sullivan Show*, in which he was allowed to perform some numbers full-figure, the tide changed.

Ironically, it was Sullivan, one of Elvis's most outspoken critics, who set the singer on course for mainstream acceptance. After his third appearance, which featured seven songs, Sullivan joined Presley on stage after his touching rendition of the gospel standard "Peace in the Valley." He put his hand on Elvis's shoulder and said, "This is a real decent, fine boy, and we want to say we have never had a more pleasant experience on our show with a big name than we have had with you."

While Elvis beams, Sullivan adds "You're clearly all right," a message to parents watching at home that it's okay if their kids love Elvis, because it won't set them on the path to juvenile delinquency. "That speech came directly from Ed's heart," producer Andrew Solt told Elvis historian Peter Harry Brown. "It was not rehearsed. He had been surprised, in the end, that he had such tremendous liking for this young man."

85
WHO'S SORRY NOW?

The $10,000 Pyramid
ABC, July 1977

Sometimes the best intentions result in disastrous consequences. Dick Clark, host of *The $10,000 Pyramid*, thought he was helping an old friend when he invited singer Connie Francis to be a celebrity guest on his game show. The two had become close after Francis's many appearances on *American Bandstand*, and Clark had been one of

Connie's few confidantes after she was victimized by a sexual assault in 1974. The emotional trauma left her unable to sing, and she had all but disappeared from the public eye when Clark extended the invitation. *The $10,000 Pyramid* would be Francis's first network television appearance in nearly two years.

But a game show is hardly the most stress-free way of staging a comeback, with its inherent pressures to win money for contestants, and to not look foolish in the playing. *The $10,000 Pyramid* was not a silly celebrity fest like *Match Game* or *Hollywood Squares*. Each game was a tense head-to-head contest between pairings of celebrities and their playing partners, who took the battle seriously. It also didn't help that Connie was matched against Nipsey Russell, who seemed to be there every other week and was one of the show's most accomplished celebrity guests.

As a result, what might have been a feel-good story was memorable only for the discomfort it created on the set, as it quickly became evident that being paired with Connie Francis on *Pyramid* was like being paired with Calista Flockhart in a pie-eating contest.

Mark Guerra, an expert on the show, reviewed the tapes of Connie's episodes and reports that she admitted being nervous in the Monday wrap-up. "Dick Clark said that this was her first time playing a game, and the first time she appeared on TV as Connie Francis the person, not the singer," Guerra said. Nipsey Russell, who had opened for Connie in her nightclub act years earlier, was sympathetic to her plight, but that didn't stop him from easily winning both games that day.

Pyramid is played in two rounds; in the first, contestants trade off giving and receiving clues to identify words in a particular category. If the word is "dog," one might say "man's best friend, what we call poodles or collies or beagles," to prompt the correct response. Each side plays three such games, and the team with the higher score advances to the Winner's Circle, where they play a slightly different word game for $10,000. In five days and ten games, the closest Connie would get to the Circle was when she walked past it at the start of each show.

On Tuesday, Nipsey again dominated the first round and nearly picked up a $10,000 win as well, though he ran afoul of the judges in the category "Padded Things" with his clue "A cell in an insane asylum." As fans will recall, prepositional phrases are verboten in the Winner's Circle.

Contestants who win their game but fall short in the Circle are then matched against a new player, but must also change celebrity partners. By Wednesday, the pattern had become clear; contestants knew they either had to win with Nipsey, or they'd be going home after the next game. When their fate was sealed, they tried to disguise their dread as they made the Bataan Death March to Connie's table. New contestants entered with a big smile and a jaunt in their step, knowing that the first game was just a formality and they'd soon be a step closer to ten grand.

On Thursday, Connie came close. Nipsey stumbled out of the gate with a flustered contestant and only posted a score of 2 in the first round. Connie's team actually had the lead at one point, to the utter astonishment of her playing partner who seemed resigned to her fate. But a calamitous second round put Nipsey's team ahead for good, after which they scaled the Winner's Circle pyramid for a $10,000 win on "Things That are Stacked" (no record on whether "Suzanne Somers" was used as a clue). The Friday show ended like the previous four, with Nipsey Russell winning every game and Connie, who put on a brave face through every loss, saying goodbye to two more contestants.

One year later, Connie Francis made a proper comeback, again with Dick Clark by her side, on *Dick Clark's Live Wednesday*. She performed a medley of her hits to a standing ovation that left both the singer and the host fighting back tears. Since then she's returned to both the concert stage and the recording studio, but has never appeared on another game show, where her name had become synonymous with lovely parting gifts.

84
THE WONDER WOMAN MOVIE THAT WASN'T

Wonder Woman
ABC, MARCH 12, 1974

Superheroes on television aren't always super. In the past 50 years there have been a handful of classic treatments: *The Adventures of Superman* in the 1950s, Adam West's inspired pop art take on *Batman*, and the WB's *Smallville*; some that deserved a better fate, such as the *Flash* series that sped to cancellation in 1990; and a few complete misfires, like *The Trial of the Incredible Hulk* (1989), featuring *Tiger Beat* cover boy Rex Smith as the grim vigilante Daredevil.

But the genre's nadir was a 1974 pilot for a series featuring Princess Diana of the Amazons, known to those outside Paradise Island as Wonder Woman. The last of DC Comics' "big three" to earn a TV show (*Superfriends* cartoons notwithstanding), and the most popular female superhero in history, Wonder Woman deserved a grand live-action debut, but this wasn't it.

If it weren't for the title, it's doubtful anyone would make the connection between the heroine on screen and the character created in 1941 by William Moulton Marston. There is no physical resemblance between sandy blonde star Cathy Lee Crosby and the raven-haired heroine of the comics. Her "transformation" from Diana to Wonder Woman involves nothing more than taking the bobby pins out of her hair. Crosby also doesn't wear the character's familiar star-spangled tights, red and gold bustier, and metallic headband, opting instead for a zip-down retro number that makes her look like a patriotic stewardess.

Writer John D.F. Black created memorable scripts for shows like *Star Trek* and *Charlie's Angels*, but his efforts on *Wonder Woman* offer scant evidence of any familiarity with the character. It's possible that the only comics he consulted dated from a few years before the movie aired, when DC had revamped the Princess after the Amazons left Paradise Island to restore their immortality. Diana relinquished her costume and her powers, and for a time became a secret agent reminiscent of *The Avengers'* Emma Peel.

The experiment proved short-lived, but if that's where Black did his research, it was a grievous miscalculation to ignore the three decades of continuity that preceeded it, and the only version of the character that would be known by the viewing public at large.

The movie opens with the theft of a set of books that list the locations and cover identities of U.S. government field agents. The case is assigned to Steve Trevor (Kaz Garas). Crosby plays Diana, Trevor's secretary and top agent with the code name Wonder Woman. A brief flashback depicts Diana leaving her tropical island home, and her mother's exhortation to "take our pure and true love, justice and right to that world beyond ours, and open closed eyes in the world of man."

She traces the theft to Paris, home of criminal mastermind Abner Smith (Ricardo Montalban). Meanwhile, a live burro is delivered to Trevor's office with ransom instructions for the safe return of the books. Trevor is to put the money in the burro's saddlebags, and have it shipped to a ghost town in Alba, Nevada.

After several failed attempts on Diana's life Smith hires the disgruntled Amazion Ahnjayla, but Wonder Woman defeats her and traces Smith to Alba and then to his luxurious hideout in the Grand Canyon. After a long chase, the villains are captured and the books are returned.

The intelligence level of Black's script is best summed up by a scene preceeding the climactic chase. When Smith escapes with the money, Diana looks around for a way she can follow him. By a stroke of luck, there just happens to be a motorcycle parked in the middle of Smith's living room. Such amazing conveniences are a regular occurrence throughout the movie.

It would not have been difficult to rise above this material,

At least they got the bracelets right; Cathy Lee Crosby as TV's original Wonder Woman.

but the cast still cannot manage it. Crosby emerges best, and would go on to better things, including a six-year stint on *That's Incredible*. Anitra Ford, who plays Ahnjayla, would have actually made a better Wonder Woman if she could act. And if you're lucky enough to have the exotic, charismatic Ricardo Montalban in your movie, don't cast him as a character named Abner Smith.

Wonder Woman wasn't Diana's first shot at a series. In 1967, at the height of Bat-mania, *Batman* producer William Dozier commissioned a Wonder Woman pilot script in the same campy style that turned the Caped Crusader into a national phenomenon; the result, "Who's Afraid of Diana Prince?", was so awful that only a few scenes were filmed before the studio pulled the plug. We can be equally grateful that this second attempt never materialized, or we would never have seen the Lynda Carter TV movie that followed one year later, which inspired a successful series. Carter's resemblance to the Amazon princess is flawless enough to fool the guards at the gates of Olympus.

The success of the *Spider-Man* and *X-Men* films has sparked talk of a big-budget Wonder Woman feature. But with names like Sandra Bullock and former pro wrestler Chyna mentioned as candidates for the role, it seems the daughter of Hippolyta's run of bad luck may not be a thing of the past.

83
MONKEY BUSINESS

Me and the Chimp
CBS, JANUARY 13–MAY 18, 1972

"This has got to be the giant mistake of my life."
—*Me and the Chimp* star TED BESSELL

Actors are happier when they're working than when they're not, which is why they sometimes say yes to television shows that damage their sense of self-worth. Part of the job is displaying a brave face for the press, and talking about how exciting it is to be in a wonderful new series. Mortification beats unemployment and who knows? *Gilligan's Island* proved that even the dumbest shows can find an audience. There will be time enough later to own up to the embarrassment.

But Ted Bessell was having none of that. After five years as Donald Hollinger on *That Girl*, he had enough experience in a popular series to recognize a loser when he read it. That was his assessment of the pilot script for a sitcom called *The Chimp and I*, and he wisely turned it down. Bessell's agent begged him to reconsider, asserting that the show's creator, Garry Marshall, wrote for *The Dick Van Dyke Show* and was also used to success. So Bessell overruled his better judgment and signed on to play Mike Reynolds, suburban family man, dentist, and adoptive parent of a chimp. However, he demanded the series be retitled *Me and the Chimp*, so he wouldn't have second billing to a lower primate.

A cast was assembled around Bessell, led by game show veteran Anita Gillette as Mike's wife. Scott Kolden (*Sigmund and the Sea Monsters*) and Kami Cotler (*The Waltons*) played the kids. In the first show, the precocious duo find a chimpanzee wandering in their Southern California neighborhood, and bring him home. The family keep him as a pet, over Mike's objections. They name him Buttons, from his tendency to push any buttons he can find, unaware that their new pet has escaped from an Air Force research center.

That might make a cute one-shot TV movie, but it was ridiculous to think there's enough in the premise for a series. And yet, when the pilot was screened by programming executive Fred Silverman, he was certain this was the show that would pull CBS out of the ratings cellar on Thursday nights.

Perhaps Silverman was inspired by the success of CBS's *Lancelot Link, Secret Chimp* (1970–1972) on Saturday mornings. The series was a live-action parody of *Get Smart*

Ted Bessell illustrates how the phrase "having a monkey on your back" came into being.

and other espionage adventures, featuring an all-chimpanzee cast voiced by actors Dayton Allen, Joan Gerber, and *The Love Boat*'s Bernie Kopell. Lance, agent of APE (Agency to Prevent Evil) battled the sinister simians from CHUMP (Criminal Headquarters for Underworld Master Plan). He was assisted by femme fatale Mata Hairi, and reported to Commander Darwin, which often prompted the classic query "What's your theory, Darwin?"

The writing was never that clever on *Me and the Chimp*, and Ted Bessell knew he was in trouble and didn't hide his indignation. He described Buttons, real name Jackie, as "rude, dirty, and untalented." "That monkey is a savage," he complained. "If we get canceled in thirteen weeks my life might be saved."

It takes patience and understanding to work with animals, who cannot always perform on cue. Perhaps if the vehicle had been more deserving, Bessell might have accommodated his knuckle-dragging costar and the frequent shooting delays that resulted from trainers taking him through the scene. But he knew the show was lousy with or without a polished simian performance, and vented his wrath on the most convenient target. "I'm tired of all the puddles on the set," he griped. "I've ruined three pairs of shoes already."

Fortunately for Bessell, his assessment of the show's chances proved accurate. After 13 episodes in which Buttons makes a mess and the family cleans it up, even younger viewers had seen enough. Critics shredded *Me and the Chimp* on first sight, and ratings for the series trailed behind *The Flip Wilson Show* and *Alias Smith and Jones*. The series was cancelled and Ted Bessell received most of the blame, not surprising given his public displays of chagrin. Said Tom Tannenbaum, head of production at Paramount, "Bessell saw it one way, we saw it another. He felt he should always be against the chimp staying in the house, while everybody else wanted the chimp to stay. I think the chimp should have stayed and Bessell should have left."

82
MEXICAN MISADVENTURE

Battle of the Network Stars #18
ABC, MAY 23, 1985

Here's the first instance where this book will depart from previous volumes profiling the worst of TV. Most critics won't have anything kind to say about *Battle of the Network Stars*. In this book, we honor the memory of these biannual specials, and sigh wistfully at the cherished memory of Heather Thomas's tight Lycra swimsuit growing more transparent every time she was plunged into the baseball dunk. But the anomalous 18th *Battle* deserves a place on this list, as a reminder to network programmers to know when to leave well enough alone.

For the uninitiated, the *Battle of the Network Stars* was fought twice a year from 1976 to 1985, and again in 1988. The formula, once they worked a few bugs out in the first three installments, stayed the same. America's three television networks, ABC, CBS, and NBC (that was it back then) would field a team of eight stars from their primetime schedules, who would compete in sporting events, including swimming, kayak racing, tandem bike riding, a running relay, an obstacle course and a climactic tug of war.

Today, such an event would be held for charity, with stars representing their favorite causes. But in the 1980s TV stars were apparently underpaid, because the celebrities kept their prize money, divided into $20,000 for each member of the winning team, $15,000 for the runners-up, and $10,000 for the losers.

The erudite Howard Cosell was an inspired choice as host. He added a sense of urgency to the frothy competitions, and could reference both Green Bay Packers coach Vince Lombardi and poet Dylan Thomas while William Shatner outpaddled Mr. T in dueling kayaks. The impossible dream is that one day all television will be this good. Sports purist that he was, Cosell may have seemed an odd choice for such an assignment, but he clearly enjoyed himself, being around the pretty starlets and teasing Billy Crystal and Gabe Kaplan over their athletic ineptitude. He also genuinely admired the effort and joy of competition put forth by the actors, having already become jaded by the attitudes of many professional athletes.

The show drew impressive ratings for 17 consecutive installments, and then someone at ABC forgot the cliché "If it ain't broke, don't fix it" and instituted sweeping changes in the format, the games, and the personnel involved. The result was proof that even a sure thing can be screwed up by someone who thinks he knows better.

For the first and only time, the competition left its home on the beautiful campus of Malibu's Pepperdine University for the Camino Real Resort on the beach in Ixtapa, Mexico. The shift in venue prompted changes to several of the events, to take advantage of the sandy coastline. Replacing the kayak race were the beach relay, in which stars raced into the ocean with an inflatable boat and attempted (usually without success) to paddle against the surf, and a Mexican Fishing Boat Race, held so far offshore that viewers couldn't tell which boat was which. The three-on-three football competition was replaced by a boring beach volleyball game, and even the traditional obstacle course was redesigned, apparently about five minutes before the race. One of the "obstacles" involved jumping over twigs six inches off the ground.

The running relay, usually held on an oval track, became a shuttle race on the hotel's front lawn. Worst of all, the baseball dunk, the most enjoyable *Battle* event ever devised, was left out.

Also left out was Howard Cosell, who was replaced by cohosts Dick Van Dyke and Joan Van Ark. The link to the sports world personified by Cosell was missing, which made the show seem even more frivolous than it already was. Bereft of Howard's cultivated commentary, the hosts were saddled with forced banter and scripted schtick. "Say, what are they fishing for?" Van Ark asked before the Mexican Fishing Boat Race. "Well if they're stars, they must be fishing for compliments!" quipped Van Dyke, who also went shirtless, something Cosell never did, and thank heaven for that.

The participants probably enjoyed themselves because of the free trip to Mexico. But it was the viewers who paid for their trip by enduring frequent travelogues of the city and the resort; "So whether you're traveling with a loved one or playing the dating game, Ixtapa has just what you're looking for" raved Van Dyke in a typical plug. Viewers were also treated to footage of Mary Frann dancing at a fiesta, and Erin Gray shopping for souvenirs.

The star power had dimmed for this installment, with the three networks represented by the likes of Mary Cadorette, Ted McGinley, Jenilee Harrison, and Michael Spound (Michael Spound?). For what it's worth, the NBC team emerged victorious; hopefully Philip Michael Thomas and Patricia McPherson invested their winnings wisely, because they haven't worked much since the 80s.

It would be three years before the next *Battle of the Network Stars*, but when the show finally returned it was back at Pepperdine with Cosell at the helm, and once again all was right with the world. Sadly, *Battle* #19 would be the last of these epic confrontations until 2003, when NBC peddled a forgettable update. There's still talk of another revival, but with FOX, UPN, the WB, and a zillion cable stations, you'd need a lot more swimming lanes in the Pepperdine pool.

81
SAY IT AIN'T SO, SANTA

Woops!
FOX, December 6, 1992

Just about every sitcom does at least one Christmas-themed show, the best of which have become as much a part of America's holiday traditions as maxed-out credit cards and unwelcome relatives at dinner. From the 1950s through the 1970s, these Yuletide shows specialized in family values and heartwarming sentiment. From the 1980s to the present, Christmas episodes often reflect our more cynical age, with stories in which one or more characters gets a wake-up call that the old values and beliefs still matter.

And then there was *Woops!*, a short-lived FOX comedy that unfortunately survived long enough to shoot their admittedly unique version of a Christmas show. It was the last episode to air, which is hardly surprising given that it portrayed Santa Claus as a mass-murderer. And you thought Heat Miser could be nasty.

Built around the premise that "The total destruction of civilization can really ruin your day," *Woops!* begins at a military parade, where a child's remote-controlled toy accidentally launches a nuclear missile, setting off a chain reaction that results in armageddon. Gradually, six strangers find their way to a remote farmhouse: everyman teacher Mark Braddock (Evan Handler), who survived the missiles because he was in his Volvo (talk about product placement); feminist bookstore owner Alice McConnell (Meagan Fay); preening yuppie stock analyst Curtis Thorpe (Lane Davies); jolly homeless drifter Jack Connors (Fred Applegate); plainspoken pathologist Frederick Ross (Cleavant Derricks); and sexy valley girl manicurist Suzanne Stillman (Marita Geraghty).

The survivors' attempts to put aside their differences and work together are chronicled by Braddock, whose diary entries are heard in voiceover ("And that's how it began—six of the unlikeliest people trying to build a new and better world") like a post-apocalyptic *Wonder Years*. Each character in this strained, overwritten series is a walking '80s cliché. The cast attempts to compensate for poor material by shouting as loudly and emphatically as possible; poor Lane Davies sounds like he's using a megaphone to deliver every ineffective punch line. Stories involved the occasional appearance of giant mutant insects, irradiated crystals that cause womens' breasts to grow, and the use of garbage bag twisty ties as currency.

Woops! wouldn't be worth remembering at all were it not for "Say it Ain't So, Santa," one of the most grotesque holiday shows ever hatched, and one that still induces nightmares in the Atari generation. The story opens with Santa Claus (Stuart Pankin) being pulled from the farmhouse chimney, having been stuck there for an indeterminate time. The survivors doubt that he's really the man he claims to be, until he tells Alice about the vibrator he put under her tree the Christmas after her divorce.

Invited to join their happy band, Santa tries to fit in but is prone to fits of depression and weeping. Asked where he was when the missiles hit, he talks of surviving by being up in his sleigh, and then adds, "I'm sure it was over fast for Mrs. Claus and the elves." They throw a Christmas party in his honor, but jolly old St. Nick just slumps in a chair in his red underwear, getting drunk on eggnog. Finally, no longer able to stomach any more holiday cheer, a distraught Santa confesses, "I killed Mrs. Claus and the elves!"

In fevered tones he recounts that fateful day, and his dash for the North Pole bomb shelter, located under a gingerbread house. He locked himself inside expecting his wife to already be there, but it turned out she and the elves arrived afterward. Santa, frozen with fear, could not open the door. "The screams, the horrible screams!" he wails, as the other survivors stare at him, appalled. "You have no right to judge me!" he cries. "I'm not a monster, I'm Santa Claus!"

FOX, perhaps realizing that there's no way the scene could be sweetened with a laugh track, lets the shocked, silent audience reaction speak for itself. Jack, who is traumatized the most by his confession, fantasizes about cutting off Santa's "candy cane."

The next morning, Santa tries to distance himself from his past by donning overalls and taking up the farming life under the name "Clem." But when he

To reluctant Flying Nun *star Sally Field, the role of Sister Bertrille was a hard habit to break.*

can no longer handle the group's ostracism, he agrees to leave. He heads for the front door, but finds himself unable to figure out the lock. The incident triggers a flashback from the bomb shelter, and as Santa pounds on the door and screams "Mrs. Claus! Patches!" the survivors realize that Santa Claus, who had been sliding down chimneys for centuries, had forgotten how to use a door. So it really wasn't his fault that his wife and the elves perished. See, kids, Santa isn't a killer, he's just mentally challenged. How's that for an uplifting Yuletide message?

His Christmas spirit now restored, Kris Kringle's reindeer return and he sets off to bring joy to other survivors. The tacked-on happy ending seems as incongruous as everything else in this bizarre episode, which induced children to flee in terror from department store Santas for years. Say what you will about Billy Bob Thornton's *Bad Santa*, for millions of traumatized couch potatoes that dubious title still belongs to Stuart Pankin.

80
SEE SALLY SOAR

The Flying Nun
ABC, September 7, 1967–September 18, 1970

Focus if you like on its merits; the inherent delight of watching Sally Field in just about anything, the fact that it ran for three years, the positive messages conveyed in nearly every episode. But there's no avoiding the inescapable truth that *The Flying Nun* may be the dumbest concept ever for a television series. So they managed to find something watchable within that premise—it's still a show about a nun that flies.

Yes, it was the 1960s, when situation comedies were built around all manner of fantastical characters. So why should *The Flying Nun* being singled out from a prime time schedule that also featured *Bewitched*, *The Munsters*, and *I Dream of Jeannie*? Because everyone grew up reading stories about witches and genies, and were familiar with their powers and abilities. To see such fairy tale creatures transplanted into a contemporary setting was a clever idea that obviously proved very successful.

But there's no precedent for a flying nun, except for the few people who read Tere Rios' *The Fifteenth Pelican*, the book on which the series was based. For the rest of us, it seems an oddly random mix of ability and occupation; why a flying nun and not a swimming tax attorney, or a psychic landscaper? Flying is usually associated with superheroes, and that might have been an idea—Sister Bertrille as Super-nun, defender of Catholicism, dive-bombing out of the sky to exact vengeance on those who haven't said all their Hail Marys. Certainly that's no less bizarre than the show we watched.

Of course Sally Field is utterly charming, and what's regrettable is how ABC didn't recognize that before canceling *Gidget*, a much better show and a more appropriate vehicle for her talents, after just one season. Audiences discovered *Gidget* during summer reruns, but by then it was too late to bring it back, so programmers scrambled to find another series for its perky teenage star. And however ridiculous it seemed to put the former beach bunny into a nun's habit, the idea worked well enough for three years of aerodynamic adventures.

The problem was getting Field to sign on. At one point, her reluctance to play Sister Bertrille prompted ABC to green-light a pilot with their second choice, Ronnie Troup (best known as Polly Williams on *My Three Sons*). But when Sally finally acquiesced, the pilot was reshot with Field as Elsie Ethrington, a teenager inspired by her aunt's stories of missionary work to become a nun. At the Convent San Tanco in San Juan, Puerto Rico, Elsie is ordained as Sister Bertrille.

Soon after, she discovers a hidden, and not always welcome, talent. Because of the tradewinds surrounding the convent, and the design of her wing-tipped coronet, the 90-pound nun can fly. "When lift plus thrust is greater than load plus drag," is the only explanation given for Sister Bertrille's tendency to take off, which became a source of amusement and occasional frustration for her friends, among them Sister Jacqueline (Marge Redmond), Sister Sixto (Shelley Morrison), and the Mother Superior (Madeleine Sherwood).

The flying sequences were accomplished with the standard wire harnesses and blue screens, and were about as convincingly executed as Frankie Avalon's surfing exploits in *Beach Blanket Bingo*. The gimmick ran its course early, and as it turned out the better episodes of *The Flying Nun* are those in which Sister Bertrille never left the ground. The only episode anyone remembers was the one in which she and the other nuns council a little girl who wishes to join the order; at one point Sister Bertrille shows home movies of herself before she took her vows, and the footage is of Sally Field surfing in scenes from *Gidget*.

Field never warmed to the role or the show, but when *The Flying Nun* became a minor hit she knew she was in trouble. "I was 19, 20, and 21 years old at the time and was dressed in a nun's habit all day long," she once said. "I didn't want to be a nun. How much fun could that be?" But studio executives tried to keep her spirits up; her wish to one day be able to drive a Ferrari was overheard by a Screen Gems representative, and on her birthday she was given a Ferrari 330 convertible.

After three seasons and the prospect of another coming up, Field finally had enough, and found a way out of her contract—she became pregnant. That's a tricky condition to pull off as a nun, unless they wanted to pay off the flirtation between Sister Bertrille and Carlos Ramirez (Alejandro Rey), owner of the local disco. But that would not have pleased the Catholic church, one of the series' most staunch supporters. Back then the church was happy to have any positive portrayal of religion in prime time, even if it involved flying nuns. Having Field's character leave the convent was out of the question, so the series was cancelled, much to its star's relief.

The stigma of *The Flying Nun* haunted Sally Field for years, costing her several film roles including the one played by Kim Darby in *True Grit*. It would take another television project, the 1977 movie *Sybil*, to finally establish Field as a formidable actress.

79
NEW DARRIN, OLD SCRIPTS

Bewitched
ABC, SEPTEMBER 17, 1964–JULY 1, 1972

This is a difficult chapter to write, because it's hard to say anything disparaging about *Bewitched*. Its magical premise created magical television for eight seasons, and despite multiple cast changes, most notably the oft-debated replacement of Dick York for Dick Sargent as Darrin Stephens, the series thrived in its original run and remains popular in syndication. Much of the credit belongs to Elizabeth Montgomery, whose Samantha Stephens was both role model and crush, liberated woman and traditional housewife, sorceress and seductress. She never won an Emmy, but she won the hearts of so many viewers that Sam remains one of the most beloved sitcom creations of all time.

Some people take *Bewitched* seriously; its saga of a witch marrying a mortal has been interpreted as an early examination of mixed marriage on television, with a supernatural rather than racial separation. There was also an anti-witchcraft crowd who feared that Sam's sexy smile might lead children into Satanism.

But for those of us who don't find hidden messages in our rice pudding, *Bewitched* was simply an impeccably cast, cleverly written, well-crafted situation comedy with a trio of likable leads (Sam, Darrin, and Agnes Moorehead as Endora) and a delightful assortment of visiting characters. Any episode with Maurice, Serena, Aunt Clara, Uncle Arthur, or Doctor Bombay was always worth a look.

The Sargent-York (ha) substitution was harmful but not fatal; where York's Darrin was more animated in his frustration with Sam's relatives and her use of magic, Sargent relied on the sardonic slow burn, understating his reactions but suffering the same consequences for his complaints. York will always be Sam's most fondly-remembered husband, but the recast was unavoidable given the actor's chronic back pain, which had already caused him to miss several shows.

There were 254 episodes of *Bewitched* in all, though that number is misleading. Viewers who tuned into the seventh and eighth seasons experienced a recurring déja vu—"Is this a rerun?" they'd ask after watching Sam and Darrin deal with a familiar-looking predicament. What they were watching was a repeated story from an earlier season of the series, in which the only significant difference was the presence of Darrin #2. If there's any reason to be mad at Sargent, it isn't for his performance, but for the excuse he apparently gave the producers to slack off.

In episode #5, "Help, Help, Don't Save Me," Sam tries to help Darrin with one of his advertising campaigns, then he accuses her of using witchcraft when his ideas are rejected. It happens again in #252, "A Good Turn Never Goes Unpunished." In "It Takes One to Know One," Darrin hires a feline beauty as a model for a perfume campaign, who threatens to come between he and Samantha. In "The Eight Year Witch," Julie Newmar plays the same role, replacing Lisa Seagram in the original.

Even the series' two most memorable episodes received second treatments; "Divided He Falls" has Endora splitting Darrin into two men, so his fun-loving half can take Sam on vacation, while his work-obsessed side finishes a job for Larry Tate (David White). "Samantha's Better Halves," the first story Dick Sargent filmed after his sixth-season arrival, follows the same plot. And "Speak the Truth," a hilarious first-season show in which Endora creates a charm that forbids anyone in its vicinity to tell a lie (the inspiration for Jim Carrey's *Liar, Liar*, perhaps?), is remade as *Bewitched*'s final episode, "The Truth, Nothing but the Truth, So Help Me Sam".

"Even when I was in seventh grade I noticed it," said Herbie J. Pilato, author of *Bewitched Forever*. "I kept thinking, 'Is this a repeat of a remake of a repeat?'" In total, sixteen episodes of *Bewitched*, a half season (nearly a full season by today's standard) were either total or partial remakes of earlier shows. "I asked Bill Asher (*Bewitched*

Dueling Darrens: Dick York (left) and Dick Sargent.

producer, then married to Elizabeth Montgomery): 'Why did you do that? Why didn't you just hire some new writers?' And the first thing he said was, 'You noticed that?' He didn't think people would!"

"When you produce 254 scripts," Asher told him, "you're constrained to remake episodes no matter what you're doing. You can't help but dig back and rework old scripts. There's a limit to the situations you can come up with and still be able to maintain your premise."

But with all due respect to one of the giants of situation comedy, that's simply not the case. Other long-running classic series—*The Dick Van Dyke Show, I Love Lucy, Friends, Frasier, Cheers*—never resorted to repeating themselves. And given the show's expansive premise, when you've got several characters who can conjure up anything or anybody, fresh ideas were certainly still possible. "The premise lent itself to imagination and to any kind of plot. They really could have gone the extra mile, expanded the budget, and brought some new material in," Pilato believes.

Enough said. *Bewitched* has given generations of fans too many happy moments and memories to be maligned any further for these late-season lapses. And admittedly the chance to compare two actors' takes on the same material, rare on a TV sitcom, is intriguing as far as it goes. But it's still no substitute for original stories.

78
THE WARDROBE MALFUNCTION

Super Bowl XXXVIIII
CBS, FEBRUARY 1, 2004

1.5 seconds. That's how long Janet Jackson's right breast popped out and waved to America during the Super Bowl XXXVIII halftime show, before CBS quickly cut from close-up to long shot to commercial. By the time viewers could ask "Was that…" the network and the National Football League were already in damage control. References to the incident were verboten in the second half in the hope of erasing suggestive ideas from football fans, though the promotion of four-hour erections in the Levitra ads didn't help.

And while it's too early to assess the extent of the fallout from Jackson's fall out, as we're still in the stage of dueling recriminations and escalating overreaction, it's not too soon to wonder whether the Jackson flash will turn out to be the most significant 1.5 seconds of television in decades.

The episode overshadowed an entertaining game between the New England Patriots and Carolina Panthers, which further riled the NFL, though amidst their wounded remonstrations they should have accepted some responsibility. Hoping to make their halftime shows more cutting edge, the League turned over the event to MTV, the network that brought us Diana Ross feeling up L'il Kim and Madonna kissing Britney Spears. After lyrically indecipherable performances from Kid Rock, Nelly and P. Diddy, headliner Janet Jackson was joined by Justin Timberlake for a duet on "Rock Your Body." "I'm gonna have you naked by the end of this song," cooed Timberlake, before reaching across Jackson's red-and-black gladiator outfit and pulling off part of the bodice, revealing her breast.

Within minutes screen captures were all over the internet, and TiVo received a bigger publicity boost than any company that advertised during the game. A TiVo press release reported a 180 percent viewership spike, as hundreds of thousands of households used the system's capabilities to pause and replay live television and view the incident over and over.

Others weren't as pleased. Several members of Congress, the Parents Television Council and the Traditional Values Coalition expressed outrage. "This was done completely without our knowledge," said Chris Ender, entertainment spokesman for CBS, which was deluged with angry calls. "It wasn't rehearsed. It wasn't discussed. It wasn't even hinted at.... This is something we would have never approved. We are angry and embarrassed."

"We were extremely disappointed by elements of the MTV-produced halftime show," NFL executive vice president Joe Browne said. "They were totally inconsistent with assurances our office was given about the content of the show. It's unlikely that MTV will produce another Super Bowl halftime." Though the show's choreographer promised "shocking moments" in an MTV.com interview prior to the show, MTV described the incident as "Unrehearsed, unplanned, completely unintentional."

In Tennessee, concerned citizen Terri Carlin filed a proposed class action lawsuit "on behalf of all Americans who watched the Super Bowl", naming Jackson, Justin Timberlake, MTV and CBS as defendants. Carlin claimed Jackson's exposure caused her and millions of unsuspecting viewers to suffer "outrage, anger, embarrassment, and serious injury."

President Bush was asked for his thoughts, but told reporters that he fell asleep after watching the first half of the game. But Federal Communications Commission Chairman Michael Powell was still awake, and denounced the halftime show as "a classless, crass, and deplorable stunt." "Our nation's children, parents and citizens deserve better," he said, before instructing the commission to open an investigation.

Obscenity laws as applied to broadcasting warn that over-the-air (as opposed to cable) TV networks cannot air material considered obscene, or air material dubbed "indecent" between 6 AM and 10 PM. The FCC defines obscene material as describing sexual conduct "in a patently offensive way" and lacking "serious literary, artistic, political, or scientific value." Which, let's face it, describes half the networks' combined prime-time schedules.

But even by liberal standards the Jackson incident had crossed a line. Janet Jackson issued a videotaped apology and appeared on *Larry King Live* to explain that while a costume reveal was added after final rehearsals, the idea was for Timberlake to pull away her bustier and expose a red-lace bra underneath. What happened, to the delight/disgust of 100 million viewers, was described as a "wardrobe malfunction," a phrase destined to enter the lexicon alongside "bimbo eruption" and "dimpled chad."

To some the explanation was suspect, given Timberlake's lyrical intimation and the fact that a new Jackson CD was imminent. Screen captures, which were scrutinized like some peep show version of the Zapruder film, revealed her leather outfit to have been modified to add a row of easy-opening snaps; according to newspaper accounts

44

in the Super Bowl host city of Houston, Jackson had purchased a special red bra but returned it, saying it did not fit. She also purchased a sun-shaped nipple shield from a piercing shop. Usually the items are sold in pairs, but Jackson curiously asked for just one. The matching shield later went on display in the shop window.

As a result of the public outcry, both Jackson and Justin Timberlake were banned from the *American Music Awards* the following week, though Timberlake was later allowed in. The show was aired with a 60-second delay, which has become standard procedure for every subsequent Jackson appearance (including *Good Morning America* and *On-Air with Ryan Seacrest*) and most live telecasts. Even the Academy Awards aired with a five second delay, in case Dame Maggie Smith got any ideas.

But just as the controversy should have relaxed, it inexplicably picked up steam. A glimpse of an elderly woman's breast was edited out of an episode of NBC's *ER*; Janet Jackson was uninvited from the Grammy Awards, where she was to present an award to Luther Vandross, and plans to star her in a TV biography of Lena Horne were scuttled; Justin Timberlake's 'NSync bandmate JC Chasez, who wasn't even at the Super Bowl, was cut from the halftime show at the NFL's Pro Bowl. Meanwhile, LaToya Jackson, who bared both breasts and more in a *Playboy* pictorial, still couldn't get arrested.

Jackson's antics evolved beyond a self-contained incident and changed the climate of broadcasting in the United States. Apparently hers is a magical breast, for as soon as it was revealed the FCC Chief realized that Howard Stern sometimes talks about sex on the radio. At Chairman Powell's urging, Congress approved a bill that raised the top indecency fine from $27,500 to $500,000 per infraction, enough to drive any offending broadcaster off the air. The first victim was Florida based shock jock Bubba the Love Sponge, who was fired after his employer, Clear Channel, was hit with $755,000 in fines.

Make no mistake, this could get real scary real fast. There are no shortage of Pax Network-viewing puritans in power who have been waiting for an opportunity to clean up Hollywood, and the FCC now has a weapon potent enough to eliminate any content they find objectionable. "It's time to return the public airwaves to the taxpayers who support them," said House Majority Whip Roy Blunt, conveniently forgetting that it's the public's support of entertainers like Howard Stern that have kept them on the air for so long.

If those who would castrate the entertainment industry succeed at bringing down the easy targets like Stern, what next? *NYPD Blue*? *Will and Grace*? Rap format radio stations? NBC's decision to no longer air the Victoria's Secret Fashion Show may be the first of many programming changes made in our post-wardrobe malfunction world.

Predictably, the overreaction on the family values side has now inspired an equally fervent wave of warnings from free speech advocates. Beware, they say, lest we regress to an era similar to the 1950s, when Senator Joe McCarthy unleashed a Communist witchhunt that ended the careers of several prominent actors and screenwriters. This, coincidentally, was the last time one boob had so much influence over public policy.

It's possible that cooler heads will prevail and both programmers and politicians will reach some common ground of responsibility, and if that happens I'm content with ranking Janet Jackson's Super Bowl escapade at #78; but if the issue of government censorship builds further to exert influence over the presidential election and beyond, you may want to cut and paste this entry into the top ten.

77
THE SURVIVORS IS VOTED OFF THE NETWORK

Harold Robbins' 'The Survivors'
ABC, SEPTEMBER 29, 1969–JANUARY 26, 1970

In 1964, ABC introduced *Peyton Place*, an attempt to transfer the soap opera format into prime time. The series launched the careers of Mia Farrow and Ryan O'Neal and ran for five successful years. Before its popularity faded, the network had already developed another sudsy property for the same time slot, in the hopes of holding onto viewers who never missed a Monday night appointment with the Mackenzies.

For a concept they turned to author Harold Robbins, master of the trashy potboiler. Robbins submitted a one-page outline about the jetset family of a banking tycoon, and received a million dollars for his efforts, as well as name-above-the-title recognition. Given how the series turned out, he might have paid the money back to have his name removed.

The Survivors was hyped with much fanfare, particularly after the casting of Hollywood screen queen Lana Turner as matriarch Tracy Carlyle Hastings. But the drama of events behind the scenes proved far more compelling than anything in the scripts, which made for great press copy but lousy television.

The first shock was that Turner and Robbins would work together at all, given Lana's anger toward the author for his earlier dramatization of the most traumatic event in her life. In 1958, Turner's mobster lover Johnny Stompanato was stabbed to death by her teenage daughter. A jury returned a verdict of justifiable homicide, but just as the sensational publicity began to subside Robbins released *Where Love Has Gone*, a book that changed the names but not the situation. The book became a movie and the case remained entrenched in the public consciousness. "I hate that man," Turner wrote of Robbins in her autobiography.

Apparently, they make paychecks big enough to soothe any grudge and Turner signed on for 26 episodes. After that, nothing much happened. "Many months went by but not a single script was written. Writers were hired and fired every day, it seemed," Turner recalled. "Before anyone ever developed a single show, we set off for the Riviera to shoot background scenes for the stories that would somehow evolve."

Despite the inactivity, *The Survivors* still generated juicy copy, particularly for Turner's rants against various production people and network executives. In her first week of shooting, a disagreement with producer William Frye turned into a slap-fight that resulted in Frye's dismissal. Lana next vented her wrath against costume designer Luis Estevez, whom the former glamour-girl complained was making her look too "matronly." Estevez followed Frye out the door, but not before delivering a parting shot: "Perhaps it was not my designs that made her look matronly. After all, nothing is forever."

Turner also took exception to being paid less than George Hamilton, who played her playboy half brother, Duncan Carlyle. You have to go with Lana on this one; her name certainly brought more viewers to the show than the Coppertone guy, but Hamilton received $17,500 per episode to Turner's $12,000.

If she wasn't going to be paid like a superstar, Turner still expected to be treated as such, with a limo at her disposal even for trips from the soundstage to her dressing room. The bean counters grumbled but authorized the expense. They were already upset over extensive changes in the storylines that rendered the previously-shot European footage obsolete.

Finally, after two years in development, three producers and one year of shooting, *The Survivors* debuted on ABC. It seemed to have all the elements; Tracy had a bed-hopping husband (Kevin McCarthy), a troubled teenage son (Jan-Michael Vincent), and an old flame (Rosanno Brazzi) later revealed to be her son's real father. Boardroom machinations pitted Tracy's terminally-ill father (Ralph Bellamy) against greedy relations, and there was a South American revolution thrown in for good measure.

But viewers preferred the more wholesome appeal of *Mayberry RFD*, and *The*

Despite prodigious use of the smoldering stare, George Hamilton and Lana Turner couldn't salvage The Survivors.

Survivors proved so unpopular that it was cancelled after 15 weeks. *Variety* called it "one of the most expensive flops in television history." The network took a multi-million dollar budget hit, but recouped some of its losses by recutting several episodes into TV movies that aired over the summer. Lana Turner emerged unscathed from the negative publicity, and made a successful return to prime time soaps ten years later on *Falcon Crest*.

76
PAUL LYNDE IS BACHELOR #1

The Dating Game
ABC, JUNE 1, 1968

The Dating Game—innocent matchmaking or the perfect cover for CIA agent Chuck Barris's covert assassination missions? Depends on whether you believe Barris's fanciful autobiography, *Confessions of a Dangerous Mind*, but even if his allegations are false there was still plenty of violence associated with the show, given how many guys were shot down by the bachelorette contestants.

Before *Elimidate*, before *Love Connection*, there was host Jim Lang in his puffy shirts and powder blue tuxedos, introducing eligible women to Bachelors # 1, 2, and 3, whom she did not see until after making her choice. The contestant asked titillating questions, scripted by the show to elicit racy responses. The prize was a chaperoned vacation date, and what the couple did after that was their own business.

What's surprising about *The Dating Game* is how many celebrities, either before or after they became famous, appeared as date-hungry bachelors. The list includes Wally Cox, Arnold Schwarzenegger, Steve Martin, Burt Reynolds, and Tom Selleck, who you'd think would be capable of getting his own girls.

But the most unlikely celebrity to accept the title of Bachelor #1 would be Paul Lynde, a comic genius best remembered as the center square on the original *Hollywood Squares*, where he stretched the censor's tolerance with some of the most risqué double-entendres ever aired on a game show. Lynde also appeared on nearly every sitcom of the 1960s at one time or another, including several episodes of *Bewitched* as Samantha's practical joke-loving Uncle Arthur.

What made *The Dating Game* appearance so amusing was that Paul Lynde was gay. Back in the day such things were not openly discussed, but there was no mystery here. Lynde was so obviously gay that people who didn't know what "gay" meant knew he was gay. Not that there's anything wrong with that, to paraphrase Jerry Seinfeld; the more flamboyant aspects of his persona only accentuated his brilliance as a comedian. With his infectious laugh and sardonic smirk, Lynde could made the straight lines funny and the punch lines funnier. But when he was introduced on *The Dating Game*, there was clearly something wrong with this picture.

The contestant, a pretty blonde who looked like an upper-crust Wellesley product, opened the game by addressing Lynde: "Bachelor #1, let's hear the sound a woman makes after you've kissed her for the very first time." Lynde's response, a dramatic "Oh, my goodness!" is hilarious in context, and drew a huge laugh from the studio audience. Some of the responses on the show were as scripted as the questions, but in this case Lynde was obviously hearing the question for the first time, to provoke his genuine sense of bemused discomfort.

After similar questions to the other two bachelors, Lynde was asked, "You're shipwrecked on an island all alone. What would you do between 4 and 6 o'clock?" "I'd start looking around for something for dinner," answers Lynde, a response that falls flat. But he got the crowd back with the last question: "Bachelor #1, I've just given you Bachelor #2. What are you going to do with him?" There was much laughter all around as Paul looked at the burly, bearded guy seated next to him, stretched the moment for all it's worth, and finally uttered, "Go dancing!" The audience exploded with laughter, and even Bachelor #2 chuckled a bit, though he seemed to wonder whether Lynde was serious.

Paul Lynde was not chosen for the dream date that day, and no records survive to indicate whether he went dancing with Bachelor #2. But Lynde actually returned to *The Dating Game* in 1972, to publicize *The Paul Lynde Show*. The short-lived series had Lynde in the role of a traditional family man, cracking jokes about his wife and kids. Perhaps Elizabeth Allen, who played the missus, could provide an answer to the sound a woman makes when he kisses her. Oh, my goodness.

75
SWEET GINGER BROWN

The Harlem Globetrotters on Gilligan's Island
NBC, May 15, 1981

I was never a fan of *Gilligan's Island*, beyond it's famous theme song, but there's no denying the show's enduring appeal. Creator Sherwood Schwartz has a knack for creating iconic characters, both here and in *The Brady Bunch*, whose adventures have brought laughs to millions of people for more than 40 years. As achievements go, that's more valuable than praise from critics or Emmy Awards.

I've always thought of *Gilligan's Island* as baby's first TV show. The silly but good-natured escapades of its seven castaways are a live-action facsimile of the cartoons that little tykes watch through the bars of their crib. Start a young pop culture consumer with Gilligan and the Skipper and eventually they'll be ready for Jerry, Elaine, and Kramer.

Schwartz's *Inside Gilligan's Island* is one of the very best television companion volumes. Fans and detractors alike would agree that *Gilligan's Island* is one of the most weightless bits of fluff ever broadcast, so its astonishing to read about all the decisions that went into every aspect of its production. Every character and situation was analyzed by network executives. Dozens of people worked 20-hour days, discussed, debated and fussed over context, content and exposition, and yet the end result is still just *Gilligan's Island.*

But the series is loved, and I'm glad fans received some closure when the castaways were rescued in a 1978 TV movie that drew an enormous 52 share of the audience. And shame on Tina Louise for being the only cast member not to return; if Robert Reed could make the *Brady* reunions, given his feelings about that show, Tina certainly could have slipped into Ginger's cocktail dress one more time.

The high rating for *Rescue from Gilligan's Island* inspired a second, less successful film, in which the castaways return to their tropic island nest to run a hotel. *The Castaways on Gilligan's Island* drew a respectable 26 share, prompting a third and final reunion, suggested by Fred Silverman, in which the *Gilligan* cast would meet the Dallas Cowboy Cheerleaders. "The Dallas Cheerleaders had done a special some months earlier that had done a great rating," Schwartz explained. "I told Fred I'm sure I could work out a story for the cheerleaders on Gilligan's Island. In fact, I thought that was a very attractive idea, all those beautiful girls in a tropical setting."

"I wrote an outline for the show, (but) even before I finished the script Fred called me to say he couldn't get the Dallas Cheerleaders because the special they did was on CBS, and CBS had an exclusive contract with them," Schwartz said. "He asked me if I could change the outline from the Dallas Cheerleaders to the Harlem Globetrotters." This is logic found only in the upper echelon of television programmers.

And so, after a few script changes necessitated by substituting large African-American athletes for nubile young women, Bob Denver (Gilligan), Alan Hale (Skipper), Russell Johnson (Professor), Mr. Howell (Jim Backus), Lovey Howell (Natalie Schafer), and Mary Ann (Dawn Wells) gathered for one more encore. Backus was in poor health at the time, so most of his scenes went to David Ruprecht, who played his son, Thurston Howell IV. And Tina Louise was a no-show again, replaced this time by Constance Forslund.

The villains of the piece are J.J. and Olga Pierson, a husband-wife team of mad scientists played by Martin Landau and Barbara Bain. Yes, there's an Academy Award-winning actor in *The Harlem Globetrotters on Gilligan's Island.* The Piersons discover a powerful new element—Supremium—on the island, and to control the supply they must get rid of the castaways. To watch Landau play scenes opposite a Walmart-quality robot named George, and to hear Bain utter, "Whoever controls Supremium—controls the world!" in a kill-moose-and-squirrel accent, it's enough to make a *Mission: Impossible* fan weep.

The Globetrotters' plane makes an emergency landing near the island, while Pierson tries to drive the castaways away. When we first see Gilligan and the Skipper, they're still sleeping in hammocks, one above the other, in the same hut. Since the Howells made them all limited partners in the hotel venture, you'd think they could at least afford bunk beds.

Halfway into the film, as Pierson swindles Gilligan, the Skipper, and Mary Ann out of their ownership shares, the Globetrotters play a pickup basketball game against the seven castaways. The image of 80-year-old Lovey Howell guarding Sweet Lou Dunbar in the low post is one that I had thought could be induced only by the most potent hallucinogens.

When Pierson fails to secure the Howells' shares, he suggests a wager for the prize—the Globetrotters vs. a team of robot players, winner take all. The silliness of robots garbed in shorts and white socks is a ridiculous distraction from the Globetrotters' basketball wizardry, and if the scene wasn't already surreal enough, the climactic game is called by legendary Lakers announcer Chick Hearn. While the Trotters run circles around the robots, Pierson has another team of androids loading Supremium into his yacht, unaware that the element is unstable at higher temperatures. The Professor fills him in, but not before his yacht explodes. The end.

The cast still looks good, and perform their groan-inducing punchlines and slapstick pratfalls with undiminished enthusiasm. Even by *Gilligan's Island* standards it's all pretty foolish, but that never bothered fans before.

The Harlem Globetrotters on Gilligan's Island drew a 26 share, same as the last movie, but not enough to green light another project. A pity, as Sherwood Schwartz had one more idea: *Murder on Gilligan's Island*, a whodunit in which famous detectives from history and fiction would gather to solve the murder of one of the castaways. I bet he'd have knocked off Ginger just to get back at Tina Louise.

74
NICK AT NITE TURNS NASTY

NICK AT NITE
NICKELODEON, NOVEMBER 1994

It started with *Taxi*.

To casual viewers of Nick at Nite, the addition of *Taxi* didn't seem like an evil portent—it was just another classic sitcom joining the schedule of a network that specialized in the best of television's past. But for those who cherished Nick at Nite as their last remaining lifeline in a pop culture that celebrated the crass and cruel, *Taxi* was the first step in the crumbling of the happiest little corner of the cable dial.

Since its debut in June 1985, Nick at Nite focused on the broadcast equivalent of comfort food, the kinds of shows that went well with warm blankets, pajamas, and graham crackers on a TV tray: *The Lucy Show, Get Smart, The Patty Duke Show, Bewitched, The Donna Reed Show, The Adventures of Superman, Dobie Gillis, The Mary Tyler Moore Show.*

Most of these shows had been in syndication for years, but Nick at Nite was the only network to make a fuss over them. For the first time, these weren't just reruns, but television classics worthy of celebration and proper presentation. Episodes were aired in their original order, even those in quaint old black-and-white, and introduced with original broadcast dates, background and interesting trivia.

"Dedicated to preserving and protecting America's precious television heritage" was Nick's slogan, and while it may have just been marketing there were certainly people at the network who got the same warm fuzzy feeling that viewers did every time Dick Van Dyke tripped over that ottoman. You had to love this stuff to come up with the whimsical promos and publicity stunts still fondly remembered by fans, such as the celebration of *Get Smart* by introducing Don Adams to 99 women dressed as Agent 99 in New York City, and sponsoring a "Jeannie vs. Samantha" viewer's poll to determine who's powers were greater. For the record, Samantha won with more than 810,000 votes, to Jeannie's 614,000.

But *Taxi* was a different kind of show, that stood out amidst the network's wholesome lineup like a loud drunk at Disneyland. A decidedly adult situation comedy, the show featured an outstanding ensemble cast portraying a memorable array of outcasts, losers and eccentrics. The show explored the seedy underbelly of urban life. There were sex jokes, drug jokes, and an assortment of colorful barbs and assaults. No one could question its brilliance in writing and performance, but characters like tyrannical Louie DePalma and spaced-out Reverend Jim seemed out of place amidst the escapist fare on the Nick schedule, most of which predated *Taxi* by at least ten years. For the first time in the network's decade-long history, it was no longer possible to watch Nick at Nite from 8 PM into the wee hours and not see something that could be objectionable to some viewers.

To some, change is inevitable, but the original appeal of Nick at Nite was in how it thumbed its nose at change and proudly lived in the past. Most viewers back then would have been content if the network rotated a core group of about two dozen shows from now until eternity.

But once *Taxi* opened the door to the contemporary sitcom, it led to the debut of *All in the Family*, Norman Lear's groundbreaking series that ushered in a new era in television comedy. The Nick at Nite start time was moved up from 8 PM to 8:30, then 9 PM. The quirky "better living through television" promos and distinctive musical bumpers were quietly removed, and the status once attached to a series joining the Nick lineup became nonexistent. After building a successful brand name as the home of classic TV, Nick at Nite kicked Donna Reed to the curb and invited Roseanne in for cold pizza and beer. In its current incarnation, the prime time schedule consists of shows so recently departed that we hardly had time to miss them.

Thankfully, the dissolution of Nick at Nite has coincided with the arrival of TV Land, where most of the original Nick shows now reside. But as delightful as it is to have a 24-hour channel devoted to the great shows of the past, the network hasn't been able to create that sense of community that made Nick at Nite so beloved. You can still watch *Leave it to Beaver*, but you can't go home again.

73

ROSEANNE SALUTES AMERICA

San Diego Padres Baseball
Fox Sports West, July 25, 1990

After fourteen years, it's time to reassign some blame. Roseanne took serious heat from sports fans, music lovers, and patriots for her horrendous rendition of the National Anthem before a San Diego Padres home game. What began as *Sportscenter* ridicule escalated into a national news story that drew the wrath of President George Bush, who described her performance as "disgusting" and "a disgrace".

There's no way to defend Roseanne's actions that day at Qualcomm Park. The sounds she discharged during that performance have been classified as torture by Amnesty International. But not enough people have asked how she came to be there in the first place. Roseanne didn't volunteer to perform the anthem, she was invited by Padres owner Tom Werner to appear at the game as part of a promotion called Working Women Night. The anthem was initially not part of the deal, but somewhere along the line the idea was suggested, by Roseanne's then husband Tom Arnold according to most sources.

This would have been the time for prudent reflection. Perhaps it's not wise to allow a woman who can't sing to perform the Star Spangled Banner, a song that has induced nightmares in professional singers. And what might happen when the musical shortcomings of a famously insecure comic are exposed before 44,000 fans and a national television audience? Might she try to get laughs to combat the rejection? Ah, the benefits of hindsight.

After being introduced, she strolled onto the field, garbed in a wrinkled, untucked pink men's dress shirt. That was the first indication that Roseanne might not have recognized the Star-Spangled Banner as a national institution worthy of one's respect, if not reverence. To focus even more attention on her voice, the performance would be without musical accompaniment.

Her first act was to put her fingers in her ears, obviously aware of the awful noise that was about to be unleashed. The rendition was dreadful from the first line, and the boos began just after Roseanne reached for but missed the high note in the line "What so proudly we hailed…" Call her Francis Scott Off-Key. "I knew it wasn't going to be good," recalled Padres hall-of-famer Tony Gwynn, who was watching from the tunnel near the clubhouse. "If she hit a bad note, I was going to run up the tunnel. She started and I flew up the tunnel."

And, just to be certain that even the deaf would be offended by the incident, Roseanne finished the song, then grabbed her crotch and spit. That last bit was an attempt to parody the most common gestures of baseball players. Had Roseanne performed them before the song, she might have gotten a laugh. But coming so soon on the heels of murdering the National Anthem, the gestures were perceived as further signs of disrespect, and engendered only more hostility.

The next day, Iraq invaded Kuwait, and a US retaliation seemed imminent. With patriotism rapidly on the rise, the timing of Roseanne's antics could not have been worse. When the Veterans of Foreign Wars started a "Boycott Roseanne" movement, Tom Werner expressed his regret over the incident, but one couldn't help wondering if he was secretly happy, because Roseanne was getting all the hate mail and it was the first time anyone outside of San Diego had paid attention to the Padres.

"That's how she sings. She didn't mean any disrespect." Tom Arnold told reporters who had gathered outside Roseanne's home. The comedian did not respond well to her critics. After watching coverage of Dodgers baseball on the local news, in which a reporter, following the performance of the Anthem, looked into the camera and said, "And that, Ms. Barr, is the way the National Anthem should sound," she called the station and demanded to be put on the air. "I'll sing that damned song any damned time I want to sing that song," she told anchorman Jerry Dumphy.

Roseanne's defiance hadn't dimmed when she covered the incident in her 1994 book *My Lives*. "What, only the best voices can sing that song? You gotta be Pavarotti, or Liza, or Barbra to sing the National Anthem? It's gotta be elitism if you have to have perfect pitch or be an opera singer to sing the National Anthem. And tell Bush I'd like to see his ass sing it better than I did ... you know what else? We got the only anthem that's about war and killing people. Now where's that at? Huh?" I'll take clueless for 200, Alex.

But the comedian got her comeuppance in the months following her performance, when she was greeted in restaurants, sporting events and grocery stores by folks assaulting her eardrums with their own screeching renditions. While Tom Arnold threatened to punch men, women and children after they bellowed "And the rockets red glare!", Roseanne finally realized what she put the rest of us through.

72

SHUTTING UP BABY

Happy
NBC, June 8, 1960–September 8, 1961

Baby Talk
ABC, March 8, 1991–July 3, 1992

Baby Bob
CBS, March 18, 2002–June 20, 2003

Some gimmicks, no matter how ghastly, have proven surprisingly resilient. Take the talking baby ... please. The idea of having a toddler's thoughts expressed in voiceover is something that Carol Burnett could turn into a marvelous ten-minute sketch on her variety show. But Burnett would also realize that the bit was only good for ten minutes. If you're creating a series, you'd better have something else to offer.

All three networks have launched variations on the talking baby show, with results utterly lacking in imagination beyond the voiceovers. NBC tried first with *Happy*, starring Ronnie Burns and Yvonne Lime as hoteliers Chris and Sally Day. Their son Happy would comment to the viewers on the guests and day-to-day activities. Burns had experience with breaking the fourth wall on a sitcom, after appearing on the ingenious series hosted by his parents, George Burns and Gracie Allen. But where George's humorous addendums to the scripted scenes added a delightfully surreal element to an already fine show, Happy's contributions weren't any more helpful than the ones he left in his diaper.

The 1989 film *Look Who's Talking* brought big-mouthed babies back in a big way. "Utterly, painfully embarrassing, to the actors and the audience," raved the *New York Post*, but the film topped the box-office charts for more than a month, and revived the careers of John Travolta and Kirstie Alley. Bruce Willis provided the voice of baby Mikey. Its success inspired two sequels, but despite the recruitment of Roseanne, Damon Wayans, and Mel Brooks to voice new rugrats, both sank without a trace.

Faring better, but just slightly, was *Baby Talk*, ABC's unofficial adaptation of the films that borrowed everything but the cast and the title. Molly (played by Alley) was now Maggie (played by Julia Duffy); James (Travolta) became Joe (George Clooney, whose work here made his season on *Facts of Life* look like Emmy material). Mikey was now Mickey, and voiced by Tony Danza, marking the first time he played a character with a name other than "Tony".

The network was certain it had a heartwarming winner, and promoted the series as the biggest potential breakout hit of the Fall 1990 lineup. But all *Baby Talk* inspired were terrible reviews and several cases of child abandonment that no district attorney would prosecute. Connie Selleca, originally cast as Maggie, bailed after shooting the pilot. Duffy lasted one season before leaving to replace Delta Burke on *Designing Women*, and Mary Page Keller became Mickey's third mommy. George Clooney left after the first few episodes, and when ABC inexplicably brought the show back for a second season, Scott Baio was cast as the new love interest. Nothing worked, and *Baby Talk* earned the title of "Worst Series on Television" by *Electronic Media* magazine.

You'd think after that, any programmer who suggested another take on the talking baby would have a pacifier jammed in his yap. But in 2001 a company called freeinternet.com used a talkative tot in a series of popular commercials, and CBS announced plans to adapt the concept into a series. For the first time, a character on a commercial was given his own show; had TV been this desperate a decade earlier, we might have seen *Scarecrow and Mrs. Olsen*, and *Hangin' With Mr. Whipple*.

Instead, we got *Baby Bob*, the story of first-time parents Walter (Adam Arkin) and Lizzy (Joely Fisher) who are shocked to discover their six-month-old baby can speak like an adult. This is a departure from previous treatments, in which the baby's comments were thoughts heard in voiceover; Bob actually talked, his computer-enhanced

After seven successful seasons on Newhart, Baby Talk's *Julia Duffy (left) ponders how her career came to this.*

moving lips resembling something out of a Clutch Cargo cartoon. They were shooting for adorable, but the result was a kid that appeared a victim of demonic possession.

Lizzy, the proud mother, wanted to show off Bob's aptitude, but Walter was afraid of the repercussions and determined to keep his son's abilities out of the newspapers. Grandpa Sam (Elliot Gould) is also in on the secret, as is Teala the babysitter (Marissa Tait). Arkin, Fisher, Gould, and Holland Taylor (as the bragging grandmother of one of Bob's baby friends) are experienced sitcom vets, but all the punch lines went to the baby, who spoke in a voice that sounded like Chuckie in the *Child's Play* films. Among the more memorable examples of Bob's "wit": "Held a raisin in my fist for almost two seconds, but then I dropped it, then I picked it up, then I dropped it— they're so darned little!", and "I wasn't born yesterday—recently, but not yesterday."

It was depressing to watch talented actors on a series this bad, and unsettling that one of the running jokes was Bob making sexual advances toward his mother. When Fisher would lean in toward Bob, her abundant cleavage prominently displayed, Bob commented about his excitement at the thought of another helping of breast milk. Was his middle name Oedipus? By the second season, he had set his lecherous sights on the comely babysitter, which I guess represents progress. Ratings were actually high for the first few episodes, but the brain-numbing stories provoked an outcry from critics and appalled viewers that ultimately sealed the series' fate.

There's always the possibility that one day the concept will again be resurrected, a particularly excruciating thought to those of us who wish all babies came with mute controls, especially in restaurants and movie theaters.

71
SPOCK'S BRAIN

Star Trek
NBC, SEPTEMBER 20, 1968

"Brain and brain! What is brain!"   —KARA

From 1966 to 1969, *Star Trek* brought sophisticated science fiction to television ... and languished in obscurity. But after being canceled by NBC, the series that had already broken its share of rules rendered the rulebook obsolete. Through nonstop reruns and subsequent film adaptations, *Star Trek* has become so firmly embedded in our consciousness that it has practically become the official story of our distant future.

Dozens of television series have introduced characters that have become part of the culture, but the Enterprise crew have soared past even that lofty status. They have added expressions to our language and created technology that has been debated in scientific journals. They have been honored by NASA and inspired the name of a US space shuttle. But what is perhaps most significant about the 23rd century as envisioned by series creator Gene Roddenberry is that it gives mankind a goal to work toward, and illustrates what we are capable of achieving if we don't screw it up.

The devotion of *Star Trek* fans is well-documented and oft-ridiculed, but they get a bad rap. Attend a convention and you'll find a diverse assortment of creative, imaginative people, and a higher overall I.Q. rating than at most public gatherings. And there's something to their belief that even a bad *Star Trek* is preferable to a good episode of most television shows, though the adventure that unfolded at Stardate 5431.4 strains that theory to its limits.

"Spock's Brain" has earned the distinction of being the worst episode in Trek Classic's 79-show run. Emerging from the show's third season, when NBC's lack of interest in the series was reflected in slashed budgets and pedestrian scripts, the episode featured situations so ludicrous and dialogue so foolish that it could not be saved even by the always reliable chemistry among the stalwart crew.

The story opens as the Enterprise approaches a mysterious craft of obviously advanced technology. But before they can run any scans a beautiful woman in a tinfoil bathing suit beams over and knocks out everyone on the ship. As she surveys the unconscious crew, she walks over to Spock, strokes his forehead, and smiles.

An unspecified time later, the crew revives and discovers that Spock's body has been moved to sickbay. After an examination, Dr. McCoy (DeForest Kelley) delivers the shocking news to Captain Kirk (William Shatner): "His brain is gone." Kirk reasons that the girl must have taken it, and "if it was taken out, it can be put back in." But McCoy cautions that it must be done in 24 hours. When the material was weak, the actors—especially Shatner—would try to overcompensate by manufacturing drama with those oddly-punctuated line readings that are so much a part of the show's legacy. So when Uhura asks why anyone would want Spock's brain, Kirk replies, "Yes ... why ... would ... they ... want it?"

They trace the ship to a primitive planet, where Kirk and a landing party beam down and are accosted by a tribe of bearded cavemen wearing fuzzy blue skirts. One of them speaks of "the others," and Kirk reasons this is where Spock's brain must have gone. McCoy beams down with Spock's body, which he manipulates by remote control. Ah, if only he had one of those for Yeoman Rand.

The crew is lured into a cave that turns into a giant elevator ("3rd floor, housewares, sporting goods, Spock's brain"). When the doors open they discover themselves surrounded by more tinfoil-clad lovelies who claim to know nothing about their mission. "We only know here below, there above." Even Kara (Marj Dusay), the woman who appeared on the Enterprise, appears to have no knowledge of her previous actions.

Suddenly, Spock's voice is heard from their communicators, which leads Kirk to a shocking discovery. "Spock's ... brain ... controls ... this!" he says, looking around the settlement. He falls to his knees in front of Kara and pleads to be taken to their leader, as Spock is informed of his fate. "You are a disembodied brain," Kirk tells him, revealing their plan to reinsert his brain back in his body. "We brought it along with us," he says. "Thoughtful," replies the brain.

But Kara and her people won't go down without a fight. They strap metal belts to the crew and shoot high voltage into their bodies. Kirk's paroxysms of pain are particularly amusing. But eventually the crew defeat their captors and discover that the means to restore Spock can only be found in the "Great teacher of all ancient knowledge," a clear plastic device that looks like an old-fashioned hair dryer.

McCoy dons the helmet and learns the procedure, but forgets a few key steps midway through the operation. Fortunately, he reattached Spock's vocal chords, and the patient talks the doctor through his own operation. As soon as the procedure is complete, Spock pops up and starts spouting off on the fascinating cultural development of the locals. "I knew it!" says McCoy. "I knew I shouldn't have reconnected his mouth!" in a final scene more suitable to *Holmes and Yoyo*.

"Spock's Brain" was written by Lee Cronin, a pseudonym for producer Gene Coon, who made several more distinguished contributions to the *Trek* mythos, including the Klingons and the Prime Directive. And according to some *Trek* experts the original script was not without merit, before being subjected to rewrites by less talented individuals. That Spock could undergo two brain surgeries in 24 hours without losing a hair on his head is only slightly less believable than Kirk failing to get busy with a miniskirted hottie like Kara. But if episodes like "Spock's Brain" and "Plato's Stepchildren" have become camp classics, they also stand as a testament to the original series' willingness to take bold chances with its storytelling. That's a lesson later *Trek* incarnations would have done well to learn.

70

HE'S CHEVY CHASE, AND WE'RE BORED

The Chevy Chase Show
FOX, SEPTEMBER 7, 1993–OCTOBER 15, 1993

That *The Chevy Chase Show* never had a chance seems obvious in retrospect, and yet the certainty of its failure somehow eluded anyone in a position to prevent the trainwreck before it left the station.

Though it doesn't justify the FOX network's confidence, two things to keep in mind: Johnny Carson's departure from *The Tonight Show* one year earlier left the impression that for the first time in three decades late night viewership was up for grabs; and Chevy Chase had not held a regular TV gig since the first year of *Saturday Night Live*, which had only grown more legendary as subsequent *SNL* casts fell short of the standard that Chase, Aykroyd, Belushi, and Radner set in those early shows. Thus, though he had made a thousand horrible movies in the interim, the return of Chevy Chase to television still had the air of an event.

But while FOX knew Chase was funny, they never really examined how he made people laugh. His was a comedy borne of arrogance, of acting the smartest person in the room and belittling anyone who crossed into his field of vision. Wearing a permanent smirk, he laughed at you, not with you. Such traits are anathema to a talk show host, who must suffer fools on a regular basis. The job is to establish a connection with each guest, whether they're a celebrity plugging a movie or a housewife from Iowa with a collection of butter churns.

That's why Carson was the king; he not only found a rapport with everyone from presidents to punk rockers, he made it look effortless. David Letterman was more neurotic, yes, and perhaps it was his success that sold FOX on Chase, another comic with a sharp edge. But Letterman's hostility was directed inward, where it became a source of self-deprecating humor. Chase, by contrast, would seem mad at everyone but himself.

To his credit, Chase was smart enough to book Goldie Hawn, his *Foul Play* costar and a famous person who actually likes him, as the first guest on his first show. This should have been Chevy's equivalent of Johnny Carson with Dyan Cannon, or David Letterman with Drew Barrymore. A few laughs, a little innocent flirting, and the comfort level of chatting with a friend rather than a guest, and sharing that friendship with viewers across America.

But as the interview began, Chevy seemed nervous. His smarmy public persona seemed to struggle against any genuine impulse to enjoy the moment. A prearranged bit of Goldie serenading the host with "Look at That Face" fell flat, which only put Chase further off his game. What followed were awkward pauses, incoherent asides, and poor Goldie doing her best to shake Chevy out of his stupor.

The segment concluded with another bit, as Goldie brought out her 17-year-old son Oliver to celebrate his birthday. It appeared Oliver would have preferred to be anywhere else, but he and his date smiled gamely as mom and Chevy sang "Happy Birthday," and wheeled out a cake. Chase then reverted to his *SNL* days, performing a pratfall into the frosting. Oliver figured the cringe-worthy segment had ended, but then another cake was brought out and set on his lap, pinning him to his chair.

What should have been a slam-dunk opening proved uncomfortable to watch, and one had to wonder how Chase would fare when he'd be forced to interview an actor he didn't know about a movie he had no plans to see. It was a recipe for

Good evening. I'm Chevy Chase, and you're watching something else.

disaster, that was served cold night after night for five weeks until the show was quiety cancelled. The network ate the $3 milion guarantee it paid the host, and the Chevy Chase Theater changed its name to protect the innocent.

Long forgotten is the fact that, in its other aspects, the show was more than competently envisioned. The handsome woody set was warm and inviting, and the basketball hoop, where Chevy would try to sink one at each show's open, was a clever touch; the band was led by sax man Tom Scott, a member of the famed Blues Brothers band. And the "News Update" segment, adapted from Chase's "Weekend Update" spots on *SNL*, showcased the comic in his natural element.

But Chase's inability (or refusal, take your pick) to relate to his guests was a death sentence. At least he tried early on, but by week three Chevy was back to relying on his safety valve of nastiness. When Martin Sheen appeared to promote his performance as Robert E. Lee in *Gettysburg*, and mentioned what an intelligent, well-read man Lee was, Chase observed that was surprising, "because we normally don't think of Southerners as readers." It was impossible to tell whether he was making a joke or expressing an opinion.

Chase's comeuppance came not with inevitable cancellation, but when he tried to match wits with Burt Reynolds, who had gone hundreds of rounds at verbal sparring with Johnny Carson. Reynolds' withering stare backed the host down from several smart remarks about his failed marriage to Loni Anderson. At one point, Burt expressed his disappointment that Loni had gone public with the details of their breakup. "Aren't you doing that now?" asked Chevy. "Yeah," said Burt. "But nobody's watching."

69
ERASING HISTORY

Lost Television Classics
1949–1967

Would you like to watch Johnny Carson's first *Tonight Show*? How about James Dean's portrayal of an angel opposite the great John Carradine in *Hound of Heaven*, a 1953 drama presented on *The Kate Smith Show*? Or perhaps the first Super Bowl? Well, you'd better settle for a *Perfect Strangers* rerun, because to the best of our knowledge these events no longer exist.

Sure, somebody taped them when they happened, but some time later, whether it was weeks or months or years, the tapes were either thrown away or used again, and as a result what would now be considered historic broadcasts have most likely disappeared forever.

How could this happen? There were economic justifications, and there's a little stupidity thrown in as there usually is, but the main reason so much of our early television heritage is gone is that no one thought it was worth saving.

"In the beginning a lot of stuff was lost because it went out live and was never put on tape in the first place," explained Robert Thompson, Director of Syracuse University's Center for the Study of Popular Television. "Videotape doesn't come into regular use until TV had been around for several years. If the program wasn't put on Kinescope, which essentially means they made a movie of it, it just went out into the ether."

Kinescopes are the reason we have much of what survives of television from the 1940s. In 1951, a company owned by Bing Crosby introduced the first magnetic video recordings, a format soon adopted throughout the industry. At about the same time, *I Love Lucy* star and executive producer Desi Arnaz opted to shoot his series on conventional film, a practice later picked up by other producers and one that explains why the reruns still look so good. But when kinescopes (created by placing a motion picture camera in front of a television monitor and recording the image off the monitor's screen) were the only game in town, they weren't always used because of cost concerns. "It was expensive to put a kinescope on; generally you did that only for the sake of the advertiser, who wanted evidence that their commercial messages had been properly played," said Thompson. "They were also used sometimes for time-delay broadcasts to the west coast."

What has been lost as a result? Countless news broadcasts; Steve Allen's early shows, including *The Tonight Show*; hundreds of episodes of TV's first daytime dramas; the first television address from the White House, delivered by President Harry S. Truman; *Actor's Studio*, a live anthology series featuring performances from Kim Hunter, Julie Harris, Jessica Tandy, and Marlon Brando; *Time to Get Ready*, Ernie Kovacs' first television series; Don Larsen's perfect game in the World Series; and the first network coverage of a National Football League Championship Game, a 1951 contest between the Los Angeles Rams and the Cleveland Browns. Even the very first commercial television broadcast, chronicling the opening of the 1939 World's Fair with David Sarnoff and President Franklin D. Roosevelt, no longer exists.

"In the 1950s things started to change, but then economics kicked in," Thompson said. "You've got limited space in facilities, and all this stuff stacked up. In some cases tapes were re-recorded over, in others they simply had to clear out a room. People didn't even know what they were destroying. There was no sense of any value there."

Thompson drew a comparison with the way we treat our email today. "Very few people archive the emails they get. Somebody is going to write a great novel, and 200 years from now people will want to study their lives. (But) instead of writing letters during their formative period that can be studied in museums, they're writing emails. The future great people of the world are casually deleting their correspondence. Television back then was like email. It was useful, people liked it and needed it, but nobody had the sense that this was history."

Ah, you say, but what about reruns? Didn't the networks see any value in running these programs again? No they did not, because back then the concept of the rerun was as alien as the concept of pay-per-view Jello wrestling. With a few prominent exceptions, such as *I Love Lucy*, the belief was that once a program aired, why would anyone want to see it a second time?

"Before we kicked into the notion of a regular TV season, and a summer season of reruns, television played new episodes for 39 weeks, followed by a 13 week replacement series over the summer. There were no reruns," Thompson explained. "TV was perceived as a disposable art form. It played once, it filled the schedule. Nobody imagined that someday someone would want to study this stuff, that people would write histories about it."

That perception was slower to change than perhaps it should have been, which is why we continued to lose shows into the 1960s. Fans of the long-running British science fiction series *Dr. Who* still hope that several missing episodes will be discovered in a vault in one of the 80 countries where the show aired; *Open End*, David Susskind's 1958–1966 talk series, has been almost completely lost, including such episodes as "The Young Giants" with directors John Frankenheimer and Sidney Lumet, and "Television Tempest" with Ernie Kovacs, Rod Serling and Sheldon Leonard. Super Bowl I, played on January 15, 1967 between the Green Bay Packers and Kansas City

Chiefs, was recorded by two networks and subsequently erased by both of them, which seems astonishing given the prestige surrounding the event today.

"Now we have a Museum of TV and Radio, and we think anything that plays on television has a value because it played on TV in the first place," Thompson said. In some ways, that concept is just as insane as destroying shows, but at least this way we don't take any chances.

68
FAWLTIER TOWERS

Amanda's
ABC, FEBRUARY 10–MAY 26, 1983

Payne
CBS, MARCH 15–APRIL 28, 1999

British sitcoms have inspired several successful American shows, including some of the most fondly remembered of the classic TV era. *All in the Family* was an adaptation of a British series called *'Til Death Do Us Part*; *Three's Company* was inspired by the similarly saucy *Man about the House*; and *Sanford and Son* took its working class themes from the original *Steptoe and Son*.

In each case, American audiences were unfamiliar with the original series. Thus, the networks could adapt freely, and change what they wished in concept and characters with no one the wiser.

By the 1970s a few British series had crossed the pond courtesy of PBS, most notably *Monty Python's Flying Circus* and *Fawlty Towers*. The latter has been celebrated as one of the masterpieces of the sitcom format, and there are those who would tell you there has never been a funnier show on television. John Cleese starred as Basil Fawlty, the manic, social-climbing owner of a seaside inn. Basil's explosive temper is regularly exercised on his guests and the cowering Spanish bellman, Manuel (Andrew Sachs), but retreats at the sight of his wife Sybil (Prunella Scales). Polly, the maid (Connie Booth, Cleese's wife and collaborator at the time) was the only level-headed employee on staff.

Only twelve episodes were made, but they became such a pledge drive staple for decades that generations of viewers can still quote favorite scenes. Every aspect of *Fawlty Towers* was so expertly crafted that it's impossible to imagine these characters and stories being done any better. But that didn't stop the American networks from trying. Twice.

In *Amanda's*, Bea Arthur played Amanda Cartwright, acerbic owner of an oceanside hotel. "It looked like a very hot property," recalled Rick Hurst, who played Earl

It takes more than a bumbling bellhop to follow Fawlty Towers, *as Tony Rosato (left) and Beatrice Arthur discovered in* Amanda's.

Nash, the fast-talking chef. "I was a big fan of *Fawlty Towers*; it was hysterical, and I was so excited when I heard they were redoing it. With Bea Arthur as the star, I thought it was going to run for seven years."

Though *Amanda's* adapted several *Fawlty Towers* scripts, they took multiple liberties with the material, the most obvious being a gender switch in the main character. "That was part of our undoing," Hurst admits. "I figured if anyone could pull it off, Bea probably could, but she wasn't as physically comedic, not nearly as manic; Cleese was a master at that. He can play five different kinds of insanity and befuddlement."

If viewers had been unfamiliar with *Fawlty Towers*, *Amanda's* might have found an audience. But the series couldn't avoid comparison, or paling next to the brilliance of the original. It's biggest misstep was not the casting of Bea Arthur, but the introduction of stereotypical greedy banker Mr. Mundy (Keene Curtis), who was always threatening to foreclose on the property, and inevitably caused the quick-tempered Amanda to appear more sympathetic. Basil Fawlty needed no outside enemies, as he was gifted at creating his own disasters.

"I didn't know what the audience reaction would be, but I thought the show itself could be done as well as the one in England," said Hurst. The audience disagreed, and *Amanda's* closed in 1983 after just eight episodes.

Those who don't remember history are doomed to repeat it, and 16 years later CBS unveiled *Payne*, starring John Larroquette as—no kidding—Royle Payne. This time an attempt was made to stay closer to the source material, right down to the set design; Payne's Whispering Pines, a Victorian inn on the northern California coast, had the same floor plan as its British counterpart.

Larroquette had Cleese's height and imposing stare, and his Emmy-winning work on *Night Court* proved he could play smarmy and unctuous. JoBeth Williams played his wife Connie, Rick Batalla portrayed the incompetent foreign-born bellhop and Julie Benz (later of *Buffy the Vampire Slayer*) played a ditzier variation on the Connie Booth role as chambermaid Breeze O'Rourke.

When writer/executive producers Judd Pillot and John Peaslee appeared on the BBC, they were told that an American adaptation of *Fawlty Towers* was like "hawking the crown jewels in a Baghdad bazaar." "Our initial instinct was to stay very close to *Fawlty*," they once said of their pilot script, "to prove that we weren't afraid of it, and that we could do it."

Ultimately, however, they failed after just nine episodes for the same reasons *Amanda's* did—an untouchable predecessor and an inability to build a series around an uncompromisingly obnoxious main character. Amanda Cartwright and Royle Payne were loud and gruff, but deep down you felt their hearts were in the right place. That was not the case with Basil Fawlty, a irredeemable, unapologetic tyrant who audiences loved anyway. The British have a knack for characters like this, but nervous American programming executives can't resist softening their rough edges. Now you know why that U.S. take on *Absolutely Fabulous*, which was to star Carrie Fisher and Barbara Carrera, didn't clear the development stage in 2001.

67

THE DEVIL MADE HER DO IT

Days of Our Lives
NBC, NOVEMBER 1994–JULY 1995

Dark Shadows set the standard for supernatural soap operas, but every so often another soap will take a break from love in the afternoon and wander into creature feature territory, with varying results. *Days of Our Lives* has been set in Salem since the show premiered in 1965, but it wasn't until 1994 that they acknowledged the legacy of their town as a battleground for good and evil, with a controversial story-line that polarized fans.

At its center was Dr. Marlena Evans, played by Deidre Hall. One of daytime's loveliest and classiest stars, Hall had maintained her grace while guiding the character through multiple marriages, affairs, murder mysteries and even a crazed twin sister storyline. But would she survive with dignity intact when Satan came to Salem? Nope.

Marlena's troubles began when the villainous Stefano DiMera became infatuated with the comely doctor. He fed her mind-altering drugs and took her out each night, and by morning Marlena wasn't sure if what she had done was fact or fantasy. The drugs weakened her system, allowing for an infection by something even more sinister. As her health deteriorated, other strange events occurred throughout Salem; a Christmas tree burst into flame; Father Francis, the local priest, received a strange wooden box in the mail, containing ancient scrolls. Another character, Kristen, was found naked and handcuffed to the church altar, with pentagrams painted on her back.

The newspapers attributed these acts to an entity called "The Desecrator," but no one was certain if they were dealing with a human madman or something far more dangerous. One night, the Desecrator appeared as a beast in Marlena's bedroom and took control of her body. Between demonic possession and Stefano's obsession with

65

making Marlena his "Queen of the Night," the poor doctor was busier after dark than she was during office hours.

At times she could still pass for normal, but when she was alone, her eyes grew larger and glowed a brilliant green, as if she were about to turn into the Incredible Hulk. In her demon state, Marlena had schizophrenic conversations with herself, in which her normal voice was replaced by one that sounded like Marvin the Martian. Her face contorted into evil twisted torment, but this being the soaps she never had a hair out of place. Deidre Hall fearlessly threw herself into the odd dual role, grunting and barking with fanatical fury, even as she must have wondered how this stuff was going over with the *Days of Our Lives* faithful.

After she had set churches on fire, displayed superhuman strength, and shown up naked at the wedding of daytime supercouple Bo and Billie, District Attorney Pat Hamilton finally made the connection between Marlena and the Desecrator. They were still wary of the 'S' word, as in Satan, perhaps out of concern for offending some viewers.

The doctor spent long stretches at the police station and the hospital, but her struggles continued for months. Any time a character would find a means to help, Marlena's devil would reemerge to deal with them. Father Francis was rendered unable to communicate, but managed to get the one-word message "succubus" to another priest. Meanwhile, the Desecrator figured out that his green glowing eyes were a dead giveaway, and bought a pair of contact lenses! Satan comes to Lenscrafters, weekdays on NBC.

Father Francis made several attempts to help Marlena, while three religious scholars arrived in Salem to translate the scrolls that had turned up months earlier. They discovered that a terrific evil was about to be unleashed on the town, which wasn't news to anybody by that time. Still, Satan didn't like his plans being discussed, and turned Marlena into a panther to hunt down the scholars.

After further skirmishes between the devil and the people of Salem, Father Francis convinced the local bishop that an exorcism was the only way to rid Marlena of the Desecrator, and rescue the town from Satan's clutches. Marlena agreed to the ritual, though her life would be placed at risk. On the fateful day, Satan conjured a strong wind to keep the participants out of Marlena's bedroom, and tormented the priest and the witnesses with nightmare images. But eventually they persevered.

Marlena went into cardiac arrest as the demon was driven from her body, and died. But Father Francis explained that when you're dealing with Satan, things aren't always what they seem. John, Marlena's boyfriend, visited her body in the morgue and discovered she was still alive; unfortunately, so was the Desecrator. He grabbed John by the throat, and jumped into his body, hoping to begin a new reign of terror. Marlena, alive and finally free from demonic possession, turned up at her own memorial service, and eventually Satan was dispatched for good.

Days of Our Lives didn't do well at the Daytime Emmys that year, and when a clip of the series was shown at the awards ceremony, in which a possessed Marlena floated over her bed, there was muffled snickering in the audience of soap stars and creative talent. Some viewers embraced the story arc, and coverage of the events in *Soap Opera Digest* and the mainstream press probably attracted a few new viewers. But it's been ten years and Satan hasn't showed his green eyes in Salem again, a sign that perhaps the risk of revisiting such stories may not be worth the reward.

66
PILL-POPPING SUPERHEROES SIDELINED

Roger Ramjet
SYNDICATED, 1965–1968

Underdog
SYNDICATED, 1964–1973

As long as there have been cartoons, there have been debates about the effect cartoons have on young minds. If the Road Runner drops an anvil on Wile E. Coyote, is a boy more likely to drop an anvil on his little sister? And where would he get an anvil anyway?

To some, the links between television viewing and behavior are indisputable; to others, the very idea seems nonsensical. As usual, the truth probably falls somewhere in the middle. But sometimes the self-proclaimed protectors of young minds go too far.

Take the Reverend Donald Wildmon, grand poobah of the American Family Association, who could find deviant behavior in the Small World ride at Disneyland. In 1987, Wildmon accused Mighty Mouse of snorting cocaine in Ralph Bakshi's *Mighty Mouse: The New Adventures*. The scene depicted Mighty Mouse smelling a flower, but Wildmon claimed that, when viewed in slow motion and extreme close-up (which of course is the way every child watches cartoons) a cloud of what might be dust or powder was visible; thus, the Mouse had a habit, and was teaching kids that cocaine will get you higher than Sugar Smacks.

When confronted with this foolishness, many Saturday morning fans recalled two earlier, equally silly instances that kept two very good shows off television for a long time. *Underdog*, which debuted in 1964, featured Wally Cox as the voice of the title super-pup, who always spoke in rhyming couplets and disguised his heroic identity in the guise of a mild-mannered shoeshine boy. Though crudely drawn the show was cleverly written and featured a marvelous collection of characters, from villains Simon Bar Sinister and Riff Raff to TV reporter Sweet Polly Purebred.

Underdog's costume, which looked like baggy red and blue pajamas, also came with a special ring that contained a powerful vitamin pill. When our hero was in jeopardy, he opened the compartment, swallowed the pill and leaped back into the fray.

More than 100 *Underdog* adventures played in syndication throughout the country, but after their initial run they were rarely broadcast. Occasionally an episode would pop up on a local station, but any scenes of Underdog swallowing his vitamin were deleted. When Nickelodeon aired the series in the early 1990s, it was the first time the episodes were broadcast uncut for two decades.

Underdog was also victimized by a rights dispute that kept all but 20 shows out of circulation, so while the pill-popping scenes certainly contributed to its problems, there were other factors at work as well. The same cannot be said for *Roger Ramjet*, another hilarious superhero parody that has never received the accolades it deserved.

The show is a benchmark for today's top animators, including *Simpsons* creator Matt Groening and *Ren & Stimpy* creator John Kricfalusi, both of whom rank the adventures of the "All-American hero, daredevil and flying fool" alongside the Jay Ward stable in the quality of its writing, and its capacity to entertain children and adults on completely different levels. But until Cartoon Network began airing *Roger Ramjet* in the late 1990s, he had been missing in action for decades.

The reason? Roger's secret weapon was a Proton Energy Pill, which gave him the strength of 20 atom bombs for a period of 20 seconds. "The Proton Pill was designed as a 60s update of Popeye's spinach," said Blake Synder, son of Roger's creator, Ken Snyder. "Originally it was Roger who had invented the pill himself, but Gary Owens' brilliant personification of Roger made him a much less scientific type and much more feckless."

When the series first aired in the early to mid-60s, no one said anything about the source of Ramjet's superpowers. "Pill awareness and parental control of TV for kids was not as stressed—that's one reason why so much of early 60s TV like *Bullwinkle*, *Roger*, and even some of the puns and inside jokes of Hanna-Barbera were so much funnier," Snyder said. "It wasn't until the end of the decade when drugs became a mainstream topic that anyone noticed Roger and his innocent little Proton Energy Pill."

Parents and teachers took a closer look at kids' TV, and lobbied for shows that emphasized education as well as entertainment. Ken Synder became one of the creators of *Sesame Street* and *The Big Blue Marble*, but his first television triumph was caught in the backlash. "Roger was rejected because many thought 'seeing a hero pop a pill to solve his problems' would be imitated by kids who would grab for mom's Halcyon by mistake," said Blake Snyder. "You'll note no one every objected to Super Chicken drinking a martini to gain his super powers, but who's counting?"

"It wasn't until shows like *Ren & Stimpy* brought some much needed anarchy back to kids' programing that the 156 episodes of *Roger Ramjet* began to play again on U.S. airwaves. Keep in mind, Roger was playing worldwide unabated for 40 years," Snyder noted. "It was only in the United States that there was an interruption."

Snyder can laugh about the situation now, but still feels the objections were ridiculous. "I think it's silly. Kids overall know the difference between reality and fantasy. My father felt the same. You could never meet a children's TV producer more sensitive to the kids in the audience and their hopes and dreams than my father. Roger was fun. The pill was fun."

Blake Snyder is developing a revival of *Roger Ramjet*, and reveals that the once-controversial pill will be a key element. "I like the idea of Roger discovering all these years later that the Proton Energy Pill was a placebo—part of a positive thinking program developed by Pentagon scientists—and that Roger had the ability all along without the pill. That's my ideal solution. And with any luck that's how we'll handle it."

65
ONE SPINOFF TOO MANY

Joanie Loves Chachi
ABC, MARCH 23, 1982–SEPTEMBER 13, 1983

"You don't build a TV show around Chachi."
—HENRY ROLLINS, *I Love the '80s*

Joanie Loves Chachi is what happens when television networks refuse to let go of a good idea.

ABC's *Happy Days* was a top-five hit for much of its run, and in Fonzie (Henry Winkler) it introduced a character as iconic as any to emerge from a sitcom. The series inspired two equally successful spinoffs in *Laverne & Shirley* and *Mork & Mindy*, and soldiered on even after the departure of Ron Howard. Familiar characters were replaced with the likes of Roger Phillips, K.C., Flip, and Jenny Piccalo, in a desperate attempt to keep the money flowing.

The term "jumping the shark" was inspired by the series' painful decline, a reference to the three-episode story arc set in Los Angeles that opened the 1977 season, in which Fonzie thwarts the arrogant California Kid by waterskiing over a live shark. However, the show still had its full cast that season and had only just started to overstay its welcome. Some fans opt instead for the "black t-shirt" theory, which states that *Happy Days* tanked when Fonzie switched from a white t-shirt to a black t-shirt.

Regardless, ABC's reluctance to allow *Happy Days* to bow out gracefully resulted in Fonzie serving as Dean of a boys vocational school, and one last attempt at a spinoff featuring Joanie "Shortcake" Cunningham (Erin Moran), who got maybe one storyline a year in the show's heyday, and the Fonz's cousin Chachi Arcola (Scott Baio), who divided *Happy Days* fans between the squealing teenage girls who loved him, and everyone else who wanted him on the next bus out of Milwaukee.

Joanie Loves Chachi was a show hatched not in Programming but Marketing: take two established characters, add a standard wacky supporting cast and another familiar face in Al Molinaro, who played Arnold's owner Al Delvecchio. Finally, take advantage of Scott Baio's teen idol status and make him a singer, never mind the fact that he can't sing.

In the pilot, Al has married Chachi's mother, Louisa (Ellen Travolta) and moved to Chicago to open a new restaurant. Chachi lives with mom and stepdad while he tries to launch a music career. Louisa's blowhard brother Rico (Art Metrano) acts as Chachi's agent. Rico's erroneous referrals to Al as "Sal" and "Cal" typify the humor level in the first episode, though his lapses prompt screams of hilarity from the over-enthusiastic laugh track.

Joanie arrives for a surprise visit and finds Chachi surrounded by female admirers after his singing debut in Al's restaurant. When she joins him on stage the following night, she wears a provocative outfit that draws whistles and party invitations from the guys in the crowd, thus teaching Chachi a lesson about flirting after a show.

Joanie and Chachi sang at least once in each episode, not counting the show's theme, "You Look At Me," a sappy ballad performed over the opening credits that must have cost them viewers before the episodes even began. Erin Moran can carry a tune at least as well as Lynda Carter, but Baio's off-key warbling delivers a fierce assault on the eardrums.

Tom Bosley, Marion Ross, and Henry Winkler all dropped in to reprise their *Happy Days* roles during the show's 17-episode run, and the merchandising machine churned out *Joanie Loves Chachi* books, guitars, tambourines, and microphones. But after encouraging ratings as a midseason replacement, the series was canceled after being trounced by *The A-Team* in 1982, sending Moran and Baio scurrying back to *Happy Days* for that show's final two seasons.

It's not that *Joanie Loves Chachi* was measurably worse than a hundred other short-lived sitcoms, but it seemed worse because it took characters that had already surpassed their expiration dates in our affections and cast them adrift in a thankless setting. Sure, we remember Joanie's first date with Fonzie's nephew Spike on *Happy Days*, the crush she had on Potsie and the time she almost ran off to sing backup for Leather Tuscadero, but our fondness for Shortcake only extends so far. Whatever reaction ABC hoped would greet this new chapter in the lives of Joanie and Chachi, the one they got was "Why are you still on my television?"

Joanie (Erin Moran) and Chachi (Scott Baio) chat with the winner of their "Most Intelligent Viewer" competition.

An odd postscript to the series' brief history is its status as the highest-rated American program in the history of Korean TV, supposedly because "Chachi" is Korean for "penis." Thus, the title translates as *Joanie Loves . . .* well, no wonder people tuned in.

64

MADONNA BURNS A CROSS FOR PEPSI

"Like a Prayer" music video
MTV, March 3, 1989

Before MTV contaminated both movies and TV shows with its stylistic excesses, the network's influence had already manifested itself in television commercials. Since music videos are really just ads for songs and artists, it was inevitable that someone would use the same sparkle and flash format to sell something else.

First to try were Coca-Cola and Pepsi, two soft drink giants engaged in a never-ending battle for the hearts and minds of America's youth. The "Cola Wars" reached new heights of intensity in the 1980s, as both companies capitalized on MTV's popularity with music video commercials, featuring the top recording stars of the day. Pepsi recruited Michael Jackson, Tina Turner, and Lionel Richie; Coke countered with Sting, Whitney Houston, George Michael, and Cyndi Lauper.

On January 25, 1989, Pepsi scored a coup when it signed Madonna to a one-year, $5 million endorsement contract. The announcement was front-page news the next day: Madonna would appear in a series of commercials, and Pepsi would sponsor her next tour. But the company was so determined to recruit another superstar that it overlooked Madonna's affection—some would say obsession—for stirring up controversy. Had they been familiar with the Material Girl's history, Pepsi would have realized she wouldn't be content to just sell the product; she would make certain her campaign induced yet another media event with herself at the center. What happened as a result was not so much a "What were they thinking" as a "What did they expect?"

During the Grammy Awards telecast on February 22, a commercial aired announcing that the world premiere of Madonna's Pepsi ad was scheduled for March 2, during *The Cosby Show* (yes, a commercial for a commercial), to be followed one day later by the MTV debut of her new music video, *Like a Prayer*.

At first, Madonna balked at dancing in the ad, and she refused to change any lyrics in her songs to mention Pepsi. Joe Phytka, who had directed Michael Jackson's Pepsi spots, convinced her to perform, believing that dancing was one of the main attributes the public associated with Madonna (she was associated with other things as well, but you couldn't put those in a commercial).

The resulting two-minute clip, entitled "Make a Wish," opens with Madonna watching a home movie of her eighth birthday party; she changes places with the little girl on the screen, and while Madonna revisits her childhood, the girl tours Madonna's sumptuous home. A church choir plays "Like a Prayer," and Madonna joins them, while her young alter-ego finds her favorite doll, still in the adult Madonna's bedroom. The two then switch back to their original locations, and toast each other through the video screen with a Pepsi. "Make a wish," Madonna tells her eight year-old counterpart, and as the little girl blows out her birthday candles, the Pepsi logo appears with the slogan "A Generation Ahead."

The commercial aired in 40 countries to an estimated viewership of 250 million people. So far, so good. And then the "Like a Prayer" video debuted on MTV, in which the lingerie-garbed singer witnesses a murder, and flees into a church where she makes love on a pew to a black man who could be Jesus. As the choir takes up the melody, Madonna dances in a field of burning crosses and displays the stigmata—bloody wounds on her palms that symbolize the Crucifixion.

"The treatment for the video is a lot more controversial," Madonna explained. "It's probably going to touch a lot of nerves in a lot of people." The volatile mix of sex, violence, and religion touched off a firestorm of controversy, and Madonna was again front page news. Pepsi never asked to see the video before its premiere, though Roger Mosconi, senior creative director at BBDO Worldwide advertisement agency, remembers an early conversation with the star in which she asked, "Hey Roger, are you going to have the burning cross reflecting in the Pepsi can?" When Mosconi asked what she was talking about, Madonna smiled and said, "You'll see".

Like the swastika, a burning cross was a perfectly legitimate symbol that became so corrupted by its association with a hate group that it would be foolhardy to expect any reaction other than outrage to its display. But Madonna has always derived a perverse pleasure in baiting the nation's self-appointed defenders of virtue, and once again they couldn't resist giving her exactly what she desired.

First up was the Reverend Donald Wildmon and his American Family Association, who complained that the commercial "puts Madonna up as a clean, wholesome role model" while her video "ridicules Christianity." Neither of which were true, but common sense never stopped him from attempting to boycott something. Then Catholic groups from around the world also issued formal protests, culminating in a statement from the Pope that banned Madonna from appearing in Italy.

Pepsi attempted to differentiate the "Make a Wish" commercial from the "Like a Prayer" video in the public's mind, but once the Pope calls you out there's no going back. The company pulled the ad, and dropped its sponsorship of Madonna's tour. For her part, Madonna kept the $5 million advance from Pepsi, and watched as both "Like a Prayer" and the album of the same name topped the charts in thirty countries. Game, set, and match to the Material Girl.

You'd think Pepsi would learn their lesson, but in 2002 they released a commercial starring rap star Ludacris, the artist responsible for such immortal lyrics as "I'm DUI, hardly ever caught sober, and you about to get ran the f—— over. Grab the peels, cuz we robbin' tonight. Beat the s—— outta security. We startin' a fight." Pepsi pulled the ad after complaints from the usual suspects (as well as a few music lovers), and opted instead for a more wholesome pitchman: Ozzy Osbourne.

63
LOST AND FOUND

Land of the Lost
NBC, September 11, 1976

At 43 episodes, *Land of the Lost* was Sid and Marty Krofft's most successful daytime series. Given how often they've been rerun, some fans are still surprised to learn that most of their classics (*Pufnstuf, The Bugaloos, Lidsville*) ran for less than 20 shows.

As with every Krofft creation, *Land of the Lost* had a catchy theme song ("Marshall, Will, and Holly/On a routine expedition") and a trippy premise unlike anything on Saturday morning television. The Marshall family, Rick (Spencer Milligan), his son Will (Wesley Eure) and daughter Holly (Kathy Coleman) are caught in an earthquake during a rafting trip. Their craft is thrown off-course and plummets down a waterfall, into a strange land that time forgot. There they must survive amongst carnivorous dinosaurs, a malevolent race of bug-eyed reptiles called Sleestaks, and the apelike Pakuni tribe.

With its impressive stop-motion special effects and scripts from *Star Trek* veterans David Gerrold and Dorothy Fontana, *Land of the Lost* was a hit with both kids and their older siblings. There was an admirable attention to detail in creating the lost world, from its authentic dinosaur designs to the creation of an actual language for the Pakuni. For two years all was well, but when the series returned for its third season in 1976, the unthinkable had happened—someone had been found in the Land of the Lost.

"I hadn't even seen the show before I was cast. I had no idea what it was about," said Ron Harper, who played Uncle Jack after the departure of Spencer Milligan. "I cannot really say why they let Spencer Milligan go. I was told very little about it, which is understandable. They had to be very diplomatic. One always assumes it's one of two reasons—they were not pleased with his work, or they were not pleased with the amount of money he was making, or wanted to make. I don't know which it was."

Whatever the cause, the Kroffts were faced with an impossible dilemma. Having created a fictional world from which there was no escape, how do you remove one character, and replace him with another? When viewers tuned in to the season premiere, they saw Rick departing through one of the mysterious 'pylon' devices introduced in an earlier episode. At the exact same instant, Uncle Jack arrived in search of his lost family.

"It was a simple transition for the children," Harper believes. "My brother, niece and nephew had disappeared and I had to find them. So I was trying to trace their route, and I'm in a canoe, go over a waterfall and I'm dropped into the Land of the Lost." Though it looked as if Milligan had appeared in that episode, Harper reveals that wasn't the case. "When they made the change our producer, Jon Kubichan, did the shot. He put on a black wig and khaki clothes, and you saw him in the pylon from the back. He was tinkering with it, something went wrong and poof, he disappeared."

Though most viewers accepted the switch and praised Harper's performance, the confirmation of an escape route undercut the drama of the Marshalls' situation. And the kids didn't seem all that upset about being separated from their father. "We can't bring dad back, and we can't follow him," Will tells Holly, neither showing much emotion. And the coincidence of dad getting sucked into a portal just as Uncle Jack dropped in from the waterfall was a stretch even for the series' youngest fans. It was explained that because of the delicate balance in this alternate universe, no one could leave without someone else entering, but that only further taxed the suspension of disbelief.

Even the show's theme song had to be altered as a result, the familiar lines changed to "Will and Holly Marshall, as the earth beneath them trembled/Lost their father through the door of time/Uncle Jack went searching and found those kids at last/And now they're looking for a way to escape." No one remembers that version.

But even if *Land of the Lost* wasn't as scary after the discovery of an exit, it remains one of the most imaginative children's shows ever conceived. "I had just come off of doing the short-lived *Planet of the Apes* series," Harper recalls. "I thought those stories were rather boring, and apparently the audience did too. So I was delighted to be cast on *Land of the Lost*. The stories were infinitely better. I've done six series (five of which ran in prime time) and probably I am still known best from that show."

62
LENDING A HAND

WWF Raw
USA Network, February 28, 2000

Between 1949 and 1951, it was possible to watch professional wrestling on television six nights a week. Broadcasting matches from New York's Jamaica Arena or the Marigold Garden in Chicago was cheap programming for the networks, and transformed wrestlers into household names. When pre-match interviews became an integral part of the presentation, wrestlers who could "work the microphone" found themselves booked in main events regardless of their grappling skills.

George Wagner, a.k.a Gorgeous George, became the first superstar of the television era by establishing a character that fans either loved or hated. He'd prance to the ring while a formally-dressed valet spread rose petals at his feet and sprayed the ring with perfume. Such flamboyant antics are still evident in the sport 50 years later, as the popularity of professional wrestling rises and falls on the personalities of its featured characters.

The task of inventing personas for its athletes falls to the promoters, who don't always strike gold the first time out. The Rock began his career as a guy named Flex Cavana; Stone Cold Steve Austin once wrestled as The Ringmaster. Some wrestlers try out several characters before finding one the public notices, and sometimes the ones that fail are just as memorable, though not for the same reasons.

R.D. Reynolds launched the Wrestlecrap web site on April 1, 2000 to salute the goofy characters and storylines created by the various wrestling federations over the years. The site inspired a book of the same name, published in 2003. Reynolds' most frequent supplier of Wrestlecrap material is World Wrestling Entertainment chairman Vince McMahon, for whom nothing is apparently too outrageous.

One of the worst victims of McMahon's fevered imagination was Mark Henry. "Mark Henry was an Olympic weightlifter, who had a legitimate claim as the world's strongest man. He was an incredible power lifter," Reynolds explained. "The WWF signed him to a ten-year deal, which is unheard of. They were desperate to get this guy because they thought he had charisma, but he knew nothing about wrestling. They figured we'll sign him now, and train him later."

After nearly a year the company saw that Henry wasn't developing the way they wished, so they gave the African-American strongman a new persona—Sexual Chocolate, a guy with an unquenchable sexual appetite. "They would do all kinds of crazy stuff. There were skits with a sex therapist, where he said he lost his virginity at age six to his sister," Reyonlds remembers. "And then they paired him up with Mae Young."

Mae Young, then 78 years old, had been a prominent wrestler herself in the 1940s. "She was brought back by the WWE as a stereotypical drunk, horny grandma. She would smoke cigars, and tell the crowd 'I know everyone came here to see my puppies (breasts)'. During one pay-per-view telecast she went topless. "It's something you never want to see," Reynolds recalled with horror.

So who else but Mae Young would be cast as the only woman able to satisfy Henry's insatiable desire? Between wrestling matches on *WWF Raw*, viewers were treated to scenes of the lust-filled couple in bed, supposedly just after they had consummated their passion.

"There was a feeling from a lot of people that the WWF was trying to get out of Henry's ten-year deal any way they could, and one way was to do things to him from a storyline perspective that he would just say 'Forget this, I'm not kissing an 80-year-old woman!' But to his credit he took it all in stride and happily cashed his checks," Reynolds said.

As for Young, she had already proven herself to be up for anything. The septuagenarian sex kitten had stripped in a bachelor party skit, and been bodyslammed through tables by wrestlers in their prime. She took some bumps in the ring that guys like Hulk Hogan wouldn't suffer, which is either admirable or disturbing depending on one's perspective.

After several on-screen trysts, Mae Young announced she was pregnant. This despite an interview in which she was asked when she had her last period, and she replied "1957." And just as it appeared the story could not get more bizarre, she went into labor after a three-month gestation period.

"Someone within the company, speaking under the condition of anonymity, told me they were trying to figure out what she would give birth to," Reynolds recalls. Vince McMahon suggested something so disgusting that the USA Network refused to air it, so no one knew how to pay off the story. "They had a prop department, and Vince reportedly went back to find something else for her. He found this plastic hand, and thought that would be the greatest idea ever." And on a now famous episode of *Raw*, Mae Young gave birth to a severed hand covered in slime. "People who saw it will never forget it, and that is absolutely not a compliment," Reynolds said.

The obvious question here is "What were they hoping to accomplish with this storyline?" "A lot of times the WWE will present something that is outlandish for the mass media, hoping someone somewhere will be so appalled that it will make the news," according to Reynolds. "In 2002 they had the gay wedding of two wrestlers named Billy and Chuck, and the ratings spiked. They tried a necrophilia storyline after that, and no one covered it."

The Mark Henry-Mae Young story suffered a similar fate, as the world outside wrestling failed to take notice of McMahon's romantic geek show. Henry remains with the company, still serving his ten-year sentence, while ratings for WWE shows have plummeted to historic lows. "There was a time when you had to watch *Monday Night Raw* because you never knew what was going to happen," said Reynolds. But wrestling fans have grown weary of stunts, and hope the company will really shock the masses by presenting something rarely seen in the WWE these days—a good wrestling match.

61
DULL SHADOWS

Dark Shadows
ABC, NOVEMBER 18, 1969–MARCH 6, 1970

General Hospital's Luke and Laura may have snagged a *Newsweek* cover and a guest appearance from Elizabeth Taylor, but no daytime drama can claim a more loyal, enduring fan following than *Dark Shadows*. Though its five-year run (1966–1971) is minimal by soap opera standards where success is measured in decades, its characters and stories have been revived in numerous incarnations ever since, and have influenced other Gothic soaps such as *Passions* and *Port Charles*.

Dark Shadows remains the only soap to be adapted into a motion picture (twice), an off-Broadway play and a primetime television series. Its entire run, more than 1,200 episodes, has been released on homevideo, and more than 35 years after its debut attendance continues to rise at the annual Dark Shadows Festival.

"It's hard for me to understand myself why it's still so popular," says Marie Wallace, who played three characters on the show. "At the 2003 Festival, 60 percent of the attendees were new, and most of them were really young. They just started watching the Sci-Fi Channel reruns and buying the DVDs. That amazed me, but it just keeps going."

The reasons for its popularity are many and varied, but the most obvious is the series' unique blend of romantic melodrama and every horror film ever released. The character of Barnabas Collins, a 240-year-old vampire, made an unlikely sex symbol out of 43-year-old Shakespearian actor Jonathan Frid, who suddenly found himself sharing the cover of *Tiger Beat* alongside Davy Jones and Bobby Sherman.

The show is also celebrated for its bloopers and mishaps, an unfortunate result of a rigorous shooting schedule. Like *Star Trek, Doctor Who,* and other sixties cult shows with a fantasy angle, the special effects are woeful by today's standards, but the quality of writing and performance transcended the limitations of the budget. And when it was right, *Dark Shadows* was as good as anything on television.

After stumbling out of the gate as a standard soap in 1966, the series hit upon its supernatural hook out of desperation, and by 1969 had become ABC's more popular daytime drama. The talented cast, particularly Frid, Kathryn Leigh Scott, Nancy Barrett, and Lara Parker, developed into a seasoned stock company, displaying their versatility in several different roles in stories set at various points in history. But after a triumphant extended flashback from 1897, *Dark Shadows* gambled on a new kind of supernatural plot, that turned out to be the beginning of the end.

As Barnabas Collins reemerges in present-day Collinsport, Maine, he falls under the spell of Oberon and Haza, two mysterious hooded figures called the Leviathans. Inspired by the H.P. Lovecraft story *Leviathan People*, the story has Barnabas transporting a wooden box from the past to the present, which carries the essence of the supreme Leviathan, that will open the doorway to earth for their ancient race to rule the world.

Unaware of its contents, Barnabas leaves the box at an antique store owned by Megan Todd, played by Marie Wallace, and her husband, Phillip. "The first scripts were very straight, and I certainly didn't know where it was heading," Wallace recalled. "That was my first normal character on *DS*, but then it started to get very wild, even wilder than the things I had done before." That's saying something—Wallace's previous two *DS* characters were Eve, a 'Bride of Frankenstein'-like creature, and Jenny Collins, a violent crazy woman who imagined herself the mother of two dolls.

The Todds take possession of the box, and the box takes possession of them— before long they find themselves acting as parents to a succession of rapidly aging children, each more annoying than the last, all of whom represent maturing incarnations of the Leviathan leader. Meanwhile, confused viewers were treated to endless scenes of the door to a room in the Todds' attic, from which was heard the sound of heavy breathing. "I followed where my own character was going, but the whole storyline? I never got the whole storyline," Wallace admits. "People still ask me what was in the box, and I tell them 'I don't know.'"

The story was dull, was poorly-paced even by soap standards, and relegated many of the series' most popular characters to the sidelines, including the werewolf Quentin played by David Selby, and Lara Parker's sexy sorceress Angelique. As for Oberon and Haza, they were forgotten as the Leviathan leader grew into Jeb Hawkes (Chris Pennock) who was too distracted by pretty Carolyn Stoddard (Nancy Barrett) to worry about taking over the world. The story took several confusing turns before ending as an afterthought, when Jeb destroys the Leviathan altar.

Having already cribbed from *Frankenstein, Dracula, The Wolfman, The Turn of the Screw*, and *The Picture of Dorian Gray*, it was inevitable that *DS* would have to move beyond traditional horror fare to avoid repeating itself. But its initial foray into science fiction would prove fatal. The series managed a few late bursts of creativity after the Leviathan arc, including a unique parallel time story, but the ratings never recovered. One year later *Dark Shadows* was cancelled, though thankfully it never really went away.

60
GOODBYE ARSENIO, HELLO…WILTON NORTH?

The Wilton-North Report
FOX, DECEMBER 11, 1987–JANUARY 8, 1988

In the beginning there was Joan Rivers and *The Late Show*, the FOX network's first contender in the late-night talk show wars. In 1986, the network lured Rivers away from her permanent guest host gig on Johnny Carson's *Tonight Show*, causing a rift between the two comedians that never mended. As it turned out, the abrasive Rivers was better handled in smaller doses, and a nightly serving of Elizabeth Taylor jokes proved more than most viewers desired.

So Rivers left her show after seven months of declining ratings, and was replaced by a rotating lineup of guest hosts, including Robert Townsend, Arsenio Hall, and Suzanne Somers. Hall emerged best from the field, more from his sheer likability than any particular talent he had at comedy or celebrity interviews. Though no official announcement was made, Hall was at some point made the new permanent host of *The Late Show*, and a buzz was building that the young comic just might be the next big thing.

But just as Hall seemed destined to actually put a small dent in *The Tonight Show*'s decades-old dominance, FOX canceled *The Late Show*, and introduced a new series with the odd name of *The Wilton-North Report*. The timing could not be worse, and neither could the new series, which lasted just four weeks.

"I want this show to be unlike anything else that's ever been on television," said producer Barry Sand. "I want it to be controversial, opinionated, provocative. I don't care if it offends people. We'll open each show with a review of that day's news, using actual footage, and we'll comment on it. I want that segment to be funny and hard-hitting, with a really strong point of view. It will be the signature of the show."

Sound familiar? Turns out *Wilton-North* was envisioned as the first attempt at a formula John Stewart perfected in his Emmy-winning *The Daily Show*. But whatever its intentions, the series failed to follow through on its promise, and what it became even regular viewers had trouble describing.

They had no shortage of good intentions. With less than three months before its scheduled debut, ideas were developed for a dozen different segments: they'd put two people together with nothing in common (the first suggested pairing—Rodney Dangerfield and Margaret Thatcher); they'd also put together groups of people with a common denominator, such as Sonny Bono and Ike Turner. What they hadn't considered was that none of these people wanted to be on the show.

The hosts were not named Wilton and North, as might be surmised. After considering and rejecting such names as "Nightcap" and "Ha Ha Goodnight," they settled on *The Wilton-North Report* after one of the writers noticed a sign in his elevator in the Wilton North Building.

Among the contenders for the anchor desk were journalists Forrest Sawyer and Judd Rose, comedians Ellen DeGeneres, Rick Doukamin and Mark Blankfield, actress Marcia Strassman and MTV host Nina Blackwood. But Barry Sand hired Phil Cowan and Paul Robins, a pair of morning drive-time deejays from Sacramento with no television experience. The young comedy team looked good in suits and could deliver a dry punchline with the appropriate understatement, but their approach was not what the series' writers had in mind, resulting in an ongoing battle that would have forced resignations from somebody if the series hadn't been canceled so quickly.

When FOX executives saw an early run-through, they described the show as "unfunny, mean-spirited, and too often resorting to cheap jokes about people's looks." One week before the debut, the opening news segment which was to be *The Wilton-North Report*'s signature was cut, and Jodie Foster, scheduled as the show's first guest, canceled to go to Paris. Nothing was working, and it would only get worse on December 11, when the show finally aired.

The hosts introduced themselves: "I am Paul, I'm not as tall. He is Phil, he's got the big bill." Okay. Segments included an interview with a Pee Wee Herman doll, a report on an electric toaster possessed by the devil, and a visit to an alligator farm. "If it wasn't my show," Sand admitted, "I'd be laughing at me." Nothing, it seemed, would go right for *The Wilton-North Report*. When correspondent Jake Haselkorn filed a report on a high school basketball team in Wallace, South Carolina that had the worst record in history, the team won the next night.

The *Wilton-North Report* was canceled, and proved a career-ender for Sand, Cowan and Robins, none of whom worked in television again. In its place *The Late Show* returned, now hosted by comedian Ross Schaefer. Arsenio Hall built upon the momentum that began with his *Late Show* stint, appearing in *Coming to America* opposite Eddie Murphy and then hosting his own syndicated talk show, which landed him on the cover of *Time* magazine as the only man to launch a genuine challenge to Johnny Carson in 30 years.

After taking a few years to regroup, FOX reentered the talk show wars with *The Chevy Chase Show*, confident that nothing they'd broadcast could possibly be worse than *The Wilton-North Report*. Oh, well.

59

GO WEST, YOUNG GILLIGAN

Dusty's Trail
SYNDICATED, SEPTEMBER 11, 1973–MARCH 12, 1974

If they gave Emmy Awards for chutzpah, there'd be one with Sherwood Schwartz's name on it for bringing *Gilligan's Island* back as a Western, when scientists are still trying to figure out why the show worked in the first place. *Dusty's Trail* wasn't just an attempt to transfer the Gilligan character played by Bob Denver into a wild west setting; the series was an exact copy of its predecessor, from the personalities of the supporting characters to the broad slapstick plots that substituted cattle rustlers for headhunters. "It was the same show," said costar Lori Saunders, "just no coconuts."

"*Dusty's Trail* was an enormous creative blunder on my part," Schwartz admits. "And it taught me a very valuable lesson. Don't ever do the same thing twice, if you did it right the first time."

In place of desert island castaways, *Dusty's Trail* followed the adventures of a wayward wagon train, lost in the wilderness thanks to Dusty, its inept scout. The backstory is explained in the Gilligan-esque theme song ("Dusty's the reason for their plight/Thanks to him, nothing's right"). The "Skipper" role is handled by Forrest Tucker as Mr. Callahan, the wagonmaster. He doesn't refer to Dusty as his "little buddy," as that would be just plain stealing; he calls him his "little pal" instead.

The millionaire and his wife? That would be wealthy travelers Mr. and Mrs. Brookhaven, played by Ivor Francis and Lynn Wood. The Professor was Andy the engineer, played by Bill Cort. Sexy starlet Ginger Grant became sexy dance hall girl Lulu McQueen (Jeannine Riley), and Lori Saunders played Betsy, the sweet brunette schoolteacher inspired by Mary Ann. "Dawn Wells (Mary Ann) and I were friends, but I didn't associate the two characters as being the same. I just brought my own persona to the show," said Saunders, who had just come off a successful five-year run as Bobbie Jo Bradley on *Petticoat Junction*.

"Mr. Schwartz knew I was becoming available and offered me the part. It was interesting working with Jeannine Riley, as she was a former *Petticoat Junction* cast member." In an odd classic TV coincidence, Riley played Billie Jo Bradley for two years, opposite the original Bobbie Jo, Pat Woodell.

As with *Gilligan's Island*, some characters appeared in the same outfits in every episode, while others pulled countless costume changes from heaven-knows-where. The outdoor prairie sets, created on a double soundstage at 20th Century-Fox, were no more convincing than the desert island home of the USS Minnow crew. When the stagecoach had to be filmed in motion, the cast would pile into the wagon and the horses would gallop across the set and out into the studio backlot, then around in front of the stage and back in through the opposite doors. Bob Denver recalls seeing people from other shows turning out to watch the bizarre spectacle.

"I had always wanted to do a Western just so I could shoot myself in the foot," Denver said. "I got what I wanted. More than a few times." But one of the many problems with *Dusty's Trail* is that Denver was now pushing 40 and too old to play a man with a six-year-old's intelligence, who can still be referred to as "Kid." His clumsy, lovable buffoon act had become tired, and the scripts offered no new challenges or inspirations.

There were treasure map episodes, escaped outlaw episodes, and other stories that could be transferred to *Gilligan's Island* with no major revisions. You keep waiting for Tucker to take off his cowboy hat and bop Dusty on the head. One of the many low points has a pair of thieves demanding a date with the women, only to be met instead by Dusty and Callahan in drag. "What kind of scout wears women's clothes?" asks Dusty. "A girl scout," says Callahan. Cue the laugh track. Of course, the crooks don't know the difference, and actually try to molest a girl who looks like Forrest Tucker, until his wig falls off.

The cast turned out two shows a week, ending one episode at noon on Wednesday and beginning the next an hour later after lunch. "I was really ready for a rest, so I wasn't too sorry when the wagon train ended," Saunders admits.

Dusty's Trail lasted just 26 episodes, but three of its stories were repackaged for a theatrical release, under the title *The Wackiest Wagon Train in the West*, which didn't fare any better than the series. Not surprisingly, moviegoers resisted the urge to buy a ticket to watch something they had already rejected when it was free. "The show was so quick I really don't have many memories of it, the way *Petticoat Junction* still lives in my head," says Lori Saunders. "I did love the crew. Forrest Tucker was an interesting guy, full of life and loved to drink. I don't think he ever did a show sober, but he could handle it and God bless him."

"It ran briefly, was seen by few, and disappeared from the airwaves," said Denver. "It rests now in a vault somewhere, Peacefully, I hope." More recently, its rest has been interrupted by occasional airings on TV Land, and a video release of the first eight episodes. Full-fledged cult status remains elusive, but when the unsinkable Bob Denver is involved, anything is possible.

58

HEY, HEY, WE'RE REDUNDANT

The New Monkees
SYNDICATED, SEPTEMBER–DECEMBER 1987

In 1986, on a fateful sunny day in Malibu, Burt Rafelson called Steve Blauner and said just one word—"Monkees." "Leave me alone," Blauner replied. If only Rafelson had listened to this sage advice.

Rafelson and Bert Schneider had produced the original *Monkees* series, and felt the time was right for a revival; Blauner, the studio force behind the first show, had retired and preferred to stay that way, but Rafelson talked him into coming back as executive producer.

Granted, if there was ever a time for *The New Monkees*, it was 1987, after MTV pulled great ratings with a marathon of the 60s show, which led to the rerelease of the original Monkees albums. A reunion tour with Micky Dolenz, Davy Jones, and Peter Tork played to sold-out arenas around the world. At the Las Vegas Hilton, showroom staff reported that they hadn't seen that type of fan frenzy since Elvis last left the building.

Certainly it was a gamble, as the first *Monkees* had prospered beyond anyone's imagining and comparisons would be inevitable. In 1966 the series took home an Emmy for Best Comedy and the band's records sold millions, at one point racking up numbers even the Beatles couldn't match. To expect that type of success a second time is the longest of longshots in television, but that's what they said about *Star Trek: The Next Generation*.

Once again, the idea was to create a free-form comedy series with original music, that would appeal to the young generation. Blauner followed the same blueprint from 20 years earlier—rather than search for actors to fit preordained roles, he set out to find four unique actor/musicians, and would shape the show around their personalities. More than 5,000 audition tapes were gradually narrowed down to 500, then 200, and then 20.

When Schneider and Rafelson saw the tapes, they hit the ceiling. "Where's the counterculture"? Schneider asked. "I said, 'Burt, you're in a time warp,'" Blauner recalled. "Twenty years ago half the youth were alienated. Today, all these kids care about is when they're gonna get their first Camaro or their next Mercedes. There's maybe 5 percent out there who are counterculture, and they're slam dancing and wearing nipple rings."

So where the original Monkees scraped out a living in a ramshackle beach house, the New Monkees would reside in a mystical mansion with countless rooms and hallways. Some doors opened into a bowling alley, roller rink, and gymnasium, others were gateways to a desert, outerspace, and Ricky Ricardo's living room. In place of a kitchen, the Monkees had their own diner, with a waitress (Bess Motta) who came with the house. The surreal mansion was controlled by a sophisticated computer named Helen, who left the Pentagon to hang out with a rock band.

"The concept took me by complete surprise. I wasn't quite sure what they had in mind and how they expected it to go over," remembers Jamie Muntner, who played keyboards for the band and also worked on the series, describing his job as "second, second assistant director." "The ideas were pretty far-fetched, perhaps too much so."

Much would depend on the casting. Once Rafelson and Schneider acquiesced on finding yuppies rather than hippies, four suitable candidates emerged. Jared Chandler, a surfer dude with a James Dean fixation, whose bedroom, complete with its own grotto, looked like it was decorated by Frankie and Annette; Larry Saltis, a quiet polite guitarist with heavy-metal hair, was the youngest of the quartet. He had planned to start college at Kent State before flying to New York with his mom for an audition.

Dino Kovas, gruff and street-smart (which is tough to pull off in a fluffy pompadour), played in a number of bands in his native Dearborn, Michigan, but was delivering pizzas when Steve Blauner called. Marty Ross, a bit old for this sort of thing at age 28, was also a veteran of several bands, including The Wigs.

While rehearsing for the series, the new Monkees also headed into the recording studio to lay down tracks for their first album (also their last album, as it turned out). Warner Bros. supplied the songs, just as Screen Gems did for the original Monkees, but this time there were no Neil Diamonds or Carole Kings in the songwriting pool. "The music was very MOR (middle of the road) pop/rock," Muntner said. "No question that the songs were all recorded and produced well, it's just that nothing stood out as being great. Having a hit sure would have helped the show."

Warner Bros. hoped the show would drive record sales and vice versa, but the flip side of that scheme is if one part bombs, it takes the other with it. As it turned out, neither the music nor the series found an audience. Teenagers, no longer an underserved demographic in television, had a zillion shows directed at them from broadcast and cable networks; the arrival of one more could never approximate the impact of the first *Monkees* series, which can rightly be described as a revolutionary moment in television and in the evolution of the music video. After 13 weeks, *The New Monkees* imploded.

57
STUPID PET TRICKS ARE INTELLECTUAL PROPERTY

The Late Show With David Letterman
CBS, AUGUST 30, 1993

When exactly was the criminal justice system hijacked by the kind of frivolous lawsuits that Judge Wapner would toss out before the first commercial? I propose a new verdict called "No, that's just stupid", as a timesaving alternative to "guilty" and "not guilty." Think of how court calendars would be cleared for important, legitimate cases if all the nonsense could be dispatched before it went to trial.

Want to sue McDonald's after deciding to put a cup of hot coffee between your legs while driving? Want to sue Spike TV because your name is Spike? Want to ban Harry Potter from the school library because you think any stories about a wizard supports Satan? "No, that's just stupid." Case dismissed.

David Letterman might have appreciated such a verdict when NBC threw a temper tantrum following his departure in 1993. After 10 years of hosting *Late Night with David Letterman*, the sardonic comic expected to inherit *The Tonight Show* after Johnny Carson stepped down. The Peacock network chose Jay Leno instead, and Letterman jumped to CBS to host a new show in the 11:30 time slot.

NBC executives, frequently referred to by Letterman as pinheads, sought to live up to that label by seeking court injunctions against some of the host's most popular bits, including the Top Ten List and Stupid Pet Tricks. "There are certain intellectual-property issues that do not travel with Dave," warned NBC president Robert C. Wright. And in case that quote wasn't silly enough, he added this classic clarification: "They can certainly do things like that. But they can't do those things."

In response, CBS Entertainment president Jeff Sagansky expressed mild amusement at the Peacock's threats—"We're not really worried about the NBC suit," then fired back. "We have invested $1 billion in baseball over the last four years, which NBC is going to get now. And we feel we have a proprietary right to the nine-inning baseball game."

NBC's lawyers were of course happy to argue the case and defend its merits—like any bar-passer they'd sue Joan of Arc for fire code violations if there was a check in it. And the case was not without precedent in television; after Suzanne Somers left *Three's Company* under acrimonious circumstances, ABC threatened to sue her if she ever played a ditzy blonde on another sitcom, prompting CBS to pull the plug on a series in which she was to play a Chrissy Snow-clone.

But with Letterman, NBC had overstepped the bounds of common sense, and didn't even have its facts straight. Entertainment-themed top ten lists date back decades and appeared in countless magazines and newspapers. To co-opt such a standard format for comedic effect can hardly be described as an inspiration worthy of copyright. And Stupid Pet Tricks was created by Letterman writer (and former Letterman girlfriend) Merrill Markoe for the comedian's short-lived 1980 morning show, which Letterman owned, not NBC.

Even after the laughter over NBC's threats reached the network's executive suite, Robert Wright continued to defend his position. At a press conference held ostensibly to dismiss rumors that NBC might be purchased by an outside investor group, Wright fielded repeated questions about why Letterman couldn't show dogs opening beer cans on CBS. "You have to be consistent in these kind of matters" and "take positions to safeguard such material," he said. But viewers and critics were convinced that NBC's only intention was to punish a wayward son. "None of us wanted to see him leave," he said of Letterman. "But the reality is … he walked out of our marriage."

Even Jay Leno, soon to be Letterman's chief competition, mocked his network's sore-loser stance. "We don't have much intellectual property at NBC," he said. "We need to hang on to all we can get." A week before the debut of *The Late Show with David Letterman*, Leno read an "NBC memo" listing the network's intellectual properties that Dave would be forbidden to use. These included the letters N, B, and C ("legally they're ours") and the name Letterman ("which originated with the singing group who appeared on NBC's *Kraft Music Hall* with Eddy Arnold in 1970").

Letterman took his own shots at his former bosses. On his second CBS show the Top Ten List compiled the Top Ten Rejected Names for the New Show. At #6: "The Stolen Intellectual Property Show." "If they sue me, that's okay," he told a reporter. "And if this goes to trial, get a seat down front."

Nightmares of a high-profile trial and nightly derision from Leno and Letterman finally convinced NBC to withdraw its objections. But Merrill Markoe offered the network a chance to not walk away empty-handed. "I came up with a really good sequel to Stupid Pet Tricks," she told *Time* magazine. "If anyone wants to contact me, for $3.5 million I can tell them what it is."

56

THE RAT-INFESTED PACK

The Brothers Grunt
MTV, AUGUST 15, 1994–FEBRUARY 20, 1995

Danny Antonucci is a normal, well-adjusted artist, polite as all Canadians are, who studied classical animation techniques in college and worked for a time at Hanna-Barbera on Scooby-Doo and The Flintstones. So how did Antonucci progress from such wholesome pursuits to the creation of *The Brothers Grunt*, perhaps the most stomach-turning cartoon ever hatched? Blame MTV, *Beavis & Butthead*, and Antonucci's own desire to push the boundaries in his chosen profession.

"The piece started off as a ten-second ID that I had done for MTV, which basically had the five guys (who became the Brothers Grunt) grunting and groaning," Antonucci explains. "At the end a big MTV logo dropped into a pool of water and then there was a flushing sound, so the whole thing was about constipation (laughs). And from that Abby Terkuhle, who was the director of animation at MTV, proposed turning it into a series. Once I got off the floor with laughter, I thought, OK, let's see what I can come up with."

Having discovered an unlikely hit with the controversial *Beavis & Butthead*, MTV was searching for another edgy animated series that would cross-promote their music videos, and Terkuhle apparently thought the next big thing would be a quintet of hideous creatures garbed in boxer shorts and wingtip shoes, with pasty white skin, gray hair, bulging, jaundiced eyeballs, wart-ridden green tongues, and varicose veins that protrude along their necks, backs, and foreheads. These little charmers don't talk so much as grunt (hence the name), and amuse themselves by pulling each other's nipples.

"It was all tongue-in-cheek. I thought I'd try something surreal and see how it went," said Antonucci. "I didn't have any aspirations of getting into a television series, so I came up with the most absurd premise that I could possibly think of, not expecting MTV would say 'OK, let's try this.' But they did, so off we went."

The story, such as it was, had the five Brothers Grunt—Frank, Tony, Bing, Dean, and Sammy, living in a secluded monastery. Their species is on the brink of extinction, but a sacred ceremony could reverse that with the help of Perry, another Grunt brother who is deemed "The Chosen One." But Perry can't deal with the pressure and runs away, forcing his brothers to enter the world of humans to search for him.

Were the names of the characters a none-too-subtle shot at the musical tastes of the parents and grandparents of the average MTV viewer? Just the opposite, says Antonucci. "It was a tribute. I'm totally into all those boys. I actually approached Tony Bennett and Tom Jones, to see if they'd sing the theme song. Tony eventually said he was busy. (laughs)"

As with *Beavis & Butthead*, animated shorts alternated with music videos, but since the Grunts were incapable of commenting on the clips, the music and animation didn't exactly mix. "The format didn't work," Antonucci admits. "Plus I picked videos that had something to do thematically with what the episode was about, and that blew up in MTV's face because the things I picked weren't hip and trendy. I was using old Tom Waits stuff, and people were complaining about that."

The choice of music was the least of the series' sins according to viewers, who were so turned off by the characters that they flooded the internet with angry posts: "An exercise in creating disgusting and over-exaggerated characters." "Just from the commercial I got sick. It is the most disgusting thing I have ever seen." "Utterly revolting on every level." "Bad enough that it appears to be a seminar in applied ugliness, but it doesn't seem to go anywhere." "Other series have tried for 'ugly', but this one hit the motherlode of repulsive. I could not watch for more than 60 seconds at a time." There was even an "I Hate the Brothers Grunt" newsgroup.

You'd expect that response from parents, but not from the show's presumed target audience. Imagine how freaky your show has to be to repel the people who watch Marilyn Manson videos.

Antonucci is amused by the intensity of the response. "I wouldn't have it any other way. I was shocked at the instant hatred of the show, but I work at the far end of the spectrum. I really relished the fact that there were people who did get it, whatever there was to get, but that others didn't just dislike it, they despised it. So I touched them in a way, and to me that's successful."

And for those who didn't stick around, Antonucci maintains there was more to the Grunts than first met the eye. "I didn't get to do a pilot, so my learning curve happened in front of millions of viewers. With the Grunts people really didn't understand what was going on. I think in the third show I tried to build the backstory and explain, but each (cartoon) was only four minutes of animation, so I only had these little blocks to try to say something."

Given the average attention span of the MTV viewer, and the grotesque appearance of the characters, it's not surprising that the series didn't last. MTV proposed softening some of the extreme aspects of *The Brothers Grunt*, but Antonucci refused to have his work compromised. "As much as they wanted to save it I was still adamant about what I was doing," he says.

The artist has since found mainstream success on his own terms with *Ed, Edd and Eddy*, which has aired on Cartoon Network for four years. "Even there, I try to take it outside the world of conventional animation," he said. "To do something down the middle, I just don't see a reason." So does that mean he's got something else up his sleeve to shock and disgust us again? "Not up my sleeve," he hints with a mischievous grin, "but maybe up my pant leg."

55
NBC PITCHES A NO-HITTER

THE NBC FALL SCHEDULE
NBC, SEPTEMBER 1983

"Be There" was the simple, direct slogan created by NBC to ballyhoo its 1983 fall schedule. Maybe they should have said "Please." Nine new shows were launched that year, and not one lasted a full season, the first and only time that has happened to one of the three major networks.

The timing for such a disastrous slate could not be worse, as NBC had just started to crawl out of the cellar after years of diminishing returns. Low-rated shows *Hill Street Blues* and *Cheers* swept the Emmy awards and picked up viewers in the aftermath, and *The A-Team* was a breakout hit from its first episode. The 1983 season was a chance to build on that momentum, but NBC would have to wait until 1984 for good news, when midseason replacements *Night Court*, *Riptide*, and *TV's Bloopers and Practical Jokes* all found an audience. One can only speculate why those shows were held back until January, to make room for the slate of losers that debuted in September. Here they are, ranked in order by how much they sucked.

1. *Manimal* (September 30–December 31)
   One of the great TV punchlines of the 80s, *Manimal* has become synonymous with television at its most ridiculous. After the show was announced, David Letterman skewered it mercilessly in his *Late Night* monologues through the

summer of 1983, so by the time *Manimal* debuted it had already acquired the reputation of a laughingstock, and the first episode did little to change that perception.

Simon MacCorkindale starred as Jonathan Chase, professor of animal studies by day, shapeshifting crimefighter by night. For unexplained reasons, Chase had the ability to transform himself into any animal he wished; unfortunately, limitations in the show's budget and special effects forced him to change into the same creatures almost every week. When the dramatic music swelled, viewers knew that Chase was probably about to become a falcon, a panther, or a cobra, which made for a great drinking game but tarnished his credibility. Even Jayna the Wonder Twin had more imagination.

2. *Mr. Smith* (September 23–December 16)

As if *Manimal* didn't bring enough critters to prime time, NBC also introduced Cha Cha the orangutan in *Mr. Smith*. Cha Cha, already a star from the Clint Eastwood film *Every Which Way but Loose*, played an ordinary circus ape that drank an experimental enzyme and acquired an I.Q. of 256. Now sporting a spiffy suit and spectacles, the super-ape was hired as a presidential advisor. With Ronald Reagan in the White House the show was labeled "Bonzo Goes to Washington", but even that level of comedy was beyond its capability.

3. *Boone* (September 26–December 19)

An empty melodrama with occasional musical interludes, *Boone* starred Tom Byrd as Boone Sawyer, an idealistic boy coming of age in rural Trinity, Tennessee circa 1953. Boone dreamed of taking his guitar to the big city to sing that dangerous new music called rockabilly; but his parents urged Boone to give up his quest for fame and run the family gas station. Way to encourage the kid, parents.

4. *The Bay City Blues* (October 25–November 15)

Of the nine series destined for cancellation in 1983, no one could have guessed that the axe would fall first on this ambitious drama from Steven Bochco, which followed the fortunes of a minor league baseball team in Bay City, California. The impressive cast, including Michael Nouri, Sharon Stone (yes, Sharon Stone), and Bochco regulars Dennis Franz and Ken Olin was set adrift in boring, depressing stories. The *Blues* name was a ridiculous conceit so soon after Bochco's *Hill Street Blues*, and it left viewers wondering when someone was going to call the cops.

5. *For Love and Honor* (September 23–December 27)

The Peacock Network never did prime time soaps as well as CBS (*Dallas, Knots Landing*) or ABC (*Dynasty*). *Flamingo Road* barely lasted two seasons, but in 1983 the network launched two more variations, the first set on an army base in Fort Geller, Texas. *For Love and Honor* had enough bedhopping among self-destructive sinners for three shows, but the series never had a chance against *Falcon Crest* on CBS.

6. *We Got it Made* (September 8, 1983–March 30, 1984)

NBC programming executives are still scratching their heads over how this one missed. *We Got it Made* had the makings of a breakout hit, particularly with fresh-faced newcomer Teri Copley as Mickey McKenzie, a live-in maid for two bachelor roommates, uptight attorney David (Matt McCoy) and goofball Jay (Tom Villard). Had the network been able to build any kind of show at all around Copley's bountiful charms, she would be remembered today alongside Farrah Fawcett as one of TV's sexiest blond bombshells.

Though *We Got it Made* won its time slot through much of the fall, it lost viewers rapidly after the holidays. In fact, one could argue it was all downhill after that opening credits image of Copley in a pink t-shirt and blue jeans. But even the horniest of young males needed a little more than that from an escapist sitcom. Though the plots should have written themselves with such a high-octane setup, *We Got it Made* served up ridiculous stories about musical toilets and Mickey's whirlwind romance with a Spanish millionaire. Even *Three's Company*, the obvious inspiration for this farcical comedy, also had the slapstick talents of John Ritter and the likable Joyce DeWitt, where Copley's costars, McCoy and Villard, were dull individually and mismatched as a duo.

Still, the concept seemed so right for a winning sitcom that *We Got it Made* was brought back in syndication in 1987, with Copley and Villard reprising their roles. It struck out again.

7. *The Rousters* (October 1, 1983–July 21, 1984)

The idea was flawed from the start. Chad Everett plays Wyatt Earp III, a descendant of the legendary lawman, reduced to working as a bouncer for Captain Jack's Sladetown Carnival, a traveling sideshow. As if the job itself didn't provide enough humiliation, Wyatt was also saddled with a batch of wacky relatives, including a mother (Maxine Stuart) who worked as a bounty hunter and an imbecile brother (played by 'Ernest' star Jim Varney).

8. *The Yellow Rose* (October 2, 1983–May 26, 1984)

Audiences dismissed *The Yellow Rose* as a *Dallas* ripoff, but the series actually had more in common with the TV Westerns of an earlier era. One of the best casts assembled for any series that season (Sam Elliott, Cybill Shepherd, David Soul, Edward Albert, Chuck Connors, Susan Anspach, and Jane Russell) starred in a continuing drama set on a modern-day West Texas ranch. *The Yellow Rose* was rough around the edges but might have blossomed in its second season; unfortunately, the series was deemed too expensive to produce and the network opted to cut its losses.

9. *Jennifer Slept Here* (October 21, 1983–September 3, 1984)

This show was a guilty pleasure for me, mostly because I think Ann Jillian is a wonderful talent that deserved better than she got from TV, and also because the series was a throwback to the fantasy sitcoms of the 60s, which had fallen out of favor in a more cynical era. Jillian played Jennifer Farrell, a recently deceased movie star whose ghost still haunts her Hollywood home, now occupied by the Elliot family. Fourteen-year-old Joey Elliott (John P. Navin) was the only one who could see Jennifer, and their relationship inspired most of the stories.

54

DEAR DIARY: EVERYBODY HATES ME

The Secret Diary of Desmond Pfeiffer
UPN, OCTOBER 5–26, 1998

What is most fascinating about the brief and controversial history of *The Secret Diary of Desmond Pfeiffer* is how the series was attacked for the wrong reasons.

Weeks before the first episode was scheduled to air, the UPN show was targeted for condemnation by a variety of protest groups that specialize in being offended. Having never watched the show, these sensitive souls nonetheless declared that *Desmond Pfeiffer* poked fun at the slavery of African-Americans. "The program trivializes our suffering and pain and denigrates the bones of our ancestors," said Danny Bakewell, CEO of the Brotherhood Crusade.

None of which was true. Though the series was set in the Abraham Lincoln White House at a time when slavery remained a blight on the American conscience, *Desmond Pfeiffer* was not about slavery, did not feature any actors portraying slaves, and never found humor in human bondage. Executive producers/writers Mort Nathan and Barry Fanaro were aiming at a different satirical target—the presidency of Bill Clinton.

The series was intended as a broad political satire, in which the smartest man in the White House is the exiled black Englishman Desmond Pfeiffer (Chi McBride), who becomes a trusted advisor to a mentally-deficient Lincoln (Dann Florek) and an object of passion for the president's amorous but emotionally unstable First Lady Mary Todd (Christine Estabrook).

The jokes emerged not from race but from the transfer of contemporary presidential scandals into the administration of the Great Emancipator. In the first episode, "There's Something About Mary Todd (And It Ain't Healthy)," the Clinton-Monica Lewinsky tryst inspires lines like "The president is having sex with someone who works at the White House? Preposterous!" In the next show, President Lincoln enjoys the 19th century version of phone sex, by tapping out dirty talk with a telegraph (I kind of hate myself for thinking that's funny). When the act proves unsatisfying, Lincoln laments "I'm afraid the fire's gone out of the old Lincoln log."

But once a good protest gets rolling it's hard to derail, and the outcry over the series' insensitivity overshadowed its other sins, primarily the fact that it wasn't especially clever or interesting. The jokes were crass and obvious, the execution hit-and-miss. McBride emerged best, playing Pfeiffer as a Civil War-era Benson (as played by Robert Guillaume), who was a servant in uniform only. "I can't really say I have any bad taste in my mouth," McBride explained later. "Life is filled with things that you try. Sometimes you succeed and sometimes you fall on your ass."

Desmond Pfeiffer didn't fall so much as it was pushed. Reacting to demonstrations outside the Paramount lot, a possible advertiser boycott and charges of racial insensitivity, the Los Angeles City Council unanimously passed a special motion requiring a community screening of the series pilot, with instructions to its Human Relations Committee to report whether the show is appropriate for broadcast. Where were they when *Joanie Loves Chachi* was released?

UPN CEO Dean Valentine objected to the motion, calling it "shameful, outrageous and dangerous," and "political correctness taken to the level of insanity." "It's an outrage and a dark sign for the creative community that any government body has decided to weigh in," he told *Daily Variety*. "In a city with problems ranging from education to crime to city services, poverty, and racism—a lot of incredibly deep, pressing social issues—it's almost laughable, if it weren't so sad, that our representatives are devoting their attention to UPN's Monday night schedule."

However, the network acquiesced, agreeing to pull the pilot for another episode. "While we do not believe the series' premise or any of the program episodes are racially insensitive, we respect our African-American viewers and will review the pilot episode again before putting it on the air," said Valentine in a released statement. Undeterred, the Brotherhood Crusade, along with the Hollywood branch of the NAACP, reaffirmed their objection to the entire concept of the show, and really didn't care that one episode was pulled for another. They vowed to maintain their protest until the show was off the air.

Usually this sort of dispute is a godsend to a new series. As *Married…with Children* discovered after being attacked by housewife Terry Rakolta, the best way to get people to watch a show is to have a lot of other people tell them not to tune in. But even controversy couldn't save *The Secret Diary of Desmond Pfeiffer*, which failed to entertain the few curious viewers it did attract and was pulled after three episodes.

But lest there's any confusion, the "What Were They Thinking" here belongs not with the series, a dumb short-lived sex comedy that would have failed on its own merits without outside help, but with those who huffed and puffed over imagined affronts, and a Los Angeles City Council that should have better things to do.

53
DAN RATHER ADVISES COURAGE

The CBS Evening News
CBS, September 2–6, 1985

He's an Emmy and Peabody Award winning journalist, and one of the most respected television newsmen of his generation. He's also, to be blunt, a little wacky. In a career that spans five decades, *CBS Evening News* anchorman Dan Rather has repeatedly found himself in the midst of bizarre circumstances, some of which were self-inflicted.

Where to start? With his early days at the CBS affiliate in Houston, Texas, where he had someone at the Houston police station shoot him with heroin so he could do a story about its effects? Or his 1980 coverage of the Soviet invasion of Afghanistan, where he went undercover as a mujahadin freedom fighter, earning the nickname "Gunga Dan"? How about the incident that same year when Rather hopped into a cab in Chicago en route to an interview for *60 Minutes*, and had to holler for help out the window when the cabbie took off in the wrong direction and refused to stop?

And those are just the runner-up memorable moments in the Rather repertoire. In 1986, he was attacked by two chemically-altered hooligans, who repeatedly bellowed the bizarre question "What's the frequency, Kenneth?" Hardly his fault, sure, but this sort of stuff never happened to Eric Sevareid. The phrase was immortalized in a song by the band REM. When they played New York, Rather was in the audience.

One year later, Rather was again making news instead of reporting it, after an argument with CBS brass over shortening the newscast to accommodate the finish of a U.S. Open tennis match. When the news was supposed to begin at 6:32, Rather wasn't there, and viewers were treated to six minutes of an empty swivel chair.

Wait—just one more before introducing the actual subject of this chapter; Rather's marathon stint into the wee hours on the night of the 2000 presidential election is a performance that has become legendary. The longer the night went on, the more the anchor regressed to his Wharton, Texas heritage, and by the time CBS changed its mind about declaring Florida for Al Gore, Rather was tossing off Southern-fried epigrams like Will Rogers in a Brooks Brothers suit: "These returns are running like a squirrel in a cage"; "Bush has run through Dixie like a big wheel through a cotton field"; "This race is as tight as a too-small bathing suit on a too-hot car ride back from the beach"; and the classic "If a frog had side pockets, he'd carry a handgun."

Though he may bristle at the suggestion, such antics have become part of his appeal. "I've got a sneaking admiration for Dan Rather because I'm never sure when he's going to go bonkers on you," observed Stephen King. When the guy who wrote *The Shining* thinks you're a little crazy, that's saying something.

For all his aforementioned adventures, Rather's most famous misfire may still be his idea for a new signoff, which he introduced on September 2, 1985. Four years earlier, he had succeeded Walter Cronkite as anchor of the CBS news. Cronkite was then considered the most trusted man in America, but Rather rose to the challenge of the coveted assignment and CBS remained on top of the nightly news ratings.

Cronkite's closing line, "And that's the way it is," had become a signature, and perhaps Rather was in search of his own catchphrase when, after the final story of that Monday newscast, he looked into the camera and solemnly signed off with the word "Courage." And viewers from across the continental U.S. looked at each other and said, "Wha...?"

"Courage"? Was he sending a message to the Cowardly Lion? Did he just discover *The Bugaloos*? Or was it a sincere attempt to bolster the nation's spirits? Whatever the motivation, the signoff clearly did not have the desired effect. "A noble gesture, at once commanding and empathetic," wrote *Harper's* magazine. "But it had no more effect than if he had said, "Porridge." There was a smugness to it, a pomposity so out of character for a newsman whose biggest strength is his down-home sincerity and straight shooting style. Rather finished out the week with his new signoff, but the following Monday he listened to the feedback and reverted to a simple "Good night."

Of the incident, Rather hasn't had much to say. He covers the period in question in his second autobiography, *The Camera Never Blinks Twice* (1994), but says nothing about the infamous sign-off, though he devotes entire chapters to other topics, including his walk off the air and his controversial interview with Vice-President George Bush over the Iran-Contra scandal. Perhaps he didn't think a one-week failed experiment needed further review, but it certainly hasn't been forgotten. Few stories about Rather fail to mention the incident, and many of the nastier ones can't resist closing with "Courage."

52
SNOW WHITE AND THE SEVEN COPYRIGHT ATTORNEYS

The 62nd Academy Awards
ABC, MARCH 29, 1989

"It will be the antithesis of tacky." —ALLAN CARR

1989 was a bad year to be Rob Lowe. Bootleg copies of the Brat Packer's homemade sex video with a 16-year-old, shot at the 1988 Democratic Convention, turned him into a national object of ridicule and got him 20 hours of community service from an Atlanta judge. And that was just his second worst screen credit that year.

The Academy Award shows have a long and illustrious history of awful musical numbers, from the "Fugue for Tinhorns" performed by Telly Savalas, Pat Morita, and

Dom DeLuise to Debbie Allen choreographing a tapdance to the theme from *Saving Private Ryan*. But even these distinguished moments pale next to the extravaganza that opened the 1989 Awards, featuring a performance of "Proud Mary" by Rob Lowe and Snow White.

The story of this indelible Oscar moment begins with flamboyant producer Allan Carr, who promised an event to remember. "You don't want to miss the beginning," he teased *Daily Variety* before the show. "When the curtain goes up, you want to be in your seat."

But the fun began even before the curtain rose as Army Archerd, after greeting celebrities from his traditional post in the lobby of the Shrine Auditorium, announced "And now ladies and gentlemen, here's one of the great legends of Hollywood. She's back with us tonight—Miss Snow White."

"I'm a little late, Army," says Snow, played by actress Eileen Bowman. "Can you tell me how to get into the theater?" "That's easy, Snow," replies the slightly embarrassed *Variety* columnist. *"Just follow the Hollywood stars."*

The Disney princess does as he asks, singing "I Only Have Eyes for You," while walking down the aisle of the Shrine, shaking hands with such mortified stars as Michelle Pfeiffer, Tom Hanks, and Sigourney Weaver. "The looks of horror on their faces were unforgettable," wrote *Vanity Fair* of the moment.

At last, Snow White ascended to the stage, set to resemble the Cocoanut Grove nightclub in its 1930s heyday. Headlining at the club is that great thespian Merv Griffin, performing his hit, "I've Got a Lovely Bunch of Cocoanuts" to a crowd of golden-age stars recruited to play the supper club's audience. Among the unfortunate attendees are Roy Rogers and Dale Evans, Dorothy Lamour, Alice Faye, and Cyd Charisse.

"Isn't it exciting, Snow?" Griffin asks. "It gets better. Meet your blind date—Rob Lowe!" Snow looks thrilled, Rob not so much, as he reluctantly makes his entrance and they belt out a pro-Hollywood variation of "Proud Mary" (sample lyric: "Rollin', rollin', keep the cameras rollin'!").

The Cocoanut Grove waitresses, so moved by this spirited performance, forget to bus the tables and start dancing, while other dancers, dressed like Carmen Miranda, shimmy out to join them.

The number continued, as the supper club set morphed into Grauman's Chinese Theater, while Lowe hastily made his exit after kissing Snow White's hand. "Being asked to perform at the Academy Awards is like being asked to the White House," he gushed before the ceremony. He changed his mind after the reviews came in. "I thought it would be sort of goofy, a camp thing," Lowe told *People* magazine. Then he spotted director Barry Levinson in the audience, mouthing the words, "What the hell is he doing?"

Those sentiments were shared by nearly everyone in the Shrine that night. Lily Tomlin had the unenviable task of following Carr's debacle, and could not resist a comment before beginning her scripted "Welcome to the show" remarks. "More than a billion and a half people watched that. And at this very moment they're trying to make sense of it."

Reaction was swift, and didn't even wait for the following day's papers. At the post-Oscar press conference, Allan Carr found himself defending his vision. "But

Allan—why Snow White?" he was asked. "It's called theatrical," the producer responded, clearly miffed.

Such questions were bouquets compared to the reviews. "One of the most grotesque television broadcasts in recent memory," raved the *Los Angeles Herald-Examiner*. "The opening number deserves a permanent place in the annals of Oscar embarrassments" wrote Janet Maslin in the *New York Times*. "Can anyone who lived through it forget such gruesome low points?" asked Desmond Ryan in the *Philadelphia Inquirer*.

As for Eileen Bowman, whose big break to that point had been a role in the Las Vegas musical spoof *Beach Blanket Babylon*, she enjoyed her five minutes of fame (fifteen would be an exaggeration), telling the *L.A. Times* that she's never seen *Snow White and the Seven Dwarfs*, but that she'd like to one day play the character at Disneyland.

Her chances dimmed after the Walt Disney Co. sued the Oscars for copyright infringement, over the "unauthorized and unflattering" use of the Snow White character. The Academy avoided litigation by issuing an apology, but the memories of Carr's spectacle did not fade as quickly. The Board of Governors fielded hundreds of phone calls from its membership. Oscar winners Gregory Peck, Billy Wilder, Paul Newman, and Julie Andrews signed an official letter calling the presentation "an embarrassment to both the Academy and the entire motion picture industry."

"What really rankled the Academy nabobs was the fact that the public humiliation wouldn't go away," reported Robert Osborne, author of *75 Years of Oscar*. "Steve Martin poked fun at the show on the Tony Awards telecast later in the spring."

Not surprisingly, Allan Carr was not invited back to produce the next Oscar telecast. That role went to Gil Cates, who had headed up a special Awards Presentation Review Committee to determine what went wrong, and how to make certain it never happened again. Billy Crystal hosted the following year's telecast, and gleefully opened an old wound by responding to the audience ovation with "Is that for me or are you just glad I'm not Snow White?"

51
FALLEN ANGEL

Charlie's Angels
ABC, SEPTEMBER 12, 1979–MAY 7, 1980

When Farrah Fawcett left *Charlie's Angels* after one season, producer Aaron Spelling offered her halo to Cheryl Ladd, recalling the petite blonde from her audition for another Spelling series, *Family*. That role went to Meredith Baxter-Birney, and though Ladd had misgivings about the frothier elements of Angel duty, she couldn't pass on the opportunity for instant stardom. Her hiring was great for the series as well, which not only held its ratings dominance but actually added viewers in its second season.

But when Kate Jackson followed Farrah out of the offices of Charles Townsend Investigations after the third season, this time there was no quick fix. Hundreds of candidates were audtioned, including such future famous names as Michelle Pfeiffer, Connie Selleca, Deborah Shelton, Kathie Lee Johnson (later Kathie Lee Gifford), Christina Ferrare, Catherine Bach, *Price is Right* spokesmodel Dian Parkinson, and Kelly Collins, the younger sister of Bo Derek.

Series producer Ed Lakso, who wrote more than 40 episodes of *Charlie's Angels*, was partial to Shari Belafonte. "She was not a great actress at the time, but there was something very engaging about her," he recalled. "And at the time we felt some political pressure to hire an African-American angel." But the two favorites that emerged from the crowded field were Barbara Bach, best known as the sexy Russian agent in the James Bond thriller *The Spy Who Loved Me*, and Shelley Hack, a familiar face on TV from a series of commercials for a perfume called Charlie, no relation to the Angels' boss.

Bach was the early favorite, and some newspapers actually reported that the role was hers. But Bach's final screen test didn't impress ABC executives, and some felt she looked too much like returning Angel Jaclyn Smith. Meanwhile, Spelling continued to fight for Shelley Hack, who he envisioned as a young Kate Hepburn. Her test radiated poise and sophistication, and Spelling also loved the idea of the Charlie perfume girl becoming a Charlie's Angel. "That carried a lot of weight, believe it or not," Lakso remembers.

Spelling got his way, as he usually did, and Hack joined the cast as Tiffany Welles, the refined, scholarly daughter of a Connecticut police chief. And just as Cheryl Ladd had been introduced to viewers in a special two-part episode filmed in Hawaii, Hack would be given a similarly elaborate debut, in which the Angels would sail on the Love Boat and shoot on location in the Caribbean.

At the first line-reading, guest star Dick Sargent asked Shelley if she was excited about becoming the new Angel. "No, not really," she replied. Her nonchalance was confirmed by a *Los Angeles Times* reporter, who overheard Hack say she wasn't nervous at all about joining the series. "That wasn't arrogance," she later explained to the reporter. "It just struck me as a silly question."

But since Aaron Spelling hired Shelley Hack in part for her cool insouciance, it didn't really matter whether she appreciated the attention her casting received. But another problem surfaced—she couldn't act. As shooting progressed on "Love Boat Angels," writer Ed Lakso kept pulling lines from Shelley and giving them to Cheryl Ladd, who ultimately wound up featured in Hack's debut episode. "Jaclyn and I were saying, 'What's going on?'," Ladd remembered. "It was confusing to us, because we thought they'd make this big presentation for her." But Lakso found Hack's line-readings so abysmal he felt he had no other choice. "I danced around it because I didn't want to say that Shelley couldn't act, but I stuck with the revisions."

"Love Boat Angels" topped the Nielsen ratings, but critics attacked Charlie's newest Angel. "She is barely able to read her lines," noted *Variety*. As the season progressed, a series that had been a top-ten staple for three years dropped into the 30s, no longer even able to win its time slot.

A change in the series format, which replaced team adventures with solo outings, further limited Hack's screen time. Her brief scenes were memorable, but not for the right reasons. In "Angels on the Street," Tiffany went undercover as a slutty streetwalker, but her patrician beauty and impeccable diction rendered the role-playing ludicrous. In "Caged Angel," Tiffany and Kelly (Smith) disguise themselves as nuns to visit Kris (Ladd) in prison. Hack skewers the delivery of every line she has in one of the series' most awkward moments.

Surprisingly, she delivered a polished performance in Tiffany's first solo effort, "Angels on Campus," and by the standout episode "Angel Hunt" Hack finally seemed to have figured out the requirements of the role. Unfortunately, most of the audience was gone by then, and when the series was picked up for a fifth season, she was not invited back. The joke that made it's way around the papers was, "Can you imagine being fired from *Charlie's Angels* for not being a good enough actress?"

After seeing the photo of Drew Barrymore on page 165, Shelley Hack (left) wonders whether she's still the worst thing to happen to Charlie's Angels.

"As I recall, she wasn't terribly hurt by it," said Ed Lakso, who tried to reverse the series' declining ratings by replacing the bookish Tiffany with the streetwise Julie Rogers, played by Tanya Roberts. But America had moved on, and *Charlie's Angels* limped through one more season before ABC clipped their wings. As *People* magazine observed, the jiggle was up.

50
CANADIAN BACON

Thicke of the Night
SYNDICATED, SEPTEMBER 5, 1983–JUNE 15, 1984

Even the few folks who watched *Thicke of the Night* 20 years ago don't remember much about the program, but they probably remember how the late-night talk show was promoted, or at least how frequently it was promoted. There were many other challengers to the ratings supremacy of *The Tonight Show*, but none entered the game with more arrogance and less ammunition.

A blitzkrieg of radio, television, billboard, and newspaper advertising heralded *Thicke of the Night*'s arrival. The ferocious campaign was orchestrated by producer Fred Silverman, who was anxious to restore his reputation for developing successful shows. The legendary "Man with the Golden Gut" suffered a bout with indigestion after his stint at NBC produced both *Pink Lady and Jeff* and *Supertrain*.

The message of the campaign was that you simply had to watch this show. *Thicke of the Night* wasn't going to be just another series, it was the beginning of an extraordinary new epoch in entertainment. No other television show had ever been pushed this hard. Women in labor don't push this hard.

"It wasn't that we all thought it was a good idea to shoot off our mouth," Thicke said years later. "But when you're selling the show, you've got 125 station owners who all say, 'We've never heard of this guy, what are you going to do to promote him?' So there was this pressure to build me up big."

Silverman didn't stop at promoting his star; the spots all but guaranteed Johnny Carson's downfall, as Americans would come to know and love Alan Thicke. The only evidence offered for Thicke's magnetic appeal was his three-year stint as host of a talk/variety program that was the biggest hit in the history of Canadian daytime television. Well, with credentials like those...

A couple of things can happen when a performer is relentlessly shoved into the public consciousness, and it's amazing those doing the shoving haven't figured this out yet. Some will be so turned off by the disturbance that they'll make a point to not watch out of spite. Others will be curious enough to tune in, with great expectations and little patience. Woe to the host who demands your attention, and then wastes your time.

Through Silverman's efforts the series debuted in 80 percent of America's television markets. It was clear from the look and style of the opening broadcast that the strategy was to position the series as a cutting-edge alternative to Carson's traditional talkfest. Which makes the booking of first guests Joan Collins and Barry Manilow all the more strange. *The Tonight Show* aired a rerun opposite the new series, but despite the lack of competition *Thicke* could only muster a 2.7 rating, ten percent of the total viewing audience. Not only did the series trail the *Best of Carson*, it lost to ABC's *Nightline* and U.S. Open golf highlights on CBS.

For its first few weeks, *Thicke of the Night* struggled to find a niche. The host was so distraught over the series' performance that he reportedly fainted while watching one of the first episodes. Gradually, a format came into focus. There were running gags like Flicke of the Night, where new dialogue would be inserted into old movie footage by a group of young comics that included Richard Belzer, Charles Fleischer, Gilbert Gottfried, Mike McManus, and Chloe Webb. And Thicke himself would occasionally strap on a guitar and sing one of his soft pop compositions, which offered proof that as a songwriter he peaked after penning the theme to *The Facts of Life*.

The ratings that began in the cellar actually tunneled to even lower depths in the weeks that followed. One month into the run, *Thicke of the Night* actually pulled a zero share in Philadelphia, which suggested the possibility that in a major metropolitan area of millions, not one television set was tuned to the show.

Other cities reported slightly higher numbers. Yet somehow, at the end of 13 weeks the series was picked up for another 65 shows. Silverman clearly still had some pull in the industry, but the affiliates had had enough. Many refused to air the new shows, and even Thicke indicated that it was time to go. But the Man with the Golden Gut opted instead for a retooling that removed the supporting cast and added Thicke's wife, actress/singer Gloria Loring, and appearances from confrontational right wing fanatic Wally George. Ratings remained nearly nonexistent, and *Thicke of the Night* was put out of its misery at last, after nine months. On the same day his series was canceled, Gloria Loring filed for divorce. Now that's a bad day.

Shortly thereafter, Thicke appeared as Johnny Carson's guest on *The Tonight Show*, and proved both charming and humorous, tossing off self-depracating barbs at his show while a clearly impressed Carson buried the hatchet. He became, in his own words, a guru of failure. His advice was sought by Joan Rivers, Rick Dees, and Arsenio Hall before their late night stints. "I think all of them avoided some of the pitfalls we suffered", Thicke said.

To his credit, Thicke stayed visible, even if most of the attention he received was about a show that had already been hailed as one of the worst in TV history. "It was pretty devastating," he said. "For about a year, my kids thought their middle names were 'ill-fated'. The truth is that those kind of reactions hurt your feelings."

By showing the kind of humor, charm, and likability that captivated Silverman in the first place, Alan Thicke earned a second chance at American TV stardom, this time in a vehicle better suited to his talents. The sitcom *Growing Pains* debuted on ABC one year after *Thicke of the Night*'s cancellation, and ran for seven successful seasons.

49
NAVEL WARFARE

Gidget
ABC, September 15, 1965–September 1, 1966

Gilligan's Island
CBS, September 26, 1964–September 4, 1967

I Dream of Jeannie
NBC, September 18, 1965–September 1, 1970

In the 1960s, nothing worried a television censor more than longterm public exposure to an attractive woman's belly button. If I had a time machine I'd zip back to one of their standards and practices powwows with a copy of the *Victoria's Secret Fashion Show*, to enlighten them on what TV is like in the 21st century. Then I'd sit back and watch their heads explode.

How ludicrous navel censorship must seem to anyone who came of age in our current era of pop culture, with the barely obscured frontal nudity in *E!'s Wild On* and *MTV Spring Break*, and pop princesses who display their belly buttons as often as they display their lack of singing ability. It's almost inconceivable now to imagine what a fuss television used to make over those little round lint-catchers.

The origins of TV's trepidation can be traced back to the Hays Code, a guideline for entertainment industry censorship adopted in the 1930s. For decades, the display of a female belly button was forbidden, as it might remind male viewers of other commonly covered body parts, and create the kind of thoughts that require absolution.

By the 1960s some of the restrictions had been eased, and though navels were no longer an automatic no-no, they could still be selectively censored depending on the circumstance, as Sally Field discovered when she played beach bunny Gidget Lawrence. "The big issue was my belly button" she told *TV Guide* in 1973. "I could never show it. Gidget's bathing suit always had to cover her belly button, despite the fact that all the other girls bounced around in skimpy bikinis." Apparently, a star's navel was more prone to induce impure thoughts than that of a pretty extra.

Sherwood Schwartz fought his own navel battles with *Gilligan's Island*, after censors objected to the height of Mary Ann's hip huggers. Programming at CBS operated under the auspices of the "Intermittent Navel" rule, which stated that it was okay if a female navel appeared briefly and occasionally, but a permanent display was going too far. That was a problem for Mary Ann (Dawn Wells), who apparently packed halter tops in every color for her three-hour tour. Schwartz asked her to raise her hip huggers about an inch. At that height, the hip huggers moved up and down, revealing her navel every other step. That was satisfactory to the censors.

The most famous belly button on television belonged to Barbara Eden, though like Jimmy Hoffa its fame was heightened by its disappearance. There would be no intermittent sightings here; on *I Dream of Jeannie*, Barbara's navel was strictly off-limits. "I was told that the lady in charge of standards and practices was a retired nun, and she had probably never seen a navel before, so that was the reason it was kept off the air," recalled Larry Hagman, who played Jeannie's befuddled master, Tony Nelson.

Actually, the premise of the series probably had more to do with the network's concerns, and in retrospect it's a wonder *Jeannie* made it to the air at all. Bad enough you had an unmarried man and woman living together, but the girl was also a beautiful genie who repeatedly expressed her willingness to grant her master's every wish.

"We had to be careful," series creator Sidney Sheldon admitted. "Our premise is a half-naked girl and a young man she's after." "She was always throwing herself at me, and I was always saying 'my career' — though I don't know what the heck my career had to do with anything," Hagman says. You get the feeling that if it were Larry in charge instead of Tony, the sexual tension between Jeannie and Major

Nelson would have been resolved by episode 2.

Jeannie's sexy pink harem outfit, certainly one of television's most memorable costumes, brought the great belly button debate out of the network executive boardrooms and into the press, where reporters began asking why they couldn't see Barbara's navel. "People are beginning to wonder if I have one," she said. The network explained its no-navel policy, and viewers reflected on whether they'd seen a navel on NBC before. They had; in fact, they had seen one on *I Dream of Jeannie.*

In the first season episode "Richest Astronaut in the World," Roger Healey (Bill Daily) discovers the secret of Jeannie's existence and becomes her new master. He conjures up a backyard swimming pool and a bevy of beautiful servants, one of whom wears a two-piece bathing suit. In "Jeannie Goes to Honolulu" and "The Battle of Waikiki," two

Jeannie (Barbara Eden) pops out of her costume, with no help from Justin Timberlake.

third-season episodes shot in Hawaii, Jeannie sunbathes on the beach in a one-piece suit, amidst a sea of bikinis.

Most amusing was the fact that in 1969, *Rowan & Martin's Laugh-In* aired right after *I Dream of Jeannie*, and featured Goldie Hawn and Teresa Graves dancing in bikinis, with suggestive slogans written on their bodies. *Laugh-In* producers invited Barbara Eden to make an appearance and finally expose her navel on their show, but NBC's chief censor put a stop to that, believing the segment to be "in bad taste."

Ironically, by focusing so much attention on the coverage of Eden's navel, the censors actually turned it into an even greater object of lust among sharp-eyed viewers. The rare on-screen appearances of Barbara's belly button became the 1960s equivalent of a nip-slip. "I think it was all silliness, but It generated a lot of publicity," said Hagman. "Everybody kept waiting for it to pop out." For the curious, its most prominent appearance is in episode #131, "Mrs. Djinn-Djinn." Watch the scene near the beginning when Jeannie is on the phone.

In 1985, when Barbara Eden reprised her most famous role in the TV movie *I Dream of Jeannie: 15 Years Later*, the no-navel regulations had long since fallen by the wayside, and Jeannie was finally able to display her uncensored midsection.

48
SPORT OR SPECTACLE?

The XFL
NBC, TNN, UPN, February 3, 2001–April 27, 2001

Now that we're a few years removed from the XFL's demise, it's easier to evaluate the fledgling football league away from media prejudice and the braggadocio of founder Vince McMahon. McMahon is often his own worst enemy, and here his enthusiasm for an alternative to the National Football League could not outrun his reputation, which saddled the new venture with a bad rap long before players took the field.

It's easy to understand the appeal of a new football enterprise, given the multibillion dollar success of the NFL, but it's been tried before. The USFL, WFL, and the Arena Football League have all faded into bankruptcy or obscurity.

McMahon thought he knew better, and his track record backed him up. As owner of World Wrestling Entertainment, he took a sport viewed as seedy and corrupt and moved it into the mainstream. At the peak of its success, the World Wrestling Federation drew 90,000 fans to the Pontiac Silverdome to watch Hulk Hogan pin Andre the Giant. McMahon's arrogance breeds enemies but also makes money for his stockholders, and though previous attempts to expand his empire outside of wrestling had failed (anyone remember the World Bodybuilding Federation?) his proven ability to deliver a sizable young male demographic forced networks to take him seriously.

As it happened, he caught Dick Ebersole, Sports Chairman of NBC, at the right time. NBC lost its NFL rights in 1997, and was ready to take a chance on the new league. Eight teams were formed, including franchises in all the major markets— New York, Chicago, Los Angeles, San Francisco, Orlando, Las Vegas, Memphis, and Birmingham.

The XFL was marketed as a working man's league, for fans fed up with the NFL's crybabies and their $10 million signing bonuses. In the XFL, there were no guaranteed contracts, and all players made the same base salary. Rule changes that substituted a play from scrimmage for the extra-point kick on a touchdown, and eliminated fair catches on punts and the 'in the grasp' rule on quarterbacks, were promoted as a return to hard-hitting football the way it ought to be. Even the coin toss was violent; instead of calling heads or tails, the XFL put the ball on the 50 and had two players race for it from 20 yards away. The first to gain possession earned the choice of kicking or receiving. For the first time in football history, a player could actually be injured before the opening kickoff.

A few media outlets expressed cautious optimism: "The early buzz is strong, thanks to a popular Web site and a witty 'Gladiator'-style ad campaign," wrote *Newsweek*. "Viewers raised on MTV will feel right at home tuning in to the XFL." But some predicted that the outcome of games would be as predetermined as a Wrestlemania match between the Undertaker and The Rock. That question was answered when Las Vegas sports books consented to post odds and take bets on the league.

On February 3, 2001, the XFL debuted before sold-out stadiums in Las Vegas and Orlando. Despite all the rule changes, what really caught fans' attention were the players who opted for messages or nicknames on their jerseys. Running back Rod Smart, a.k.a. "He Hate Me," instantly became the XFL's most prominent star.

Reviews of the league's first weekend were dreadful. "A grating, gyrating, miscalculated mess" was a typical reaction, but ratings were astronomical. Having predicted a 4.5 rating for the Saturday night telecast, the XFL delivered an astonishing 9.5 (each rating point represents about one million television homes). But the numbers dropped 50 percent in week 2, and never recovered.

By midseason the league was forced to give away 30 percent of its ad inventory to sponsors whose commercials weren't reaching as many viewers as they had promised. The week 7 game is believed to be the lowest-rated primetime program ever broadcast by a major network. The XFL championship game earned a 2.1, tying for 93rd place among the week's prime time shows. Attendance figures weren't any better; the final game drew a crowd of 24,000 to the 90,000-seat Los Angeles Coliseum. League merchandise, including 12 million Topps XFL trading cards, quickly found its way into bargain bins at sporting retailers.

"We knew it wasn't going to work from early March on," said Ebersole. "The launch worked, the people were there, and we didn't answer their expectations, I guess." When the league folded after one season, the combined losses for the WWE and NBC totaled more than $70 million.

What went wrong? Start with the time slot. Any sporting event in prime time on a Saturday night is a risky proposition, especially one with no proven track record. Football and cheerleaders were not incentive enough to keep millions of young sports fans home on date night.

Critics and viewers were also unable to separate the product on the field from Vince McMahon, who has always been a lightning rod for the easily offended; after the first week mental health organizations griped about the name and logo of the Memphis Maniax, which is something they never did to Michael Sembello.

There's no question Vince crosses the line of stupidity and vulgarity, but in the carny world of pro wrestling that's a virtue. The same sensibility doesn't translate to football and McMahon knew it. His goal was legitimacy, with a dash of WWE attitude. Critics who predicted strippers on the sideline and steel cage gridiron contests were disappointed when all they got was a football game. "To Survive, XFL Must get Tackier", recommended the *Orlando Sentinel*. So in week three McMahon finally gave in and promoted a glimpse inside the cheerleaders' locker room at halftime, prompting righteous indignation from demagogues like *New York Post* columnist Phil Mushnick, who has always been quick to blame the WWE for all of society's ills. Some people were determined to be disappointed no matter where the line was drawn.

In wrestling, McMahon had the best athletes in the business on his roster. With the XFL, he had to recruit from the bottom, and the result showed. Only a handful of players were signed by the NFL after the league folded, most notably Tommy Maddox, who was picked up by the Pittsburgh Steelers, where he eventually won the starting quarterback job away from Kordell Stewart.

But as much as the NFL may have dismissed their lowbrow competition, the league was not above adopting some of the XFL's innovations in technology, such as putting more live microphones on the players during the game, mounting cameras on the heads of the officiating crew, and the remarkable SkyCam, a wire-mounted remote camera that provides a unique view from above the field. So while the XFL may have been short-lived, its influence lives on in the way television covers football.

47
THE BRADY BUNCH WELCOMES COUSIN OLIVER

The Brady Bunch
ABC, April 28, 1974–June 10, 1974

"The other kids are right—I'm nothing but a jinx!"
—Cousin Oliver

The monumental cultural significance of *The Brady Bunch* cannot be understated. When the series first aired, from 1969 to 1974, it seemed like a standard family-based situation comedy. But during the past 25 years of constant reruns and periodic reunions, an entire generation of baby boomers formed an emotional attachment to the show and all of its characters that still resonates. All of its characters, that is, except for Cousin Oliver.

In the pilot episode, aired on September 26, 1969, architect Mike Brady (Robert Reed) married Carol Martin (Florence Henderson). Mike's three boys, Greg (Barry Williams), Peter (Christopher Knight), and Bobby (Mike Lookinland), became stepbrothers to Carol's three girls, Marcia (Maureen McCormick), Jan (Eve Plumb), and Cindy (Susan Olsen). Alice Nelson (Ann B. Davis), Mike's housekeeper, completed the household.

Add a family dog (Tiger), a split-level house with only one bathroom, and an astroturf backyard, and the ingredients were in place for every classic sitcom story. The Bradys tackled family vacations, first cars, first dates, school plays, and the full menu of adolescent insecurities, and with smiles and hugs they conquered each one faster than Domino's delivers pizza.

If you're in your thirties, you know the details of the Bradys' lives more intimately than those of your own family. Maybe you can't name three Eminem songs, but you know all the words to "It's a Sunshine Day." You can't order pork chops and applesauce in a restaurant without smiling. You still break appointments by saying, "Something suddenly came up."

The Brady Bunch wasn't a ratings blockbuster in its original run; in fact, the series never ranked among the top 25 shows. But when the numbers slipped even further in the show's fifth season, the stage was set for Oliver's infamous arrival. "(The character) was added to *The Brady Bunch* over my very strong objections," said series creator Sherwood Schwartz. "The executives at Paramount thought the Brady kids were getting older and there would be nobody for the younger viewers to identify with. I didn't think Paramount's argument was valid, but there are times when you have to do what you have to do. So I added a younger boy, Oliver."

And so, in the April 28, 1974 episode entitled "Welcome Aboard," Carol explained to the kids that their cousin was coming to live with them for awhile, because his archeologist parents were dispatched to a project in South America.

The role was played by Robbie Rist, a pint-sized John Denver lookalike who had originally auditioned for "Kelly's Kids," an attempted Brady spinoff featuring Ken Berry and Brooke Bundy as adoptive parents. He lost that role (to Mike Lookinland's brother, Todd), but achieved sitcom immortality as an unwelcome intruder into the idealized American family.

Here's the thing about Oliver—he's not exceptionally obnoxious, but he's completely unnecessary, like a fifth Beatle or a third Olsen twin. Even the producers seemed to realize this shortly after his arrival; the only episode that revolves around Oliver is "Welcome Aboard," in which the Brady kids complain about having him around, and accuse him of being a jinx. This being *The Brady Bunch*, their hostility turns to hospitality before the closing credits, but for the final four episodes of the season, Oliver is reduced to the status of observer.

In "The Snooperstar," Oliver watches Cindy pretend to be Shirley Temple; in "The Hustler," he watches Bobby beat the rest of the family at billiards; in "Top Secret," he's again paired with Bobby, who misguidedly believes his father is working for the FBI; and in "The Hair-Brained Scheme," he tails behind Bobby and Cindy as they fail at separate get-rich-quick schemes.

The arrival of Cousin Oliver did nothing to reverse the series' plummeting ratings, and *The Brady Bunch* was not renewed for the 1975 season. Indeed, the reason his existence doesn't rank higher on the list is that the Bradys were headed for cancellation anyway. If Oliver performed any sort of public service, it was in helping fans see a positive side to the series' demise. What would have happened had the show continued? Would he have had his own box in the opening credits? Would the theme song be changed to "Here's the story of a lovely lady, who was bringing up three very lovely girls and a cousin whose parents were in South America"?

Thankfully, we never had to find out. Oliver was history, and the title of "Most Annoying Sitcom Kid" shifted to Ricky Segall, who polluted the last two minutes of *Partridge Family* episodes by performing such cloying self-penned ditties as "When I Grow Up."

Robbie Rist remained one of TV's most familiar preteen faces for the rest of the

1970s. He played David Hartman's neighbor, Glendon Farrell, on the short-lived drama series *Lucas Tanner*, and then found greater success as David Baxter, the adopted son of Ted Baxter (Ted Knight) and his wife, Georgette (Georgia Engel) on *The Mary Tyler Moore Show*.

Today, Rist is the lead singer for his own Los Angeles-based rock band, Wonderboy. People still approach him after concerts and ask "You were that kid, weren't you?" If they were Brady fans, it's probably best that we don't record what they say next.

46

WELL, THERE THEY GO AGAIN

The Reagans
SHOWTIME, NOVEMBER 30, 2003

No political agenda is required to view *The Reagans* for what it was—a shameless, vicious hatchet job unleashed when the Reagans themselves had been divided and debilitated by a tragic illness. Certainly the former president had as many detractors as admirers, many of whom work in Hollywood. But if you justify this portrayal then don't say a word when a Bill Clinton movie is released that spends 75 percent of its running time on Monica Lewinsky.

All film biographies exist in a heightened state of reality, and focus on the most dramatic incidents from their subjects' lives, so it's no surprise that the infamous moments from Reagan's two presidential terms are well-documented—the Iran-Contra deal, the visit to Bitburg Cemetery—but even Reagan's most rabid detractors would have to acknowledge, however grudgingly, that the man accomplished some good in his eight years in the White House. Those scenes do not appear in the film, or they're glossed over quickly as if these achievements were little more than a footnote to his legacy.

"This is a dramatization, it isn't a documentary," said director Robert Alan Ackerman. "The politics are kind of a background to the story of Nancy and Ronald and the family. It's driven by their relationship. I think anybody who sees this movie will come away with very positive feelings about both of them and that relationship." The problem with this argument is that even in its depictions of the couple that do not involve politics, the portrayal is hardly flattering.

Consider the scenes set in 1949, when Ron and Nancy were actors on the MGM payroll. Ron is introduced to Nancy and asked by a studio chief to take her to dinner, and console her after she was inadvertently named on a list of communist sympathizers. But the next scene reveals that Nancy manipulated the meeting to further her career. She rehearses flattery between dates, and Ron, big softhearted galoot that he is, falls for it every time.

The movie opens in 1987, with President Reagan watching cartoons and sitting mute on his bed while Nancy hashes out political strategy with his staff regarding Iran/Contra. The film's characterizations of the couple are quickly established; Ronnie is a simple-minded charmer, kind and compassionate but not too bright and frightened of any sort of confrontation. He's an actor turned wind-up toy politician, directed and choreographed by advisers and his overbearing wife.

Given the sensitivity of the subject, the appearance of impropriety can be just as damning as the real thing, so the producers didn't do themselves any favors when they cast James Brolin, husband of über-Democrat Barbra Streisand, as Reagan. His performance is admirable in a Rich Little sort of way, but even in those moments when Reagan is portrayed as trying to do the right thing, his good intentions are undercut by a costume choice or a gesture or a deadpan expression suggesting that no one should take this guy seriously.

As for Nancy, she comes off as a combination of Lady Macbeth, Eve Harrington and Joan Crawford in *Mommie Dearest*. Australian actress Judy Davis also revived some of the nervous tics she used in her Emmy-winning portrayal of Judy Garland. "She is often so taut that you could play Bach on her," wrote the *Los Angeles Times*.

While Nancy alienates her children and her husband's advisers, Ronnie stumbles along in his own world, causing havoc but unaware he is doing so. "They made my father look like Mr. Magoo," said son Michael Reagan. We see then-Governor Reagan refusing to meet with the mother of a death row inmate on the eve of his execution, so he can make it to the Academy Awards, and releasing hundreds of crazy people onto the streets of California after closing the mental hospitals. But we don't see Reagan's "Mr. Gorbachev, tear down this wall" speech, his teary-eyed tribute at the memorial for the Challenger astronauts, any evidence of the economic prosperity that accompanied much of his presidency, or an explanation for how he won two landslide presidential elections. If *The Reagans* is to be believed, the only two things for which the president showed any talent were public speaking and taking a bullet.

Also missing are two sequences filmed but deleted after their contents were leaked, resulting in 80,000 angry emails to CBS. One scene had Reagan speculating that AIDS was a plague from God to punish homosexuals. The other had Ronnie telling Nancy, after a disagreement over the firing of Secretary of State Al Haig, to "get off my goddamn back." Neither incident was based on any documented facts.

The timing of the film proved just as offensive as the content; Reagan was stricken with Alzheimer's Disease in 1994, and Nancy devoted herself to his care until the day of his passing ten years later. It was hard to find anyone who believed the presentation of such a portrayal wasn't hitting below the belt given Reagan's condition at the time. "I was told it was going to be a love story, that the politics would be in the background," said CBS president Les Moonves. "I didn't feel that was the case." Balancing the public outcry and his own personal misgivings against what may have been a ratings winner during November sweeps, Moonves ultimately decided to drop the two-part miniseries.

"Although the miniseries features impressive production values and acting performances, and although the producers have sources to verify each scene in the script, we believe it does not present a balanced portrayal of the Reagans for CBS and its audience," said the network in a released statement. "Subsequent edits that we considered did not address those concerns."

As a result, the miniseries was edited down to a three-hour film, and debuted on Showtime. Prior to its presentation, the network aired a taped message from Showtime Chairman and CEO Matt Blank; "As you probably know, *The Reagans* has been criticized by those who have yet to see it as an unbalanced denouncement of Ronald Reagan's presidency. We believe it is, in fact, an honest portrayal of many of the turning points in his life and in his political career.

Critics, hardly the most politically conservative bunch, disagreed. "Offensive, grotesque, unfair and ultimately trivial" (*Salt Lake Tribune*); "Belittling, derogatory and cartoonish" (*ChronWatch*); "The film... definitely makes the Reagans rather freakish creatures. At least the film acknowledges, if mostly in a postscript, that he did end the Cold War and bring down the Berlin Wall, among other historic accomplishments" (*Washington Post*); "The makers of *The Reagans* claim it isn't biased. Wrong, oh so wrong. Worse than wrong, though, the movie isn't even entertaining, except as high camp" (*Atlanta Journal-Constitution*).

In a panel discussion aired on Showtime following the movie, even the two liberal guests, Marvin Kalb and Lou Cannon, denounced *The Reagans*. "It's hard to imagine a cartoon that could be that bad," said Cannon. "I *do* know Ronald Reagan. This isn't Ronald Reagan."

To those who maintain the outrage was politically motivated, no doubt some of it was. And if *The Reagans* emphasized only the president's shortcomings, that's not to say that he didn't have any. The lesson to be learned, even moreso than the dangers of dramatic license abuse, is don't kick a guy when he's down.

45
CARPS AND ROBBERS

Fish Police
CBS, February 28–March 13, 1992

Film critic Gene Siskel had a test he applied while reviewing a movie. He asked whether the film was more interesting than a documentary of its cast having lunch. By this criteria, given the personnel involved and the caliber of the finished product, *Fish Police* may be the most flagrant waste of talent ever devised.

The lead character of Inspector Gil ("I'm a cop—who's a carp") was voiced by John Ritter, whose great comedic gifts stemmed mainly from the twinkle in his eye and the clumsy grace of his slapstick pratfalls, neither of which were of any help to him here. Ritter's supporting cast is as follows: Edward Asner, Tim Curry, Hector Elizondo, Robert Guillaume, Buddy Hackett, Megan Mullally, Frank Welker, JoBeth Williams, and Jonathan Winters. That lunchtime documentary sounds pretty good.

Apparently, this was CBS's answer to *The Simpsons*, an animated series with sharper writing than most live-action sitcoms. The Tiffany network got the animated part right, but comparisons end there. Based on a comic book by Steve Moncuse, *Fish Police* envisioned a film noir-esque metropolis beneath the sea called Fish City, where various species of undersea creatures take on the roles of trenchcoat-clad gumshoes, dames of questionable virtue, mobsters, thugs and cops. If New York was a melting pot, Fish City was a bouillabaisse. That's one of the jokes from the first episode. They don't get better.

In "The Shell Game," Gil investigates the murder of underworld figure Clams Casino. Sultry Angel (JoBeth Williams) is a suspect, a cab drivin' crab (Hackett) provides clues to the case, and diner waitress Pearl (Mullally) offers Gil a sympathetic shoulder when his boss, Chief Abalone (Asner) demands answers. Abalone, a gruff but lovable portly bit of seafood in a white shirt and too-short tie, is Lou Grant with fins, and it's surprising that Asner would lend his voice to a watered-down, water-logged variation on his most famous character.

What's supposed to be funny is that the characters are fish, but that's hardly a revelation in cartoons, where animals have walked and talked and solved crimes for decades, especially at the Hanna-Barbera studio where *Fish Police* was created. But though the animation boasts more color and detail than Hanna-Barbera's Saturday morning stable, the humor rarely descends beyond the series' basic premise. Characters with names like Muscles Marinara trade insults like 'Barnacle Butt' and 'Dorsal-Kisser,' the mob lawyer is a shark who wonders if his client will be "of-fish-ally charged"; a nightclub singer croons "Flounders in the Night"; the house of worship is the Church of the Holy Mackeral. And on it went.

Once viewers figured out that fish puns were all the show had to offer, the series floundered (sue me) as viewers switched back to the comparative comedic brilliance of Patrick Duffy and Suzanne Somers on ABC's *Step By Step*. Six episodes of *Fish Police* were made: "The Shell Game," "A Fish Out of Water," "Beauty's Only Fin Deep," "The Godfather," "The Two Gils," and—get ready—"No Way to Treat a Fillet-dy." CBS aired the first three then pulled the plug, dispatching *Fish Police* from its Friday night perch (get it? perch?) down the drain to a watery grave.

44
WHEN COUSINS ARE TWO OF A KIND

The Dukes of Hazzard
CBS, SEPTEMBER 24, 1982–FEBRUARY 25, 1983

When *The Dukes of Hazzard* debuted on CBS in 1979, creator Gy Waldron collected 200 reviews of the series—196 of them were bad. And yet, this story of two good ol' boys and their sexy cousin battling corruption in a small Southern town became a sensation, especially in what elitist Hollywood calls 'flyover country' '(i.e. everything between New York and Los Angeles). The Dukes' appeal in the South was so pervasive that high schools rescheduled the traditional Friday night football games because fans were home watching Bo and Luke outrun Sheriff Roscoe.

Confused TV critics could offer only one explanation for the series' success. "The car is the star" they wrote, a reference to a customized '69 Dodge Charger, dubbed the General Lee. In every episode, Bo (John Schneider) and Luke Duke (Tom Wopat) would race through the backroads of Hazzard county, one step ahead of the sheriff (James Best) and corrupt county commissioner Boss Hogg (Sorrell Booke). The General skidded through bootlegger turns and jumped over ravines, grain silos and two-story houses, accompanied by guitar-pickin' music and the downhome narration of balladeer Waylon Jennings.

Schneider and Wopat tested that "car is the star" theory in 1982, when they discovered *The Dukes of Hazzard* had become television's most merchandised series, generating more than $190 million from t-shirts, toy cars, posters, lunchboxes, and 400 other items. The two stars were supposed to receive five percent of merchandising revenues, but had been paid less than $25,000 each. "We started asking questions, but they weren't answered. They gave us a *Dukes* yo-yo and a lunchbox instead," Schneider recalled.

So instead of reporting to work on the series' fifth season, they filed a $25 million lawsuit. "The Duke boys wouldn't stand for being cheated, and neither will we," they declared in a joint statement. Costar Catherine Bach (Daisy) was apprised of their decision, but not asked to join the walkout. "They said 'No, this is man's work,'" she remembers, "But I'd have gone out with them in a second." Had she done so, Warner Bros. was prepared to cancel the series.

But as long as Daisy and the supporting cast remained, CBS figured it really didn't matter who was driving the car, and let the stars walk. Warner Bros. countersued Schneider and Wopat for $117 million, and announced public auditions for "cast additions" to *The Dukes of Hazzard*. Open cattle calls were held in L.A., Chicago, New York, and ten other cities for the roles of Coy and Vance Duke, cousins to Bo and Luke. Applicants without previous acting experience would be considered, but they should "be able to do light Southern dialects."

More than 2,000 contenders showed up, including some Asian and African-American candidates, which would have made for an intriguing branch of the Duke family tree. Meanwhile, attorneys for Schneider and Wopat conducted an audit on the studio ledger. But Schneider was so certain his departure was temporary he recommended his own replacement. "Whether Warner Bros. will admit this or not, I told them, 'If you want to get someone who will remind you of me, there's a guy in Atlanta named Byron Cherry.'"

Cherry, a former flight attendant for Eastern Airlines, had intended to audition for the original *Dukes* cast in 1978, until he was booked on a red-eye heading in the opposite direction. But his fortunes changed when he landed the role of Coy, opposite Christopher Mayer as Vance. "All I want to do," said the dutiful Cherry, "is keep Warner Bros. happy and show up on time."

Mayer was equally delighted at his big break, having been previously unemployed, and the victim of a robbery in the one-bedroom Hollywood apartment he shared with his pregnant wife, actress Teri Copley. Before he joined the *Dukes* cast, the couple's only means of income had been the handmade straw baskets Teri sold at swap meets. "It is the nearest a man can come to having a baby," is how Mayer described his joy.

I couldn't wait to see who they'd come up with to replace them," recalled Rick Hurst, who played deputy Cletus. "I was surprised and delighted to find they had guys that kinda looked like them. I thought they might be able to do this, but America wouldn't buy it."

As production began with the substitute Dukes, it quickly became apparent that Warner Bros. was more interested in creating clones than hiring actors. Cherry and Mayer were dressed in identical jeans and colored shirts, the same wardrobe worn by their predecessors, and played the characters without the slightest derivation from the established pattern. Hardly surprising, as the only change made to previously-written scripts was switching the names from "Bo and Luke" to "Coy and Vance."

"I thought they would have to try and come up with two different characters, but then when I saw the wardrobe, how similar-looking they were, it was obvious they were just trying to xerox Tom and John and it became pretty evident that they couldn't do that," said Hurst. Adds series writer Si Rose, "The studio figured some of the people watching over their beer wouldn't know the difference."

In the fifth season opener, "The New Dukes," balladeer Jennings explains that Bo and Luke have joined the NASCAR circuit, but made certain that Daisy and their Uncle Jesse were looked after by asking cousins Coy and Vance to run the farm. Viewers just hoped they would buy the farm. After the first few episodes, the series that had spent the previous three seasons in the top ten had dropped to 36th in the ratings.

Once it was apparent that the charisma and camaraderie of Schneider and Wopat could not be replicated, and that viewers actually did care about what happened on the show between chase scenes, a set-tlement was quickly negotiated. Just before Christmas of 1982, by which time *The Dukes of Hazzard* had plummeted into the fifties among the top 70 shows Nielsen surveys, CBS announced the return of the original Duke boys. There was a mutual dropping of lawsuits, and an agreement to keep the terms of the resolution confidential.

With Bo and Luke back, what fate would befall Coy and Vance? "We intend to keep them in the cast and take full advantage of the fact that they have created their own fan followings," said Warner Bros.

Temporary Duke boys Christopher Mayer (left) and Byron Cherry. Next, we're going to pretend to be Starsky and Hutch.

111

Television President Alan Shane, apparently with a straight face. But in the episode "Welcome Back, Bo and Luke", the doppelgangers were shuffled off before the first commercial break, and never seen or heard from again.

"Everyone was very supportive of the two guys themselves, but at the same time we were also supportive of Tom and John, because we knew what they were objecting to had some validity," says Hurst. "In fact, some 20 years later their issue with Warner Bros. is still up in the air for myself, James Best, Sonny Shroyer (Enos), and Ben Jones (Cooter). We haven't gotten any merchandising checks for 20 years and they are still licensing (*Dukes*) t-shirts and posters. So we'll be knockin' on their door pretty soon."

43

THE LIGHTER SIDE OF CHILD LABOR

Small Wonder
SYNDICATED, SEPTEMBER 7, 1985–FEBRUARY 9, 1989

"I can do anything I'm programmed to do."   —VICKI

We must take *Small Wonder* creator Howard Leeds at his word when he describes the series as a sunny situation comedy geared toward younger viewers. But however innocuous this early example of first-run syndication may seem, there's something undeniably creepy about the premise.

This is the tale of Ted Lawson (Dick Christie), a cybernetics genius at United Robotronics who creates a mechanical household servant in the form of a pretty ten-year-old girl (Tiffany Brissette). The girl is named Vicki, a modified acronym for Voice Input Child Identicant. To the outside world, the Lawsons—Ted, his wife Joan (Marla Pennington), and their son Jamie (Jerry Supran) treat Vicki as one of the family, even going so far as to formalize an adoption proceeding. But behind closed doors, she is relegated to the status of a domestic servant and household appliance. In various episodes Vicki is used as a tape recorder, food processor, blender, and popcorn popper, all of which are activated by touching her nose.

Leeds was a 30 year veteran of television when he pitched this concept, having started out as producer and head writer on *My Living Doll*, another series about a mechanical female, starring Robert Cummings and Julie Newmar. In *Small Wonder*, Victoria Ann-Smith Lawson is programmed to act like a normal child despite her stoic expression and monotone voice. The addition of a Personality Emulation Program allows her to pass for human, well enough to fool her peers at Grant Junior High.

Vicki resembles a life-sized doll, with her bobbed ponytail, lacy red pinafore, white knee socks and Mary Jane shoes. Her control panel is placed either on her front or back depending on the episode, but requires partial removal of her dress to access.

At some point the issue was settled by moving the panel to the dorsal position, to accommodate Tiffany Brissette's understandable modesty.

In the series' first two seasons, Vicki responds to questions with "I can do anything I'm programmed to do," which certainly appeals to her male classmates, who frequently ask her out. In the third season, her design is upgraded so she can eat and go to the bathroom, which may be a little too much information for the home viewer.

Vicki's relationship with Jamie is uncomfortably ambiguous. Though he's never cruel, the boy orders Vicki around at home, always having her clean up their room, though he demands she turn her back when he puts on his pajamas. But he's also protective of his "sister" at school, and enjoys spending time with her. What made some viewers squeamish was having Vicki, an anatomically-correct girl, stored in Jamie's bedroom closet overnight. Any teenage boy that age is bound to be curious, but thankfully we never get that very special episode.

One doesn't want to take a featherbrained sitcom too seriously, but the implications in its scenario are impossible to ignore. Under the circumstances it might have been wise to avoid any mention of sex, no matter how innocent, but the character of Harriet (Emily Schulman), an obnoxious flirt forever hitting on Jamie, is a constant reminder that kids their age are already attracted to each other.

The Vicki character is ill-conceived on so many levels, but the show lucked out with its casting of Brissette, a charming young actress who did the best she could with a miserable assignment. She even generates a few laughs with Vicki's ability to copy the speech patterns and behavior of others, bursting out of her frozen expression into brief moments of animation, then instantly shifting back into robot mode.

Small Wonder ran four seasons and 96 episodes. Because it was syndicated, it could be produced for less money and survive longer with lower ratings. The series generally flew under the radar after an initial round of bad reviews, never receiving a cover or even an article in *TV Guide*, rare for a sitcom that lasted that long. But some college feminist studies courses were paying attention, and incorporated the series in their classroom discussions.

The series' failure to sufficiently penetrate the pop culture explains why there wasn't more speculation about how Vicki may have been used and abused by the Lawsons, the way fans still enjoy debating about how Gilligan and Mary Ann or Jeannie and Captain Nelson passed the time between episodes. Perhaps that's for the best.

42
HOME OF THE FLOPPER

The "Herb" campaign
ABC, CBS, NBC, November 1985–February 1986

Americans love fast food, no matter how many health and nutritional studies are released by dietitians, government officials and other professional busybodies. Despite the growing market presence of Wendy's, Carl's Jr., and other regional chains, McDonald's has enjoyed a decades-long dominance of the drive-through cuisine market, with Burger King still playing Phil Mickelson to its Tiger Woods.

The home of the Whopper has been around since 1954, when James McLamore and David Edgerton opened the first location in Miami, Florida. Millions swear by the French fries and the flame-broiling of the hamburgers, but the company seems forever destined to operate in the shadow of the golden arches. Arguments among burger buffs will never be resolved, but even those who prefer the Whopper to the Big Mac must concede the superiority of McDonald's in the field of creative advertising.

From the 1960s through the 1990s, the McDonald's marketing machine was untouchable, introducing one memorable song, slogan and promotion after another. Next to Mickey Mouse, Ronald McDonald may be the most recognized company mascot ever conceived. "You Deserve a Break Today" was named the best jingle in television history by *Advertising Age* magazine, and made VH-1's countdown of television's top 100 musical moments, alongside *American Bandstand* and the Beatles on Ed Sullivan. Thanks to another catchy tune most baby boomers can still recite the ingredients in a Big Mac ("Two all-beef patties, special sauce lettuce cheese pickles onions on a sesame seed bun.") And with McDonaldland, the company created its own Disney-esque universe, complete with a line of colorful plastic toys and action figures.

Burger King, by contrast, has been hit and miss on Madison Ave. They launched a winner with the "Have It Your Way" campaign, best remembered by Debra Winger warbling "Hold the pickle, hold the lettuce, special orders don't upset us." A good song and a shrewdly-chosen selling point, directed at anyone who special ordered a Big Mac at Mickey D's and waited at the counter for 20 minutes. But other campaigns fizzled, none more spectacularly than the introduction of a mystery man named Herb in November 1985.

A brainchild of the J. Walter Thompson agency, the $40 million campaign opened with in-store ads, billboards and television commercials all asking the question "Where's Herb?" After a few weeks of teasing, we were told that Herb is the only man in America who has never had a Burger King hamburger (which no doubt came as a great surprise to the nation's vegetarians). Commercials featured mock testimonials from Herb's family and friends, who expressed amazement that Herb still hasn't tried a Whopper, and urged the wayward chump to get with the program.

To enlist the public's help, Burger King offered $5,000 to any customer who spotted Herb in one of its franchises. Unfortunately, they failed to mention what the guy looked like, hoping this would prompt widespread debate among the viewing public. Instead, it prompted customers harassing each other with "Are you Herb?" questions in Burger Kings across the country.

These were dark days for fast food employees. No one will ever know how many times contest nuts and amateur comics would single out a vagrant, who had scraped together enough change for a meager lunch, and shout "Herb! I found Herb! Where's my money?" The minimum wage-earning teenager behind the counter, who had enough problems without having to deal with wiseasses all day, would then have to diffuse the situation.

The company corrected the debacle by announcing that, never mind, they had found Herb, so stop accosting customers in our restaurants. During the Super Bowl in January 1986, while football fans watched the Chicago Bears pummel the New England Patriots, the enigmatic Whopper-hater was revealed at last. As played by John Merrick, a classically trained 35-year-old actor, he was a balding, bespectacled nerd in a loud jacket, high-water pants, and white socks. Amidst much fanfare, Herb subsequently appeared on NBC's *Today Show* and as the celebrity timekeeper at Wrestlemania II.

Hoping to finally claim its own boxcar on the fast food merchandising money train, Burger King plastered Herb's image on a variety of products, including t-shirts that read "I dated Herb." John Merrick appeared in Burger King restaurants nationwide, giving a prize to the first person who recognized him. Some customers settled for the next best thing; a group of MIT students stole a Herb poster, barely making their escape after being chased by an angry manager. Back at the dorm, they called the Burger King and announced "We have Herb." The reply was "We have your license number."

Clearly, Herb had thus far triumphed in generating customer abuse, employee discomfort and petty theft. What he failed to do was increase sales. In fact, business plummeted during the campaign, which was projected to run for more than a year, but was shut down in four months. The original message of Herb being a nerd because he never ate at Burger King was lost after he became the company's most prominent symbol. Besides, if he hated the place so much, why was he always hanging out there? Somewhere along the way, Herb became the equivalent of those creepy guys who lurk at the bus station, and Whoppers became the meal of choice among socially awkward losers.

Advertising Age labeled the Herb campaign the "most elaborate advertising flop of the decade", and its legacy endures in college corporate marketing textbooks, as an example of what not to do. Burger King's next two campaigns, "Burger King Town" and "Best Food for Fast Times" didn't fare much better, but at least they didn't kill the business. As advertising misfires go, Herb was a whopper.

41
CASABLANCA, THE SERIES?

From *The Front Page* in 1949 to *My Big Fat Greek Family* in 2002, television adaptations of feature films have always been a part of the medium's history. But successful transitions from the big screen to the big screen TV are rare. *M*A*S*H*, *The Odd Couple*, and *Buffy the Vampire Slayer* all enjoyed critical acclaim and are more fondly remembered today than the movies that inspired them, and the TV takes on *Gidget* and *Please Don't Eat the Daisies* also match up well with their theatrical predecessors. But most attempts to recapture the magic of a hit movie fail within their first season. From a field of hundreds, here are the 25 worst offenders.

Casablanca (NBC, 1983)
David Soul as Rick Blaine. Enough said.

Shane (ABC, 1966)
The reason little Joey's plaintive cry "Come back, Shane!" was so moving is that we knew Shane was never going to come back. The reluctant gunfighter could not outrun his violent past, much as he yearned to live out his days with the frontier family who . . . .hey, wait a minute, who's that riding through the valley? After 13 years, Shane comes back, and this time, he's taller. David Carradine played the role originated by Alan Ladd.

The Thin Man (NBC, 1957–1959)
It was foolish to expect that any couple could emulate the matchless chemistry between William Powell and Myrna Loy,

In NBC's remake of Casablanca, *Rick (David Soul) tells Ilsa "Don't give up on us, baby."*

who played Nick and Nora Charles in six classic *Thin Man* films. Peter Lawford and Phyllis Kirk never had a chance, though the series did last two seasons. Stafford Repp, who played Chief O'Hara on *Batman* and practically spent his entire career in a police uniform, played Nick's friend on the force.

Ferris Bueller (NBC, 1990)
Why hasn't Jennifer Aniston used some of her *Friends* money to buy up all existing copies of this embarrassment? Charlie Schlatter, trying way too hard to be cool, plays Ferris opposite Aniston as hostile big sister Jeannie. In the first episode, Schlatter had the *cajones* to run a chainsaw through a cardboard cutout of Matthew Broderick. The FOX network's *Parker Lewis Can't Lose*, a blatant Ferris Bueller rip-off, actually fared better than the authorized adaptation.

Serpico (NBC, 1976–1977)

The role of tough but honest undercover cop Frank Serpico, played by Al Pacino in the 1973 film, was inexplicably turned over to David Birney, best known as that nice clean cut Jewish boy from *Bridget Loves Bernie*. Birney's attempt to intimidate dangerous street hoods was reminiscent of Richie Cunningham's attempts to emulate the Fonz.

Seven Brides for Seven Brothers (CBS, 1982–1983)

I'll applaud almost any revival of large-scale musicals to television, but the idea only works if you hire actors who can sing and dance. Richard Dean Anderson, Peter Horton, Drake Hogestyn, and River Phoenix struggle through frontier production numbers that make Monty Python's "Lumberjack Song" look polished by comparison.

The Third Man (Syndicated, 1960–1962)

In the film, Harry Lime was a vicious, amoral swindler, albeit a charming one as played by Orson Welles. Hardly a made-for-TV hero, so in this short-lived series Lime (Michael Rennie) was transformed into a wealthy amateur sleuth with a shady past. Jonathan Harris, later of *Lost in Space* fame, played his assistant.

Freebie and the Bean (CBS, 1980–1981)

It's bad enough that television can't stop adapting good movies, here's a case where a lousy cop flick starring James Caan and Alan Arkin was transformed into an even worse action series, with Tom Mason as Sgt. Tim (Freebie) Walker and Hector Elizondo as Sgt. Dan Delgado, "The Bean."

Uncle Buck (CBS, 1990–1991)

Controversy swirled around this adaptation of the John Candy/John Hughes comedy, when CBS censors objected to the first episode dialogue, "Miles, you suck!" This was the first time that particular epithet aired on the Tiffany network, and what a proud moment that was. Parents found the humor in poor taste and kids found star Kevin Meaney more creepy than cuddly.

Conan the Adventurer (Syndicated, 1997)

From the folks who brought you *Tarzan: The Epic Adventures* and *Acapulco Heat*, *Conan the Adventurer* starred Ralf Moeller, a two-time Mr. Universe and friend of movie Conan Arnold Schwarzenegger. The German actor's accent was easier to decipher than Arnold's, but the stories were dreadful.

The Bad News Bears (CBS, 1979–1980)

Let's face it, what made the movies so entertaining was watching 10-year-old kids swear and spit and attack each other like … well, like real 10-year-old kids. Once the Bears cleaned up their act for prime time, they weren't anywhere near as much fun. Still, check out a rerun if you can for early career performances from Corey Feldman, Catherine Hicks and Christoff St. John.

Down and Out in Beverly Hills (FOX, 1987)
Let's give it up for Hector Elizondo, who appeared in no less than three failed TV adaptations of hit motion pictures. In addition to his work here as Dave Whiteman (played by Richard Dreyfuss in the film), Elizondo also costarred in *Casablanca* and *Freebie and the Bean*. He gets cancelled a lot, but at least he keeps busy.

Mr. Roberts (NBC, 1965–1966)
I suppose this must be a prequel to the 1948 film with Henry Fonda, James Cagney, and Jack Lemmon, who won the Oscar as Ensign Pulver. Roberts died at the end of that movie, but somehow made it back onto the U.S.S. Reluctant for this derivative comedy. Roger Smith played Roberts, opposite Steve Harmon as Pulver.

Born Free (NBC, 1974)
The further adventures of Elsa the lioness, with Gary Collins and Diana Muldaur stepping into the roles of game wardens George and Joy Adamson. On location filming in East Africa made this one of the better-looking failures of the year, but even in 1974 everyone was starting to get tired of that theme song.

Delta House (ABC, 1979)
Gross-out gags, gratuitous nudity, and everything else that made *National Lampoon's Animal House* a comedy classic could never be shown on television, which explains why *Delta House* folded in three months, despite the presence of several of the film's cast members, including John Vernon (Dean Wormer), Stephen Furst (Flounder), and James Widdoes (Hoover).

Barefoot in the Park (ABC, 1970–1971)
This was ABC's first unsuccessful attempt to adapt a Neil Simon play with an African-American cast; Scoey Mitchell and Tracy Reed play young newlyweds in New York City. Ten years later, they tried the same experiment with *The Odd Couple*, with Demond Wilson and Ron Glass taking over for Tony Randall and Jack Klugman (who took over for Jack Lemmon and Walter Matthau). I look forward to Bernie Mac in *Brighton Beach Memoirs* any day now.

Planet of the Apes (CBS, 1974)
After five feature outings Roddy McDowell still hadn't had enough of three-hour makeup sessions, and signed up to play sympathetic ape Galen opposite marooned astronauts Alan Virdon (Ron Harper) and Pete Burke (James Naughton). Despite the enduring popularity of the franchise, this time it was 14 shows and out for those damn, dirty apes.

Stir Crazy (CBS, 1985–1986)
The film really wasn't much to begin with, but the Richard Pryor-Gene Wilder chemistry generated enough laughs to justify the video rental. Bereft of their skills

and timing, the spinoff series had nothing to recommend. Larry Riley and Joseph Guzaldo played the leads.

Mr. Smith Goes to Washington (ABC, 1962–1963)
Actually, a better title would be *Davy Crockett Goes to Washington*; Fess Parker, who made coonskin caps a fashion statement in the fifties, plays the homespun freshman senator first essayed by Jimmy Stewart.

Fast Times (CBS, 1986)
Movie version: Judge Reinhold pleasures himself to the fantasy of a topless Phoebe Cates; TV version: Jason Hervey plays Jeff Spicoli's brother, Curtis. Not quite the same. Ray Walston as Mr. Hand was his same ornery self, and Courtney Thorne-Smith is a charmer in Jennifer Jason Leigh's role, but these *Fast Times* quickly ground to a halt.

Dirty Dancing (CBS, 1988–1989)
It's a mystery why CBS chose to de-ethnicize the romance between sweet Jewish girl Baby and her leather pants-clad dance teacher. For the series, Baby's family were conservative WASPs, which would lead one to question what they were doing in the Catskills. Patrick Cassidy and Melora Hardin played the dancing couple, with McLean Stevenson stepping into the Jerry Orbach role of Baby's overprotective father.

A League of Their Own (CBS, 1993)
With only Tracy Reiner (Betty) and Megan Cavanagh (Marla) returning from the 1992 film, this sitcom about the Rockford Peaches baseball team was the pits. Garry Marshall, whose sister Penny directed the film, appeared as the league owner.

Private Benjamin (CBS, 1981–1983)
Where the 1980 film mined comic inspiration from the difficult adjustment to army life made by spoiled New York socialite Judy Benjamin (Goldie Hawn), the series dropped its heroine into a series of slapstick adventures that had more in common with *Laverne & Shirley*. Lorna Patterson was a cute, spunky substitute for Goldie, but even with Eileen Brennan and Hal Williams reprising their film roles this *Private Benjamin* deserved a dishonorable discharge.

Working Girl (NBC, 1990)
Nancy McKeon was originally set to play upwardly mobile executive Tess McGill (played by Melanie Griffith in the 1988 film), but when she passed the role went to an unknown named Sandra Bullock. Four years before she drove a bus to stardom in *Speed*, Bullock did her best with inferior material, but the show lasted less than three months. A pre-*Deep Space Nine* Nana Visitor played Tess' demanding boss, Bryn Newhouse.

Shaft (CBS, 1973–1974)
This one could have been a contender, with Richard Roundtree back in the role of

detective John Shaft and Isaac Hayes' Oscar-winning theme punctuating the gritty urban stories. But network censors prompted too many changes in the hard-livin', hard-lovin' character.

How to Marry a Millionaire (Syndicated, 1957–1959)

Barbara Eden almost makes this one work, with her inspired take on cute but clumsy Loco Jones (played by Betty Grable in the 1953 film). But costars Merry Anders and Lori Nelson were no match for their movie counterparts, Lauren Bacall and Marilyn Monroe.

40

STILL NOT READY FOR PRIME TIME

The Dana Carvey Show
ABC, MARCH 12–MAY 7, 1996

All across Middle America the cry rang out—"But he seemed like such a nice young man when he says "Wouldn't be prudent" on *Saturday Night Live*!" Through seven seasons as *SNL*'s most valuable player, Dana Carvey created a stock company of memorable characters, from Garth and the Church Lady to his dead-on sendups of George Bush, Ross Perot, and Paul McCartney. With his tousled hair, boyish face and impish grin, Carvey appeared ever-capable of mischief, but never anything that crossed the line into cruelty. At least that's what ABC figured when they offered the comic chameleon his own prime time series.

The Dana Carvey Show was touted as sketch comedy with a subversive twist. "It's kind of a combination of *Saturday Night Live*, Monty Python, *The Ben Stiller Show*, and *Kids in the Hall*," Carvey told *TV Guide* a week before the premiere. "It's going to be my sensibility, very silly and weird. I'm executive producer, so if it stinks, you can come after me." He probably wishes he didn't add that last part.

The idea was hatched when Carvey turned down an offer to replace David Letterman in NBC's post *Tonight Show* slot, after Letterman moved to CBS. Having left *Saturday Night Live* after the 1992 season, the 40-year-old Carvey was looking for an assignment that would still leave time to spend with his wife and two young sons. Plans for a prime time stint at NBC never materialized, but ABC jumped at the chance to add such a likable proven commodity to their schedule. Carvey was given the network's most propitious time slot, Tuesdays at 9:30 between *Home Improvement* and *NYPD Blue*. "We can't wait to get the show on the air," gushed ABC Entertainment president Ted Harbert.

But before the first show aired, there were rumblings from the Carvey camp that he and co-writer (and *SNL* vet) Robert Smigel were planning to push the envelope.

"We can do a lot of weird stuff because Dana is so likable he can get away with it," Smigel told *TV Guide*.

"I don't know if the world is ready for this at 9:30," Carvey echoed. "I'm packaged in sort of a people-pleasing way ... I compartmentalize my madness. I think people would be surprised by who I really am."

One of his first inspirations was to include the program's sponsor in the title, and then take jabs at the company during the show. Thus the first episode aired with the official title of *The Taco Bell Dana Carvey Show*. An early sketch had a chorus of dancing Taco Bell employees introducing Carvey with the musical salute, "We paid him a fortune to use our name, because he's a shameless whore." Later, Carvey appeared as conservative talk show host Pat Buchanan and unleashed a tirade of derogatory remarks about Mexican immigrants, which Taco Bell must have loved.

But the most appalling moment in the first episode had Carvey as President Bill Clinton delivering a campaign speech. He announced that he had placed his wife Hillary under house arrest, as the camera cut to a black-and-white clip of the First Lady howling and snarling as she clawed at a locked door. But there's no reason for concern, says Clinton; "Without Hillary, I can be both mother and father to my country. With the development of hormone therapy, I invite the American people to suckle on my teats." Carvey then ripped open a white shirt to reveal a prosthetic of a chest with eight nipples, where he was suckling a baby, two dogs, and a cat. Milk dripping from the prosthetic was lapped up by three golden retriever puppies on the president's desk.

As a final touch, Carvey offered up a top ten list, suggesting new names for Britain's Princess Diana. Among the choices: 'slut' and 'whore.' Maybe it was a good thing he didn't take Letterman's time slot.

Taco Bell and Pizza Hut withdrew $5 million in ads less than 24 hours after the show debuted. "I think the content took everyone by surprise," said a Pizza Hut spokesman. "Maybe it's a case of what works at 11:30 on Saturday night doesn't work at 9:30 on a weeknight. The show may very well go on to be a big hit, but we're no longer comfortable as a title sponsor." Though the episode won its time slot, even ABC executives were upset. "Portions of the premiere episode went too far," they acknowledged. "We will be more careful in the future."

Among the show's major sponsors, only Pepsi renewed its support, but ratings started to drop as quickly as the level of intelligence in the material. Subsequent episodes featured skits about the nation's first ladies as dogs, and a Pakistani sex therapist who offered sleazy advice to every patient. Restricted from using any of his *SNL* characters on the new show, Carvey tried to end-around the restrictions by portraying their relatives; one sketch featured the Church Lady's gay nephew, who predictably spoke with the same nasal inflections.

What is most baffling is how Carvey rarely indulged his fondness for controversial material on *Saturday Night Live*, a more appropriate venue for such ideas. Though *SNL* stopped being genuinely subversive almost a decade before his arrival in 1986, the show was still capable of occasionally stretching beyond the margins of network broadcast standards. Inexplicably, Carvey saved his hardcore routines for prime time, when millions of kids were watching. "It was just totally silly, a total mistake" he told *TV Guide* after the series was axed.

Dana Carvey was philosophical about his show's fate; "If it bombs I'll just go back to doing movies." he told *L.A. Life*, before its debut. So if *The Dana Carvey Show* didn't already have enough to live down, it can also be blamed for Carvey's appearances in *Little Nicky* and *Master of Disguise*.

39
MORNING SICKNESS

CBS Morning Shows
CBS, 1954–present

Of all the television genres, the morning show has changed the least from Golden Age to present-day. From Dave Garroway and David Hartman to Katie Couric and Charlie Gibson, the format has remained constant—hard news, human interest stories, celebrity guests, a weather forecast, and a dash of light banter among the hosts to help ease viewers into their day.

But though CBS has aired a morning show for decades, the network has never enjoyed the same success as NBC's *Today* and ABC's *Good Morning America*. It's not for lack of trying—the web has launched a seemingly endless series of attempts, hosted at one time or another by actresses, journalists, politicians, and puppets, but always finished third in a three-horse field. Desperation has inspired bizarre experiments in this snakebitten time slot, and a couple of times they just gave up altogether, only to bounce back with yet another contender that suffered the same fate as its predecessors.

It's difficult to single out one particularly memorable era from such a crowded field, so instead I'll salute CBS morning television with a "What were they thinking?" career-achievement accolade, and review some of the highlights of their long, strange trip.

In the Beginning
The network's first foray into AM talk was titled simply *Morning Show*, hosted by Walter Cronkite and a lion puppet named Charlemane. Cronkite, long before he became the most trusted man in America and an icon of broadcast journalism, actually began his career at the Tiffany Network with five months as straight man for a sock with his own gag writer.

With Cronkite's departure, the show was turned over to Jack Paar, then Dick Van Dyke, then Will Rogers, Jr., who on one memorable morning rode a horse into a ritzy Chicago hotel, only to have the horse take a dump in the lobby. Newsman Ned Calmer, unaware his microphone was open, exclaimed "Good God, what a f—— up."

By then the name had changed to *Good Morning*, but there was nothing good about it. CBS thought so too, and turned the time slot over to Captain Kangaroo.

Hugs and Misses

From the moment CBS jumped back into the morning show race with *Calendar* in 1961, the revolving door of hosts rarely stopped spinning. First up was Harry Reasoner and Broadway actress Mary Fickett; Reasoner was replaced by Mike Wallace, but with ratings still low CBS moved the 8 AM broadcast to 7 AM, to make room for reruns of *I Love Lucy*. Several more forgettable lineup changes ensued over the next two decades until the next major relaunch in 1981. *Morning* was hosted by Charles Kuralt, whose folksy style was ideally suited to the early time slot. With co-host Diane Sawyer, they presided over CBS's first genuine contender in the field.

But network programmers panicked when ratings didn't rise fast enough, and replaced Kuralt with Bill Kurtis, a respected Chicago journalist whose no-nonsense style seemed out of place when he had to interview TV's Daisy Duke. Sawyer left to join *60 Minutes*, and was replaced by former Miss America Phyllis George. In one of the most embarrassing moments in morning TV history, George presided over a segment with a man who had served a prison term for rape, and the alleged victim who later recanted her story. "How about a hug?" she suggested to the two barely-speaking guests. Her days were numbered after that. The show was revamped yet again, first with Forrest Sawyer and Maria Shriver, then again with Bruce Morton and Faith Daniels.

Ladies and Gentlemen, the News!

In 1987, with CBS now having failed for decades to adapt the traditional morning format with any success (more than 25 anchors had come and gone since 1954), network executives decided to try something completely different with *The Morning Program*, a 90-minute talkfest hosted by newsman Rolland Smith, actress Mariette Hartley, and comedian Bob Saget. The show was performed before a studio audience. "I tried to break the mold," said producer Bob Shanks.

Though smart and personable, Hartley was woefully out of her element, and suffered more malaprops per show than Norm Crosby in Las Vegas. She introduced country singer Eddie Rabbitt as Eddie Albert, asked Trinidad-born actor Geoffrey Holder about growing up in Tahiti, asked Karen Valentine about being raised by nuns, which she wasn't, and once said to an entire audience, "I hear you're all from Japan," to which the entire audience responded, "No."

After ten months, *The Morning Program* was canceled, and replaced by *CBS This Morning*, hosted by Harry Smith and Kathleen Sullivan. When Paula Zahn replaced Sullivan, the program fielded its most stable and successful team in years. But CBS couldn't leave well enough alone, and brought back the live audience ("Let's hear it for the Secretary of Health and Human Services!"). Both anchors departed, and Jane Robelot assumed the position until the next revamp, which brought a new name, a new cast and a new studio.

The Early Show debuted in 1999 with hosts Bryant Gumbel and Jane Clayson.

Gumbel has been a polarizing figure since his successful stint on *Today*, and the bland Clayson was unable to puncture his superciliousness the way Katie Couric did on NBC. In 2002 Gumbel quit, Clayson was reassigned, and Harry Smith returned with a trio of cohosts dubbed (by me, anyway) Harry's Angels: Hannah Storm, Julie Chen, and Rene Syler. But if history is any judge they won't be there long, and as it's now been a few years since the last overhaul, CBS should be due for another experiment. I can't wait to see what they come up with next.

38

NICE GUYS FINISH SECOND

Survivor
CBS, May 3, 2001

Imagine entering a competition with a $1 million prize, and after weeks of besting the field in strength, skill and strategy winding up in a guaranteed position to win the money. Then imagine giving it all away. For Colby Donaldson, contestant on *Survivor: Outback*, no imagination is required. At the penultimate Tribal Council, Donaldson's decision to take fellow contestant Tina Wesson into the final vote over the eminently beatable Keith Famie remains the most shocking moment in the reality series' history. Depending on one's perspective, it was either an act of admirable sportsmanship or stunning stupidity.

Some background for the *Survivor*-impaired: the game begins with 16 strangers deposited into a remote corner of the globe. They are divided into two tribes, who must live off the land for the next 39 days. The tribes compete against each other in challenges for food and supplies, and for the right to keep their group together; losing an immunity challenge means a visit to Tribal Council, to vote somebody out of the game. At some point, the remaining members of each tribe merge into one group, and the game switches from one of team competition to individual advancement, though savvy players will have been thinking that way all along. The objective, of course, is to not be voted off. When just two players are left, a jury of nine former contestants vote on which finalist deserves the $1 million and the title of "Ultimate Survivor."

After the first series became a national obsession, *Survivor* returned with an Australian Outback edition that featured an even more engaging band of contestants. Fans still fondly recall foxy physical trainer Alicia Calaway, sassy retired cop Maralyn (Mad Dog) Hershey, gentleman farmer Rodger (Kentucky Joe) Bingham, cute-as-a-button shoe designer Elisabeth Filarski, now a co-host on *The View*, and aspiring actress Jerri Manthey, a seductive villainess who orchestrated a revolt against Army Intelligence Officer Kel Gleason by accusing him of hoarding a secret supply of beef jerky.

The final five consisted of Kucha tribe members Rodger and Elisabeth, and three members of the Ogakor tribe; handsome Texan Colby Donaldson, an auto customizer, Tina Wesson, a nurse and mother from Tennessee, and Keith Famie, a chef from Michigan. The Ogakor alliance held together and voted the two Kuchas off, which left Colby as an odds-on favorite to win. He had dominated many of the challenges, and played Jerri like a harp with flirting and false promises until the merger, when he helped vote her off. When it came time to vote off Elisabeth, Donaldson properly chose strategy over mutual affection. "I don't think there's any way I can win $1 million with you sitting next to me," he said at her final Tribal Council.

Famie survived to the final three through his alliance with Colby and Tina, both of whom ostensibly kept him around because they knew he'd be cannon fodder in a final vote. He had taken control of his tribe's food supply early on, but the experienced chef undercooked their rice supply and prepared vegetable paella that even the starving castaways couldn't stomach. "He's a fool. The guy's a bozo," said Colby of Keith after the rice incident.

Wesson flew under the radar for much of the game, playing peacemaker between Keith and Jerri and den mother to her (mostly) younger tribe. But after bonding with Maralyn then voting her out at the first opportunity, viewers realized there was more to Tina than her June Cleaver smile. When a flood swept through the camp, washing away all their provisions, it was Tina who braved the rushing waters to retrieve the tribe's rice supply, after Keith had tried and failed.

Colby's victory in the last immunity challenge allowed him to select the person he would take into the finals. Choose Keith, and he could start building that investment portfolio. It would be like going into Final Jeopardy against Jessica Simpson. But Colby didn't believe Keith deserved a place among the final two, even though he knew his victory would be assured. And so, as he had not done with Elisabeth and Rodger, he chose friendship over strategy, and opted to face the jury against Tina.

By listening to his heart, Colby Donaldson removed $900,000 from his wallet. In a 5-4 decision, Tina became the Ultimate Survivor. "You've been the mastermind behind all the strategies that have taken place," said Jerri, who recognized a kindred spirit in casting her vote. "The greatest (strategy) of all was getting Colby to pick you over Keith."

Tina finished 39 days in the Outback without a single vote ever cast against her, another testament to her accomplished game play. Though she professed to sharing Colby's loyalty, and suggested she would have taken him to the finals had their situation been reversed, most viewers are certain she would have chosen Keith. As she stated in the last episode, she didn't "go through all of this just to give away the prize." Colby seemed genuinely happy with Tina's victory and his second-place check for $100,000, while millions of viewers shook their heads in disbelief.

In the post-game wrap-up, host Bryant Gumbel asked Colby how he could win so many challenges, only to let the game slip away. Donaldson stood by his belief that Tina deserved the final spot. "No matter what happens, Keith Famie didn't win the million dollars," he said, completely satisfied with his choice. "I've had to live with this decision, and I haven't missed a night of sleep." Neither has Tina, but then she's sleeping on a much nicer bed these days.

37

THE DISAPPEARANCE OF CHUCK CUNNINGHAM

Happy Days
ABC, JANUARY 15, 1974–JULY 12, 1984

In 1970, on the daytime drama *All My Children*, teenager Jeff Martin walked upstairs to his room to pack for a ski trip. He hasn't been seen since. Fans still wonder if the show will ever address his disappearance; would *All My Children* have the guts to let a middle-aged Jeff descend the same staircase 35 years later, carrying a set of skis, and ask "Mom, is my ride here yet?"

Daytime television has a history of playing fast and loose with character continuity, and such incidents, while still uncommon, are not unheard of. But the unexplained disappearance of a recurring character could never happen on a prime time series, much less to one of America's most beloved television families—could it?

Happy Days was a show made in the 1970s that looked back on the 1950s with nostalgic fondness. Those who were around in the 70s recall that any other decade looked better at the time. The story centered on the Cunningham family; hardware store owner Howard (Tom Bosley), cookie-baking housewife Marion (Marion Ross), their redheaded teenage son, Richie (Ron Howard), Richie's cute kid sister Joanie (Erin Moran), and his college-bound older brother Chuck, played by Gavan O'Herlihy.

At first, *Happy Days* was similar to any other family sitcom, except for the Fabian records on the soundtrack. But as the character of Fonzie emerged from the supporting ranks to give the show its hook, the series evolved from a hit to a phenomenon.

That was bad news for Chuck, who was conceived as the older and wiser Cunningham sibling, ever ready to dispense advice about life to his naive brother Richie. As the Fonz developed into Richie's mentor, there didn't seem any reason for Chuck to be around anymore.

The rather doofus-looking O'Herlihy didn't look the advice-dispensing type anyway. His only character traits were dribbling a basketball and eating a sandwich. He appeared in six first-season episodes, but never made a contribution worthy of the plot synopsis. O'Herlihy asked Garry Marshall to be released from his contract, and if they were going to dispense with the character this would have been the perfect time. Chuck goes to college, and the family soldiers on into the second season and beyond.

But *Happy Days* wasn't ready to be rid of Chuck just yet; the character was revived in the second season, still wearing the same high school varsity sweater and dribbling the same basketball, but this time played by Randolph Roberts. Episode #17, "Richie Moves Out," finally put Chuck in the spotlight, as Richie leaves the Cunningham nest to move in with his older brother. But the arrangement proves short-lived, and Richie returns home by episode's end.

Chuck's final appearance is in episode #27, "Guess Who's Coming for Christmas," the series' best holiday show. He gives Richie a gift-wrapped basketball, then disappears for good. However, the character is mentioned one last time in episode 36, "Fish and the Fins," by Marion, who recalls how Chuck still sucks his thumb when something is bothering him. A mother never forgets.

No mention is made of Chuck's fate, and though viewers wrote letters asking where he went the producers decided to ignore the issue and hope everyone would just forget about him. In his autobiography, Garry Marshall says whenever anyone asked him about Chuck and where he disappeared to, he would say "Chuck got a 12-year basketball scholarship to the University of Outer Mongolia."

In the final scene of the final episode of *Happy Days'* ten-year run, Howard Cunningham proposes a toast at the wedding of his daughter to Chachi Arcola (Scott Baio). "Here's to happy days," he says, after reminiscing about having experienced "the joy of raising two wonderful children." The obliteration of Chuck Cunningham was now complete.

It was an ignoble fate, to be sure, but let's not feel too bad for Chuck. At least he left before *Happy Days* went off the rails in its final seasons. And though the character disappeared, the actors that portrayed Chuck have surfaced occasionally since their time in Milwaukee; Gavan O'Herlihy has appeared on episodes of *Star Trek: Voyager*, *Twin Peaks*, and *China Beach*, as well as the films *Superman 3* and *Top of the World*. Randolph Roberts (now Will Roberts) can be seen in episodes of *Pensacola Wings of Gold*, *The Invisible Man*, and *18 Wheels of Justice*, and in the Disney movie *Motocrossed*. He also works as an Education Supervisor for ITT Technical Institute in San Diego.

The legacy of Chuck Cunningham survives in TV Land reruns, and as the name of a Minneapolis rock band, who can only hope they have more staying power than their namesake.

The Cunningham family, plus one: "If we all just smile and stay very still, maybe the strange man behind us will go away."

36

DAVE AND MADDIE GET PHYSICAL

Moonlighting
ABC, March 31, 1987

It's a proven axiom that unresolved sexual tension can lengthen the lifespan of a television show, and the resolution of said tension can hasten its departure. Examples of both are plentiful, but there's never been a better test case for the theory than *Moonlighting*. No other series suffered a more dramatic collapse post-coitus, when detectives David Addison (Bruce Willis) and Maddie Hayes (Cybill Shepherd) consummated three years of foreplay in episode 39, "I Am Curious ... Maddie".

Granted, other aspects of the series suffered an inexplicable drop in quality at the same time, and the show was beset by a variety of production difficulties, from the dueling egos of its stars to a writer's strike that delayed new episodes by months. But there's no denying that Dave and Maddie's tryst transformed *Moonlighting* from whipsmart TV to a confused parody of its former self, that pushed the "aren't we clever we know it's a TV show" schtick to the point where viewers no longer cared about the characters.

Created by Glen Gordon Caron in 1984, *Moonlighting* was a groundbreaking series that defied television's unwritten rule that all 30-minute shows be comedies and all 60-minute shows be dramas. Ostensibly a detective show, *Moonlighting* bent, spoofed and flipped the format with comedy, music, fantasy sequences and winks to the audience that inspired a new word—'Dramedy', and confused the heck out of Emmy voters, who liked the show but didn't know what to do with it. In 1987, Bruce Willis won Best Actor in a Drama series, as the Academy still couldn't wrap their minds around the concept of a one-hour comedy.

Each *Moonlighting* episode packed so much into 60 minutes that the plot was almost an afterthought. But whatever cases found their way to the Blue Moon Detective Agency, the real story always revolved around the almost-relationship of Dave and Maddie, and whether the characters would ever, as Dave phrased it, go "horizontee." Sure, the wait seemed like torture—the February 1987 *US* magazine ran a cover photo of the couple with the caption "Just do it already!"—but there was much to love besides their suggestive dialogue exchanges and on-again, off-again flirtation.

At its best, this was TV for the ages. Fans still fondly recall the film noir-esque musical episode "The Dream Sequence Always Rings Twice," the cute leprechaun in "Somewhere Under the Rainbow," the "Big Man on Mulberry Street" dance number, the brilliant updating of *The Taming of the Shrew* in "Atomic Shakespeare," and the surreal mix of fantasy and reality in "The Straight Poop," in which gossip columnist Rona Barrett investigated rumors of discord at Blue Moon, Shepherd's ex-flame Peter Bogdanovich described his rebound fling with Maddie after breaking up with Cybill, and Pierce Brosnan appeared as fellow TV detective Remington Steele.

In the teaser sequence of the second season episode "Every Daughter's Father is a Virgin," David and Maddie are shown reading letters from viewers wanting to know when they would finally kiss. They did, in the very next episode, but then the relationship cooled for the better part of a year. Their prospects were further jeopardized when Maddie met Sam (Mark Harmon) a handsome suitor whose stable, low-key personality was a refreshing contrast to Dave's insanity. Sam proposed and Maddie gave it serious thought, while Dave examined his own commitment issues, scared that he might lose Maddie forever.

In "I Am Curious … Maddie," Sam confronts Dave at his apartment. "If you really care for her, you should tell her. And if you don't … do everybody a favor and just back off." Later, the two get into a fistfight, which leaves Dave bloody and beaten. Maddie realizes she needs to resolve the situation. That night she heads home and sees a man under the covers in her bed. Assuming it's Sam, she tells him that she loves him, but since she also loves David she cannot accept his proposal.

When she discovers that it's David in her bed, Maddie goes ballistic, resulting in a vicious argument that ignites passions of another kind. It was hardly the tender love scene viewers had anticipated; while the Ronettes' "Be My Baby" played on the soundtrack, the couple rolled around on the floor, shattering a glass coffee table, venting their combustible ecstasy in a scene that must have just squeaked by the censors.

The following episode, the final show of the third season, opens on the morning after. They say love changes everything, and truer words were never spoken, as the events of the previous night rendered both characters unrecognizable by the series' fans. "Dave, I think we should make a pact," Maddie says, hoping to erase the memory of their tryst and go back to being just pals. Though they tried to lighten the tension, by saying if they stayed together the home viewers would lose interest and the show would be moved to Sunday night, It was a sad and frustrating climax to a story viewers had waited three years to see.

Producer Glen Gordon Caron opted to undo the relationship, when there was no reason they couldn't become Nick and Nora Charles for a new generation. As a result, *Moonlighting*'s fourth season was a mess. Maddie heads home to be with her family, refusing to have any contact with Dave. This was done in part to accommodate Cybill Shepherd's pregnancy, which caused her to miss half the season's shows. With Shepherd gone, Willis is reduced to trading wisecracks with the obnoxious Bert Viola (Curtis Armstrong), detective in training and potential love interest for Blue Moon's daffy receptionist, Agnes Dipesto (Allyce Beasley).

On her way back from Chicago, Maddie meets Walter Bishop on the train and marries him. This was Maddie, who was always afraid of being impulsive, whose attraction to Dave was tempered by concerns over his shoot-from-the-hip spontanaity. The ridiculous plot twist was rendered less convincing with Bishop played by wimpy Dennis Dugan, one of those unfortunate actors that has compelled channels to change since his days of ruining *The Rockford Files* as Richie Brockelman.

Eventually Dave finds out about the baby, Bishop bows out and again the writers raise expectations that the couple would finally get together, only to dash them once more when, at the beginning of the fifth season, Maddie suffers a miscarriage. "I don't think I'll ever be the same," she tells Dave. "I don't think we'll ever be the same." The delicate subject was rendered in appalling taste; the episode opens with Bruce Willis playing her unborn baby, singing and dancing in the womb, and ends with the shock twist as the action jumps from an office party to an ambulance, after which the tragedy is revealed.

Moonlighting limped through its final season with long gaps between new shows, episodes built around Agnes and Bert, and clip shows in place of fresh stories. By now they're talking to the camera as often as the Monkees, but what was once bold and clever now seems like a desperate tactic to fill time. There was still a chance to end the story on a happy note, but the writers refused to let viewers leave satisfied.

In the final three episodes, Dave hooked up with Maddie's cousin, Annie (Virginia Madsen). Annie went back to her husband in the final show, "Lunar Eclipse," in which the wedding of Bert and Agnes takes center stage, and the agency closes its doors, with Dave and Maddie headed off into uncertain, separate futures. Willis and Shepherd couldn't stand each other, and both were glad to move on, rendering the chances for a reunion movie roughly equal to that of a Bert Viola spinoff series. Dave and Maddie should be together forever in TV Land, but like the song said, they're sadly destined to remain "Moonlighting strangers, who just met on the way."

35
DRUDGE-ING UP TROUBLE

The Drudge Report
FOX NEWS, JUNE 20, 1998–NOVEMBER 13, 1999

So you want to launch a new 24-hour cable news network to compete with CNN. What's the best way to establish the credibility and professionalism of your news gathering organization? Well, it might be wise to avoid offering television shows to an Internet scribe based out of his Hollywood apartment who proudly boasts of "80 percent accuracy" in his reporting. But that's what the Fox News Channel did when they recruited Matt Drudge in 1998.

The network had already raised viewer suspicions after claims by owner Rupert Murdoch that media was too liberal, and it was time to redress the balance. Mainstream news coverage may indeed lean toward the left, but they're smart enough to never admit it. To suggest that FNC may espouse a specific political viewpoint in its coverage raised some warning flags, especially among those who usually worked the other side of the street.

Eight years later, Fox News has become an established name in television journalism, ridiculed by some (who refer to the net as "Faux News") and embraced by others for their more flamboyant brand of journalism, personified by such hosts as Bill O'Reilly. But there's a line between maverick and moron that must not be crossed, and FNC lost sight of that border when they offered Drudge a weekend gossip show.

Drudge came to prominence in 1995, a time when newspapers, radio stations, and every store in the shopping mall felt their livelihood threatened by the encroachment of the Internet. The prestige then bestowed upon its pioneers resulted in Drudge being hailed as "a new kind of journalist," which in this case meant one who didn't bother with details like fact-checking and multiple sources. His Drudge Report web site was thrust into the mainstream when it broke the news of President Bill Clinton's affair with White House intern Monica Lewinsky, after *Newsweek* uncovered the relationship but opted to hold the story until all the facts could be confirmed.

But for every successful scoop dredged by Drudge, there are as many erroneous reports that must later be retracted, sometimes at the threat of a lawsuit. White House lawyer Sidney Blumenthal sued Drudge for $30 million after he published a report that Blumenthal abused his wife. Drudge also touted a "world exclusive" that Bill Clinton fathered a son after a tryst in Arkansas with an African-American prostitute; DNA tests on the boy, Danny Williams, proved negative.

"Sure, he's a journalist," said an undaunted Roger Ailes, chairman of Fox's news division. "He's a citizen journalist. I don't think Ben Franklin ever went to (journalism) school, did he?" But while the network's brass compared Drudge to one of America's founding fathers, fellow talk show host Keith Olbermann offered a less enthusiastic welcome: "He has gone from being an idiot with a modem to an idiot with a modem and a TV show on the most irresponsible network in America."

"This will be my first real media job," the 31-year-old Drudge told *Daily Variety*. "Three years ago, I was folding shirts at the CBS Studio Center gift shop." The show debuted on June 20, 1998, promising to provide the dish on the news events and the personalities of the week. Drudge's guest was literary agent and renowned Clinton-basher Lucianne Goldberg, who joined the host on a futuristic set that looked like the police interrogation room at the United Federation of Planets. Goldberg launched into several tirades about Clinton's job performance and personal pitfalls, while Drudge merely smiled and nodded, offering little in the way of follow-up questions or requests for verification.

The subject of Bill and Monica was a popular one on Drudge's show, which only provided more ammunition for the network's critics. But the honeymoon between FNC and Drudge ended abruptly in November 1999, when the network forbade him from showing a picture of a fetus undergoing surgery in the womb. At least he didn't claim the child was Clinton's.

According to the *Washington Post*, Drudge wanted to use the photo in a segment on why the United States should not help finance United Nations population-control programs. Drudge himself claimed he only planned to discuss "the miracle of life." Fox News executives believed the photo would be part of the host's ongoing campaign against abortion.

Drudge, who was not used to having to answer to anyone for his reports, was outraged by the restriction, and the demand for an apology after he had refused to do the show. "Apology? Here's my apology," he told the *Philadelphia Inquirer*. "I apologize deeply to Fox News for having a free mind ... I don't know why Fox is afraid. They're overgrown fetuses who hit the panic button."

That didn't go over too well at the network, which sent him a "See you in court" letter. "What he calls censorship is what the rest of us call editing," fumed Britt Hume. The fact that Drudge's show had lost 33 percent of its viewers may have also figured into the network's position.

Their divorce was finalized soon after, with Drudge apologizing for calling his bosses "weak-kneed suits", and FNC canceling his show and voiding his contract. Drudge returned to his Hollywood apartment, where he continues to churn out The Drudge Report online to seven million readers.

34
THE UNRAVELING OF TWIN PEAKS

Twin Peaks
ABC, APRIL 8, 1990–JUNE 10, 1991

Let's give credit where it's due: before a television series can fall as far as *Twin Peaks*, it must first rise to heights of achievement beyond the imagining of most network dramas. *Twin Peaks* attained that level from the opening moments of its two-hour pilot, with the discovery of a corpse wrapped in cellophane. "The best two hours of film you'll find anywhere these days," observed *Rolling Stone*.

The deceased was high school student Laura Palmer, an angel on the surface but a devil down deep; just the sort of character beloved by series creator David Lynch. The oddball director of *Blue Velvet* and *Wild at Heart* instilled his trademark brand of highly-stylized weirdness into *Twin Peaks*, which merits comparison to his motion pictures in its scope, depth, and conception. It was a calculated risk whether Lynch's unique vision would translate well to television, dependable purveyor of the safe and bland, but the payoff was immediate. "In one night," raved *Time* magazine, "the show had hip America hooked."

Sent to investigate Laura's murder is FBI special agent Dale Cooper (Kyle MacLachlan), the first of a seemingly inexhaustible supply of remarkable original characters introduced by Lynch and co-creator Mark Frost. Cooper, the brilliant, eccentric devoteé of cherry pie and damn fine cups of coffee, is aided in his investigation by earnest small town sheriff Harry S. Truman (Michael Ontkean) and the hilariously acerbic forensics expert Albert Rosenfield (Miguel Ferrer).

We met a selection of potential suspects—Laura's feral boyfriend Bobby Briggs, sensitive biker James Hurley, creepy shrink Dr. Jacoby, and wife-beating trucker Leo Johnson. But as the story unfolded to the strains of Angelo Badalamenti's haunting music, raw emotion mixed with grotesque horror and dry humor, and viewers suspected that this was a series that felt no obligation to follow the boundaries of what was acceptable. Once that safety net was removed, the experience was both frightening and exhilarating.

Seven episodes followed the two-hour pilot, each one quite extraordinary. Viewers became caught up in the machinations of Josie Packard and Catherine Martell at the Twin Peaks sawmill, and in saucy Audrey Horn's undercover mission at the brothel One-Eyed Jacks. But the fate of Laura Palmer was never far from our minds, and the identity of the killer was TV's most burning question since "Who Shot J.R.?"

The first season ended with Cooper being shot by an unknown assailant, the sawmill burning down with Catherine Martell inside and Ben Horn unwittingly about to sleep with his own daughter, but Laura's murder remained unsolved. Fans expected an answer before the summer hiatus, and felt cheated that they'd have to wait three months before the story resumed. "Will viewers have grown weary of the show's cliffhanging teases?" asked *Time* magazine.

The fall season premiere was appointment TV, but something was amiss. The opening scene had a senile room service waiter finding the seriously wounded Cooper bleeding all over the hardwood floor, and not noticing his condition. Cooper then had a vision of a giant who speaks in riddles ("The owls are not what they seem."). Later, Cooper shared his vision with the sheriff, and hoped to find the answers he seeks in its message.

Supernatural elements were always a part of the mix. Cooper's reliance on dreams was established early on, but as just another quirk in his personality, not his primary method of crimesolving. But suddenly the entire tone of the series had changed, as *Twin Peaks* progressed from slightly surreal to flat-out stupid.

Ridiculous new characters turned up—foppish menswear clerk Dick Tremayne, a cross-dressing DEA agent played in drag by David Duchovny, and Lynch himself as Cooper's hard-of-hearing boss. And still the murderer was not revealed. It was not until episode 14, aired six

Twin Peaks *fans couldn't wait to find out who killed Homecoming Queen Laura Palmer (Sheryl Lee). But wait, they did.*

months after Laura's body was discovered, that we learned she was killed by her father, while he was possessed by a forest demon named Bob. By then, much of the audience had become frustrated, and moved on to other pleasures. The moment had passed.

In a *TV Guide* interview, Demon Bob portrayer Frank Silva revealed that he was originally hired as the show's propmaster, and that his character was added as a whim after Lynch spotted him on the set. "The interview confirms what this column has suspected all along," the piece concluded; "the great minds behind *Twin Peaks* are just making it up at they go."

Such articles prompted Frost to respond that the series was never supposed to be about Laura Palmer, and that the media fixated on that story while ignoring their overall "vision". A ridiculous argument. You introduce a murder victim in the first scene, you follow that up with a detective, suspects, clues and an investigation, but it's not a murder mystery?

That's not to say there weren't some moments worth remembering during the show's long decline; Joan Chen revealed new facets of the enigmatic Josie Packard, the suave Jean Reault (Michael Paris) was a memorable villain, and there's a fun reunion between *Mod Squad* costars Peggy Lipton, who played waitress Norma Jennings, and guest star Clarence Williams III. But the last few episodes are almost unbearable to watch, with their messages from outer space, and the spectacle of Josie's spirit being trapped in the top drawer of a hotel nightstand. *Twin Peaks* was finally put out of its misery after 29 shows.

Whether it was their inexperience with the dramatic television format or a certain arrogance in expecting viewers to follow them anywhere for as long as they wished, David Lynch and Mark Frost captured the nation's attention and squandered the opportunity. "Lynch and Frost were like weekend fisherman, who when they tossed their lines in the water, hooked Jaws," observed Brandon Tartikoff in his book *The Last Great Ride*. "But they couldn't hold on to that big a fish."

33
MADE IN JAPAN

Pink Lady and Jeff
NBC, March 1–April 4, 1980

"It's like Tony Orlando and Dawn—except Dawn doesn't speak English." —Brandon Tartikoff

There's bad TV you watch in anger, over the span of your life that was just wasted, and there's bad TV that merely generates a sense of wonder, which is better for the blood pressure. The only appropriate response to *Pink Lady and Jeff* is a wide, goofy grin at the sheer improbability of it all. Twenty years later, it's still astonishing that NBC believed the next great variety show would be hosted by an unknown standup comic and two Japanese women who couldn't speak English.

Once again we kneel at the altar of Fred Silverman, whose name graces several other entries on this list. His stint at NBC, following successful programming revivals at CBS and ABC, produced some of the most memorably bad television ever created. Eager to jump-start the third-place Peacock Network, the "Golden Gut" spotted a golden opportunity on Friday nights, where ABC's *Donny and Marie* left the air after three successful seasons. Silverman hoped NBC could fill the variety show void, though ratings of other unsuccessful contenders suggested that viewers were looking for something different.

What we have here is failure to communicate: Pink Lady and Jeff.

Enter Mitsuyo Nemoto (Mie) and Keiko Masuda (Kei), a Japanese singing duo billed as Pink Lady. They began performing together as teenagers in 1976 and, after winning the Japanese equivalent of *Star Search*, recorded a string of hit records with titles like "Pepper Police Inspector." The music was bouncy disco-pop, and the girls' sweet good looks and short spangly dresses made them overnight sensations. From 1976 to 1978, they dominated Japanese record charts and played sold-out stadium concerts.

All of this went unnoticed in America, though a few Pink Lady stories appeared in teen and music magazines, including *Tiger Beat* and *Rolling Stone*. One single, "Kiss in the Dark," barely scratched the top 40. But Silverman was convinced that Pink Lady would be the next Sonny and Cher, a duo he propelled into mainstream stardom in their own series. The language barrier was not a liability but a gimmick that could be mined for laughs and humorous (though never offensive) outsider observations about America.

But Pink Lady could hardly carry a show on their own by singing and speaking phonetically, so NBC added a third regular in Jeff Altman, who would serve as both interpreter and comic foil. The first *Pink Lady and Jeff* episode opens with a brief monologue by Altman, who then introduces concert footage of Pink Lady in Japan. "Boy, I wish I had the tempura concession on that!" he says of the baseball stadium

135

packed with fans. Finally, the girls made their appearance in traditional flowing Japanese robes, which were peeled off to reveal mini dresses underneath.

After the opening song Altman (or "Ulta-man," as the girls call him) returned for some comic repartee. Kei was given the Cher role of cutting down the self-effacing comic, but Mie, who apparently did better in the Berlitz class, did most of the talking. Their pronunciations were clear enough, and sometimes their comic timing was better than Altman's, though to be fair he was saddled with lines like "You're just turned on by my sexy round eyes."

Each one-hour episode was divided into musical numbers and comedic sketches, many of which Altman performed with supporting player Jim Varney, in his days before *Ernest Goes to Camp*. Running bits included Mie writing a letter home about a city she visited, such as New York or Chicago, which introduced a medley of songs from Pink Lady and that week's guest stars; Cheapshot Magazine, which poked fun at the tabloid news stories of the day, and the closing scene, in which a bikini-clad Mie and Kei join Altman in a hot tub.

Both girls were talented singers, and while someone should have advised them against covering Motown hits like "You Keep Me Hangin' On," they hardly embarrassed themselves on songs like "You've Got a Friend" and "How Deep Is Your Love." Where they got in trouble was in lip-synching to their prerecorded tracks, which recalled a badly-dubbed Godzilla movie and provided a much greater source of amusement than Altman's sketches. If you closed your eyes, their version of the Beatles' "Yesterday" is lovely. If you watch the performance, it's hard not to laugh.

Suddenly, Fallon's solution to every crisis is a nice cup of tea. Jeff James and Emma Samms in Dynasty.

Occasionally they were allowed to sing in Japanese, which resulted in tighter harmonies and a more self-assured performance that provides some insight into what captivated Fred Silverman in the first place.

Pink Lady and Jeff was pulled after five episodes, following merciless reviews and disappointing ratings. But there's a certain retro charm in it now, with its eclectic batches of guest stars, from Larry Hagman at the height of J.R.-mania to Jerry Lewis and Sid Caesar, and performances from Alice Cooper, Teddy Pendergrass and Bobby Vinton. Where else could you hear Greg Evigan sing "Don't Go Breakin' My Heart," or Hugh Hefner sing (yes, sing!) "Chicago (My Kind of Town)"? If you catch it in the right mood, or after enough alcohol, it'll make you smile.

Altman went on to host *Solid Gold*, then went back to the comedy clubs. He now plays the corporate circuit. Pink Lady returned to Japan where they performed a farewell concert in 1981. Mie and Kei reunited in 1996, and in 2003 celebrated the 25th anniversary of their first hit with a sold-out concert tour. Is an American revival also possible? Jeff Altman, call your agent.

32
WORST. RECAST. EVER.

Dynasty
ABC, SEPTEMBER 25, 1985

The legacy of Dick Sargent teaches us that when a casting change fails the natural tendency is to blame the replacement, but there are times when doing so is unfair. On *Dynasty*, the selection of Emma Samms to follow Pamela Sue Martin as Fallon never had a chance. Never. It was like casting Audrey Hepburn as Batgirl. Yet it was Samms who took the brunt of the criticism, including one of the most scathing reviews ever published in *The Hollywood Reporter*.

Yes, she could have passed on the role. But after making the showbiz equivalent of minimum wage on *General Hospital*, how can she be blamed for not turning down a spot on Aaron Spelling's payroll, and a chance to wear glamorous Nolan Miller creations every week? No jury would convict her.

In this case, to paraphrase Shakespeare, the fault lies not in the star, but in the producer's daughter. Tori Spelling, who has been responsible for plenty of bad television on her own, made her first foray into casting by recommending Samms to her father. Tori had been a *General Hospital* fan, and enjoyed Emma's wonderful portrayal of Holly Sutton, swindler turned sidekick to the show's two top heartthrobs, Luke Spencer (Anthony Geary) and Robert Scorpio (Tristan Rogers).

Displaying the same judgment she showed when starring in the movie *Mother May I Sleep with Danger?* , Tori told her dad that Emma would make a terrific Fallon

Carrington Colby. For five seasons, Pamela Sue Martin portrayed Fallon as a crude, slutty spoiled rich girl, and that was how the character was familiar to *Dynasty* fans. But it's hard to imagine two actresses more different in type than Martin and Emma Samms, a beautiful English rose with a quiet charm and natural refinement. Yeah, it's called acting, but with a change this dramatic there was no guarantee of viewer acceptance.

Samms debuted in the role in the first episode of season six, following the dramatic Moldavian massacre cliffhanger four months earlier. The character of Fallon had been missing and presumed dead following an automobile accident the previous season, but it turns out she walked away without a scratch, suffering from amnesia. Having to play Fallon as a blank slate for the first few episodes, amidst recurring rumors of Pamela Sue Martin's return, was a no-win situation for an actress attempting to claim the character. It also didn't help that she was paired upon arrival with Miles Colby, played by Maxwell Caulfield, who could be the worst actor in history.

The *Hollywood Reporter* pan was picked up cross-country. "It made it sound like everybody shared that one opinion," said Samms. "Maybe they did." The actress also had to read comments from *Dynasty* co-creator Esther Shapiro about how she hated the substitution of Donna Reed for Barbara Bel Geddes as Miss Ellie on *Dallas*, an indirect swipe at how ABC handled the Fallon situation.

"People have gotten hung up on the fact that Emma doesn't look anything like Pamela Sue," said a *Dynasty* spokesman in a *Redbook* piece. "But the creators said, 'Look, that's not what we wanted to do. We needed someone who could capture the character.'"

Let's review: Fallon was a spoiled bitch with an acid tongue whose idea of fun was to sleep with her father's chauffeur. Now, she was British. Samms' accent peeked out regularly, especially on her 'r's, and despite lightening her hair color to better approximate Martin's she still looked like a European princess. "I'm always going for the sympathetic aspect of a character," said Samms upon her hiring. "The producers haven't told me all that's in store for Fallon, so I can't make predictions. But I do have a hard time playing a villainess."

After one year, *Dynasty* supervising producer David Paulsen considered replacing Samms, hoping to bring back Pamela Sue Martin. But after meeting Emma he couldn't go through with it. "I fell in love," he told the Lifetime network. That's understandable, but it might have been better for both Samms and the series had he made the switch. Martin's return would have restored the character to her true nature, and Samms certainly would have found other work in either film or television.

As it turned out, Samms never settled into the role, and could only make the best of a bad situation as her character was dropped into one ridiculous plotline after another. After one season on *The Colbys*, during which Fallon was abducted by a UFO, she returned to *Dynasty* while that once-mighty series gasped through its final seasons.

Though she worked steadily following *Dynasty*'s cancellation, including a stint in the short-lived *Models Inc.* in 1994, Emma Samms never found another project worthy of her talents. How much of that was a result of the negative publicity that arose from her stint as Fallon, we'll never know. But Samms makes the most of her opportunities, even the bad ones. Her Fallon paychecks helped to support the Starlight Children's Foundation, an organization she co-founded that helps more than 100,000 children each month in 1,000 hospitals throughout the world. Once a princess, always a princess.

31
MICHAEL JACKSON BEATS UP A CAR

"Black or White"
FOX, MTV, BET, November 14, 1991

From the moment Michael Jackson left the comfortable confines of the Jackson Five, his career can be characterized as a maddening race between exceptional talent and exceptional eccentricity. For each album sales record he shattered, for every contribution he made to the art of the music video, there was at least one "Michael Jackson Moment"—an instance of bizarre behavior that draws one's attention away from his musical gifts. At some point eccentricity won out, and turned the majority opinion of Jackson from brilliant artist to Wacko Jacko.

But that critical mass had not yet been achieved in 1991, two weeks before the release of Jackson's album *Dangerous*. Still capable of choreographing a global-caliber media event, he announced that the first music video from that album, "Black or White," would debut simultaneously on the FOX network, Black Entertainment Television and MTV, and on satellite feeds around the world. To secure broadcast rights, MTV agreed to refer to Jackson as "the King of Pop" for the next two weeks. Jackson's new nickname seemed at odds with the normally soft-spoken artist; remember, this was years before he had a giant statue of himself towed down the Thames River to promote the *HIStory* compilation.

The $4 million, 11-minute clip, directed by John Landis, would be seen by 500 million people in 27 countries. Though it's hard to believe now that any music video could create such feverish anticipation, the *New York Times* described it as "Longer awaited, it seemed, that anything without theological implications."

"Black or White" opens with a prologue sequence in which Macaulay Culkin blasts rock music in his bedroom, to the consternation of his father, played by George Wendt. When Wendt orders the kid to turn it down, he and his recliner are blasted through the ceiling by the power of rock'n'roll. A ringing guitar riff supplied by Slash from Guns'n'Roses kicked off the actual music video, a plea for racial harmony in which Jackson dances with African tribesmen, Russian cossacks, Balinese dancers, and Native Americans.

Images of babies of different ethnic heritage sitting atop a huge globe, and of Jackson singing from the Statue of Liberty, surrounded by other world landmarks, reinforce the message that we're all more alike that different. But the clip's most amazing sequence involved morphing, a computer technique now taken for granted, but at the time revolutionary and prohibitively expensive, costing $10,000 per second. Actors both male and female, white, black, Asian, and Arabic, lip-synched to the song, as their faces seamlessly transformed from one into another. Both song and video rank with the artist's very best, and the morphing sequences would have been all fans and media talked about the next day were in not for an unfortunate epilogue that negated the positive message of the music.

The sequence begins with a panther prowling a city street at night; the panther morphs into Michael Jackson, who launches into a violent rampage. The scene plays without music, except for the artist's medley of grunts and screams. His pop and lock dance moves are executed amidst much aggressive crotch-grabbing; that particular adjustment had long been part of his choreography, but here Jackson touches himself no less than 13 times in four minutes, and the hand lingers near his nether regions long enough to cross the line from dance to deviance.

Not content to stick with self-abuse, Jackson leaps onto the hood of a car, and bashes in the windshield with a crowbar. After repeatedly smashing the car, he hurls a garbage can through a store window, then drops to his knees in a puddle, while being surrounded by sparks falling from a shattered neon sign. Apparently satisfied with the carnage, Jackson morphs back into a panther and slinks away.

The FOX network received thousands of angry phone calls, many from parents who had to explain to the kids why Michael was so angry. "People couldn't believe he did that," said one network spokesman. Jackson biographer Christopher Andersen described the scene as "the most obvious expression of Michael's rage toward his father," a reference to the singer's allegedly abusive childhood.

The *New York Times* speculated whether this was Jackson's way of asserting his masculinity, having heard too many jokes about his fey voice and plastic surgery-sculpted feminine features. "Is it an outpouring of pain and frustration? A desperate cry for attention from one of the world's most famous people? Or is it simply a noisy self-indulgence?"

Just 24 hours after the video aired, Jackson issued an apology for the offending clip, and had it deleted from future broadcasts. "It upsets me to think that 'Black or White' could influence any child or adult to destructive behavior, either sexual or violent," he said in a released statement. "I've always tried to be a good role model and therefore have made these changes to avoid any possibility of adversely affecting any individual's behavior. I deeply regret any pain or hurt that the final segment of 'Black or White' may have caused children, their parents, or any other viewers."

"Black or White" established Jackson's self-destructive pattern of eclipsing artistic achievement with poor judgment. It was also the last time he captured the world's attention with his music. The Jacko headlines since 1991 have all dealt with subjects more tragic and grim than automobile abuse.

30
LIVE FROM LOS ANGELES, IT'S ... HOWARD COSELL?

Saturday Night Live with Howard Cosell
ABC, SEPTEMBER 20, 1975–JANUARY 17, 1976

"You know what's going to make this show? Me."
—HOWARD COSELL

What's really strange is, when you read the rundowns of what happened on nearly every episode of *Saturday Night Live with Howard Cosell*, the show sounds like a winner. With its eclectic lineups of comedy and music performances, some beamed in via satellite from remote corners of the world long before such technological feats became commonplace, the "other" *SNL* seemed a valiant attempt to revive the Ed Sullivan-type of variety series that had flourished a decade earlier. Certainly, a show that could boast appearances from Frank Sinatra, Muhammad Ali, John Wayne, The Bay City Rollers, and Shamu the killer whale couldn't be dull.

And yet, somehow when all the elements came together, the result was less satisfying than the sum of its parts. The lion's share of the blame was attributed to host Howard Cosell, who wavered between obvious discomfort at having to introduce the likes of Charo, and diving head first into cringe-inducing skits such as his singing duet with Barbara Walters. After hearing the Mouth that Roared and Baba Wawa crooning silly love songs, you'll have renewed appreciation for the music of Kristy and Jimmy McNichol.

Cosell at the time ranked among TV's best-loved and most-hated personalities, a result of his brash color commentary on *Monday Night Football*, which typically generated more next-day water cooler conversation than the game itself. The idea for *Saturday Night Live* was hatched by Cosell and *Monday Night Football* executive producer Roone Arledge, and developed in ABC's Sports division, which might not have been a wise decision. But on the eve of its debut, the host seemed confident in its prospects. "I'm no song and dance man. Nor am I a stand-up comic.... What I am is a performer with an ability to communicate," said Cosell with his usual lack of humility. "I have established credibility in every corner of the country. I have felt the pulse of America. I know who has something to say, what to ask, and when to ask it."

It was hard to tell where the braggadocio Cosell displayed as part of a carefully crafted public persona stopped and his genuine arrogance, which was much less appealing, began. But statements like "They didn't give me looks, but they gave me an absolute monopoly on brains and talent" further polarized potential viewers, and it was clear that the fate of his series would hinge as much on Cosell's contributions as that of his guests.

The first show opened with the Broadway cast of *The Wiz* performing "Ease on

Down the Road" through the streets of New York, followed by the American television debut of The Bay City Rollers, who were then prompting Beatle-sized teenybopper tremors. Next, a Vegas-based segment featured performances from Siegfried and Roy, Shirley Bassey, and John Denver ("That poet of the mountains," Cosell proclaimed).

But critics focused on the segments in between the superstar moments; these included the singing debut of tennis player Jimmy Connors, and a political commentary by John Wayne on the assassination attempts of President Gerald Ford. The Duke favored frontier justice for the shooters, suggesting that they be "bloodied up a bit" before being put before the news media.

Even for someone with Cosell's voluminous vocabulary, it's difficult to segue from a moment like that to the comedy stylings of Billy Crystal. Ironically, Crystal was a last-minute drop from the original cast of NBC's *Saturday Night*, but an appearance on Cosell's SNL boosted his reputation with ABC, where he was cast in *Soap*, the series that launched his career.

Too many whiplash-quick changes in tone, and odd mixtures of entertainment, sports and politics (Senators Lowell Weicker and Ted Kennedy both appeared in the first show) kept viewers uncomfortably off-balance throughout the proceedings. As a result, though the series produced many memorable moments, including a report live from Manila with Muhammad Ali and Joe Frazier on the eve of their legendary fight, it never found a formula that appealed to enough Saturday night viewers.

Two years later, during an introduction of Billy Crystal on *Battle of the Network Stars*, Cosell referred to the comic's debut on "a series that I would rather forget." That was as close to an admission of defeat as Cosell ever divulged in his career, and thankfully he is now best remembered for several groundbreaking achievements in sports journalism, and not for one lofty miscalculation.

29
FREEZE! IN THE NAME OF LOVE!

Cop Rock
ABC, SEPTEMBER 26–DECEMBER 25, 1990

"I loved it then. I love it now."
—Cop Rock *creator* STEVEN BOCHCO

Explaining why *Cop Rock* didn't last is like having to explain why Mike Tyson never did more voiceover work. The very idea seems so ridiculous that the question isn't why the series failed but why was it ever attempted in the first place? Apparently, ABC was willing to say yes to anything pitched by Steven Bochco, after the network signed the creator of *Hill Street Blues* and *L.A. Law* to a $50 million development deal. Had Bochco pitched a Western starring Liza Minnelli, the network would have rented horses and cleared a time slot.

Bochco's first ABC effort, *Doogie Howser, M.D.*, was a minor hit, but with *Cop Rock* he set a new standard for bizarre high concept. Most critics slaughtered it, but some strove to express admiration for the attempt, as if anything from such an obviously creative mind couldn't possibly be rubbish. "If interested, watch it early in the season," *Newsweek* cautioned. "It may not be there later on." Indeed, *Cop Rock* lasted just 11 episodes, by which time it had become a prime time laughing stock and a late night punch line.

The idea, admittedly a novel one, was to blend a *Hill Street*-style police procedural with a musical, featuring new original songs every week and elaborate dance sequences that periodically popped up between (and sometimes during) chase scenes, precinct confrontations, and cops and robbers shoot-outs.

The problem is that it's impossible for two such diverse genres to coexist without one being overshadowed. The drama inevitably became filler between the song cues, a situation that happens with every musical. Think of your favorite moments in *Singin' in the Rain*, *Grease*, or *Chicago*, and all of them will feature singing and dancing, and not the dialogue in between. Perhaps if the performances had been exceptional the series may have found an audience, but judging from the results the cast of 15 regulars were hired more for their acting ability than what they did when the music starts.

In the pilot, police raid a crackhouse under the glow of spotlights from hovering helicopters. As the suspects are led away, they suddenly break into song: "In these streets, we got the power, we got the power, we got the power." When the gang is later freed on a technicality, Detective LaRusso (Peter Onorati) shoots and kills one of the hoods, dividing the squadroom between supporters and detractors.

Another plot thread follows officers Andy Campo (David Gianopoulos) and Vicki Quinn (Anne Bobby), whose flirtatious banter threatens to destroy Quinn's marriage to forensics expert Ralph Ruskin (Ron McLarty). Ruskin's sappy ballad "She Chose Me," is one of the episode's low points.

Only two of the cast members would be familiar to audiences then or now: Ronny Cox plays Chief Roger Kendrick, who sports a cowboy fixation that extends to having a quick-draw arcade game in his office. Barbara Bosson plays the town's corrupt mayor, Louise Plank. Bosson was married to Bochco at the time and appeared in nearly every one of his shows until their divorce, but here the nepotism didn't do her any favors. *Cop Rock*'s fate was sealed the moment she belted out "You're the One" in the mayor's office, backed by her advisers. The song sounds like Journey-lite arena rock, and when Bosson jumps on a table to shake her groove thing, the only possible reaction is stunned silence.

In the courtroom climax, a judge asks if the jury has reached a verdict. "We have, your Honor," the foreman responds. "Hit it!" As an electric piano magically appears, the jury sings "He's guilty, judge, guilty, we can see it in his eyes," their street clothes suddenly replaced by choir robes. It's the most effective musical moment in the show, as the gospel-style number gets the toes to tapping. Even at its worst *Cop Rock* was mounted on an impressive scale, costing $2 million per one-hour episode, but glossy production values couldn't compensate for the absurdity of the premise.

"I just think that people were embarrassed by it," Bochco admitted. "You know it's like when your drunk uncle Herbie gets up and sings something on Thanksgiving." But the producer's reputation suffered no permanent damage, and his deal with ABC paid huge dividends for both sides with the success of *NYPD Blue*. But despite the public reaction to *Cop Rock* and its swift cancellation, Bochco still proudly defends his musical madness. "I loved it then. I love it now," he said. "It probably was the most fun I ever had."

Don't arrest us yet—we haven't done our pop-and-lock combo!

28
KEEP THE CHANGE

The $1.98 Beauty Show
Syndicated, September 1978–September 1980

A television producer that sets up shop on the fringe of good taste courts disaster with every new project. Such has been the legacy of Chuck Barris, who enjoyed back-to-back hits in *The Dating Game* and *The Newlywed Game*, then took the format one step too far in *Three's A Crowd*.

The Gong Show was genius, especially after it dropped all pretense of being a talent show and devolved into 30 minutes of anarchy. But when Barris applied a similar rate-the-losers formula to a beauty pageant in *The $1.98 Beauty Show*, the results were excruciating. Barris should have realized there's a difference between laughing at singers who can't sing and laughing at women just because they're not attractive. "I couldn't believe they sold it," said host Rip Taylor. "I thought it might be hurtful, (but) there was never any malice towards women or men on the entire show." Perhaps not intended, but there was a cruel streak to the ridicule that contravened Taylor's "all in good fun" hijinks, which couldn't be erased no matter how the concept was handled.

A tuxedo-clad Taylor opened each show on a stage bedecked in crushed velvet curtains, baroque filigree and a chandelier that might have been purchased at Liberace's garage sale. Six contestants of varying sizes, shapes, and ages paraded through this tacky arena to the painfully unfunny introductions of announcer Johnny Jacobs. Usually there would be one bimbo-esque contestant in gobs of makeup and Farrah hair, one cute girl next door type who look slightly embarrassed to be there, one foreign contestant trying to avoid mail-order bride status, and a couple of spirited full-figured gals, some of whom tipped the scales at more than 200 bills.

Each episode featured a swimsuit competition, a talent show and an evening gown competition, judged by a panel of three celebrities. The winner received a tacky crown, a bouquet of vegetables, and a cash prize of $1.98. This set the stage for the most memorable moment of the show, when Taylor would bring out his bags of confetti, and serenade the beauty queen in a piercing voice that sounded like a cross between Placido Domingo and Jerry Lewis: "You win the prize ... you take the cake ... you win the crown/and a dollar-ninety-eight. You ring the bell, you hit the spot/in other words, we like what you got." "Chuck Barris wrote the song, and I sang it live on every show," Taylor recalled.

One or two viewings satisfied whatever hidden desire one might have to see 60-year-olds or Jenny Craig dropouts in bathing suits, yet Barris got two years out of a one-joke show. The only real suspense was in which celebrities needed work desperately enough to sign up as a judge between *Love Boat* voyages. Says Taylor, "The biggest stars were dying to be on that show!"

Most of the *Gong Show* judges turned up—Jaye P. Morgan, Jamie Farr, Louis Nye, "Unknown Comic" Murray Langston, and Patty Andrews, along with such 70s icons as Erik Estrada, Vidal Sassoon, and Suzy Chaffee ('Call me Suzy Chapstick'). But it was sad to see golden age Hollywood stars like Gloria De Haven and Dorothy Lamour participating in such nonsense.

Of the contestants, most of them out-of-work actresses and models hoping for a career boost from the exposure, only two were ever heard from again. Comedian Sandra Bernhard, competing under the name Malvina Rae, took first place on a 1978 broadcast, which speaks volumes about whether beauty and charm actually mattered in the final judging. And comic Rhonda Shear parlayed her victory into a *Playboy* layout and a hosting stint on *USA Up All Night*.

As with every Chuck Barris Production, *The $1.98 Beauty Show* ran afoul of society's gatekeepers of decorum, though there wasn't much enthusiasm behind the outrage. Only the Roman Catholic Archdiocese of New York went one step beyond the customary condemnation, naming the series as one of the fifteen worst shows on television. The show still pops up from time to time on Game Show Network, but whatever kitsch appeal it had the first time around has not aged well.

Some revisionist historians have actually praised *The $1.98 Beauty Show* as a sophisticated satire of beauty pageants, that exposes the shallow and exploitative facets of Miss America and other competitions. Nice try. The relevance of pageants in the 21st century may be open for debate, but it won't be Chuck Barris who decides their fate.

27

HE'S GOT THE WHOLE WORLD IN HIS HANDS

St. Elsewhere
NBC, May 25, 1988

To what extent does the way a television series ends affect its legacy? Some shows left viewers wanting more—*The Mary Tyler Moore Show*, *The Dick Van Dyke Show*, *Angel*—while others endured a long and painful decline in stature and viewer interest before finally pulling the plug (Mulder? Scully?); but very few take their leave at exactly the right time.

No series began and ended better than *The Brady Bunch*. Just as Greg graduates high school in the final episode, and his life is about to become less certain as he heads to college and into the working world, the reruns revert back to the beginning, with the marriage of Mike and Carol, and we watch the kids grow up again, safe and happy. Most of the shows we love occupy a similarly secure and comforting time loop, which is certainly one of the greatest appeals of classic TV.

So when the much-lauded series *St. Elsewhere* ends its 137-episode run by telling viewers that nothing they watched and enjoyed for the previous six seasons ever happened, have the writers done their fans a disservice? Only if the fates of fictional characters have any meaning in the real world.

There's ample evidence to make that case. One could go back to 1841, when thousands of readers of Charles Dickens' *The Old Curiosity Shop* gathered on the docks of New York to await the shipboard arrival of the book's final chapters, which revealed the fate of its beloved protagonist, Little Nell. When Nell didn't make it, newspapers reported widespread public grief. Lord Jeffrey, a confidant of Dickens during the writing process, confessed he was "torn in tears over Little Nell's death". More recently, the revelation that a major character would perish in 2003's *Harry Potter and the Order of the Phoenix* prompted millions of readers to turn each page with a mix of excitement and trepidation.

People do care. They have an emotional investment in the characters they meet in books, movies and on television. *Star Trek* fans grew up to be astronauts; young

L.A. Law viewers were inspired to become attorneys. So after sharing countless moments of humor, tragedy, and heroism at St. Eligius Hospital, many *St. Elsewhere* viewers felt a rug had been pulled out from under them in the final scene of "The Last One," written by series creators Bruce Paltrow and Mark Tinker.

Following a wrap-up of the continuing stories of the sixth season—a resolution of the marital problems between Dr. Mark Craig (William Daniels) and wife Ellen (Bonnie Bartlett), the saving of the hospital from corporate ownership, Dr. Morrison (David Morse) choosing between two potential love interests—a final exterior shot of the hospital surrounded by snow was gradually revealed to be a snow globe held by Tommy Westphall (Chad Allen), the autistic son of Dr. Donald Westphall (Ed Flanders). A different father places the globe on top of the TV set, after summoning Tommy to dinner. We are left to conclude that the six-year saga of *St. Elsewhere* existed only in the imagination of a mentally-challenged child.

Some critics praised the moment for its cleverness, but at least as many criticized the idea as more of a writers' conceit than a legitimate dramatic choice. Admittedly, the snow globe climax wasn't the first time *St. Elsewhere* crossed over into surrealism; memorable episodes included Dr. Fiscus (Howie Mandel) visiting Heaven during an out-of-body experience, and discovering that God is baseball player Lou Gehrig; and when a mental patient became convinced he was Mary Richards from *The Mary Tyler Moore Show*, other cast members from that series appeared in the episode. But where those moments were sly and whimsical, the finale had a bleak and cynical semblance, and left a bitter aftertaste. And the repercussions don't stop there, as humorist Dwayne McDuffie observed:

> Characters from *St. Elsewhere* have appeared on *Homicide*, which means that show is part of the autistic child's daydream and likewise doesn't exist. It gets worse. The omnipresent Detective John Munch from *Homicide* has appeared on *X-Files*, *Law & Order*, and *Law & Order: SVU*. X-Files characters have appeared on *The Lone Gunmen* and *Millennium*. Characters from *Chicago Hope* have appeared on *Homicide*. Characters from *Picket Fences* have appeared on *Chicago Hope*. All those shows are gone (if you count cartoons, which makes this game much too easy, the *X-Files* characters have appeared on *The Simpsons*. *The Critic* has also appeared on *The Simpsons*. Dead).
>
> Characters from *Picket Fences* have appeared on *Ally McBeal*. Ally McBeal has appeared on *The Practice*. Characters from *The Practice* have appeared on *Boston Public*. Autistic daydreams, every one.
>
> But that's not all. *St Elsewhere* characters have appeared on *Cheers*, so *Fraiser* doesn't exist. Neither do *Wings*, *Caroline in the City*, or *The Tortellis*, but who cares? Well, maybe you do, because *Caroline in the City* once crossed over with *Friends*, which crossed over with *Mad about You*, which crossed over with *Seinfeld* and *The Dick Van Dyke Show*. None of them happened in our new, shared continuity.
>
> *St. Elsewhere* also shared characters with *The White Shadow* and *It's Gary Shandling's Show*. Garry Shandling crossed over with *The Andy Griffith Show* (no, really!). So *Gomer Pyle*, *Mayberry RFD*, and *Make Room for Daddy*/*The Danny*

Thomas Show are gone. *Make Room for Daddy* takes out *I Love Lucy*. And there's more; *St. Elsewhere* also shares continuity with *M*A*S*H*, so *AfterMASH* and *Trapper John, M.D.* are out of there.

Now here's a good one: *St. Elsewhere* shared a patient with *The Bob Newhart Show*, so *The Bob Newhart Show* is part of the grand daydream. *The Bob Newhart Show* crossed over with *Murphy Brown*, which in turn links to, among many others, *Julia*, *The Nanny*, *Everybody Loves Raymond*, and *I Dream of Jeannie!* Meanwhile, the series *Newhart* was revealed to be a nightmare had by Bob Newhart's character on *The Bob Newhart Show*. *Newhart* crossed over with *Coach*, which connects it to *Grace under Fire*, *Ellen*, and *The Drew Carey Show*. *Drew Carey* takes out *Home Improvement* and *NYPD Blue*. All of these shows (and many more that I left out or missed) are daydreams of *St. Elsewhere's* autistic kid."

"Someone did the math once," said *St. Elsewhere* producer Tom Fontana, "and something like 90 per cent of all television took place in Tommy Westphall's mind. God love him."

26

HE SHOOTS, WE SNORE

The Magic Hour
SYNDICATED, JUNE 8–AUGUST 7, 1998

The Magic Hour is one of the more obvious selections for a ranking of memorably bad television moments, but the show deserves a pass from the pejorative rhetorical question, "What Were They Thinking?" In this case, it's not hard to see why a lot of smart people would give a talk show hosted by Earvin "Magic" Johnson a legit shot at success.

Start with America's adoration of its sports heroes, especially those who can still muster a smile for a hometown crowd or an autograph for a young fan. We are awed by their grace and strength and skills, though we think that $10-$20 million in salary is a bit much for playing a kid's game; so if they can also manage a little humility in with the bravado, we love them even more. Magic had all the tools, both on and off the court. Affable and articulate, he was a Hall of Fame point guard and a guy who would shoot hoops with you on the playground.

In addition to his basketball prowess, Magic Johnson also became a hero to millions of people with HIV after he became its most prominent victim. Rather than shun the spotlight, as other stricken celebrities had before him, Magic put a new, vibrant and even healthy face on an illness that stigmatized its carriers and fueled a rise in prejudice and homophobia. By just showing up for a charity run or a talk show appearance, he brought hope to those who saw only a death sentence in an HIV-positive diagnosis.

The outlook for his talk show was also aided by Arsenio Hall's success in breaking the late-night color barrier. Arsenio was a mediocre stand-up comic and a terrible interviewer, whose show prospered anyway on his energy, enthusiasm, and high spirits. Why couldn't Magic, one of the most positive, upbeat guys on the planet, succeed with the same formula?

To his credit, Magic prepared for his career by scouting the competition. He appeared as a guest of *The Tonight Show* with both Johnny Carson and guest host Jay Leno, and with Arsenio Hall, picking up pointers along the way. He took diction lessons, and rehearsed with dozens of practice shows. "I want to be the Oprah Winfrey of late night," he said prior to his debut.

Former Prince drummer Sheila E. headed up the house band, and comedian Craig Shoemaker was hired as sidekick/announcer. In an interesting departure from the usual talk format, it was Shoemaker who delivered the opening comedy monologue, while host Magic supplied the Ed McMahon-esque laughter from the wings. "The show will be like myself—fun, crazy, but a good environment," he said.

But *The Magic Hour* debuted to disastrous reviews and low ratings, and it was obvious that something was amiss. "Likability and a trademark, crescent moon smile weren't nearly enough to overcome Johnson's almost shocking shortcomings as a talk show host," wrote one critic. "Namely, he couldn't carry a conversation, tell a joke, or ad lib. Magic's main contribution to the proceedings was a boisterous, all-purpose 'ha-ha-ha' that punctuated virtually anything a guest told him."

Though he turned out the A-list with guests such as Whitney Houston, Arnold Schwarzenegger, Gloria Estefan, and Michael Douglas, Magic's desire to be a charming host resulted in fawning interviews that were embarrassing in their deference. "You're a great man," he told Schwarzenegger, "You're one of my all-time favorites." When Harrison Ford appeared, Magic gushed, "You're one of my all-time favorites," to which Ford replied, "Isn't that what you said to Schwarzenegger?" Both stars were also subjected to film clips of themselves in pre-stardom bit parts, a gag that Leno and Arsenio had already done to death.

After one week, the show lost 17 percent of its audience, and could only manage a 1.5 Nielsen rating, lower even than the short-lived *Keenan Ivory Wayans Show*; apparently, the answer to the show's opening question, "Are you ready for Magic?" was, "No, not really."

Despite the shaky start, *The Magic Hour* had one chance to command the national spotlight, which ironically emerged from its ineptitude. Howard Stern lambasted Magic almost every morning on his radio show, and Magic responded by inviting the shock jock to appear as a guest. Stern appeared on the July 2 broadcast, about a month after the show debuted. The confrontation was promoted in the papers and on entertainment news shows, and as a result *The Magic Hour* drew its largest-ever viewership—a 4.2 rating, higher than both Leno and Letterman and a 110% increase over the previous night.

First-time viewers saw Stern and his posse—Robin Quivers, Fred Norris, Jackie Martling—perform a song accompanied by sounds of flatulence, after which Stern joined Magic on the couch and told him exactly why his show was tanking. The self-proclaimed "King of All Media" accused Magic of "trying to talk like the white man," and suggested he mix in a little ebonics. He praised the disappearance of Shoemaker ("the white guy comedian"), who had departed a week earlier, and predicted ratings would rise if Sheila E. would take off her top. And then he got tasteless.

Stern turned the tables on the host, who lost control of his own show. He asked Magic about the sex-fueled pool parties he used to host before he was diagnosed as HIV-positive. Magic squirmed, his ever-present smile dropping ever so slightly. "Nobody has fun getting HIV," said Magic. "Believe me brother, you did," Howard said, before asking whether he practices safe sex with his wife, Cookie.

For the first time, *The Magic Hour* had taken a side road out of its comfort zone, and there was a sense that anything could happen. Would Magic get angry? Would he take a swing at Stern? No, he laughed and took the abuse, still the perfect host, when a more honest reaction might have paid greater dividends.

As a parting shot, Magic learned about honest on-camera exchanges when he asked Robin, "How can you work with this guy?" "Now wait a minute. How can I work with you, Magic?," she replied, smiling all the while. "You didn't even pay for me to come here. You didn't get me a hotel room. And then you ask me to do the show. You have some nerve!"

"It's a part of life and it didn't work out and you just pick yourself back off the ground and keep going," Johnson said about *The Magic Hour* in a 2002 interview with *Sports Illustrated.* "One thing about me: I don't have a problem laughing at myself or criticizing myself. That's just who I am."

25

TURN-ON IS TUNED OUT

Turn-On
ABC, FEBRUARY 5, 1969

A bad television show may be cancelled in its first season. A really bad show might disappear after just one or two episodes. But how awful does a show have to be to get cancelled *while* its first show is still airing? That's what happened in several markets to *Turn-On*, ABC's attempt to duplicate the success of *Rowan & Martin's Laugh-In*, aided and abetted by *Laugh-In* executive producer George Schlatter. The series, one year in development, was yanked from the network's schedule within 24 hours of its debut, in what the *Los Angeles Times* described as "perhaps the fastest action by a network since the days of the quiz scandals."

"By the time the first show got on the air on the West Coast, it had been cancelled in New York," recalled Tim Conway, *Turn-On*'s first and only guest star. "The premiere party turned out to be a cancellation party. In Cleveland, they cut it off after 15 minutes. The station put a slide up and called an old guy out to play the organ."

To the credit of Schlatter and his partner, producer Digby Wolfe, they didn't just set out to create a *Laugh-In* clone. Though each show featured a cast of young comic talent, and a mix of slapstick and topical humor with quick fadeout sketches, *Turn-On* ventured one step beyond even *Laugh-In*'s controversial content, with frank language and sexual double-entendres rarely found on television at the time. But if it had been cancelled for pushing the prime time envelope, *Turn-On* might be celebrated as a noble failure. The real problem was the show just wasn't funny.

Digby Wolfe described the series as a "visual, comedic, sensory assault involving … animation, videotape, stop-action film, electronic distortion, (and) computer graphics." Schlatter promised *Turn-On* would be truer in spirit to what *Laugh-In* was supposed to be before the concept changed in development. The assembled cast included one *Laugh-In* vet, Teresa Graves, plus Chuck McCann, who went on to star in the Krofft series *Far Out Space Nuts*. The others—Bonnie Boland, Maura McGiveney, Cecile Ozorio, Mel Stuart, Alma Murphy, Hamilton Camp, Maxine Greene, Carlos Manteca, Bob Staats, and Ken Greenwald—all more or less disappeared with the show.

The series' frenetic pace was dictated on screen by a futuristic computer, that flashed and popped between bits while electronic music blared over the transitions. It was all a bit much for ABC programmers, none of whom were particularly enthusiastic about the new venture. But the network was starved for hits at the time and gave *Turn-On* an 18-episode commitment, and complete creative freedom to Schlatter and Wolfe.

They used this freedom to tell the kind of snickering sex jokes that were tired when most of us gradutated from the third grade. One of the computer's on-screen messages read "The Amsterdam Levee is a Dike." Richard Nixon being described as "the titular head of the Republican Party" was supposed to be hilarious because the word "titular" contains the word tit. In a sketch where a buxom spy is about to be shot, the leader whispers to her that this time, it's the firing squad that has one last request.

More disturbing than the lowbrow humor was the blatant attempt to stir up controversy with scenes like a surrealistic dance number, in which a male and female groped each other while the word "sex" pulsated on the screen. Shortly after, the general manager of Cleveland's ABC affiliate sent a telegram to the New York office with the admonishment, "If you naughtly little boys have to write dirty words on the walls, please don't use *our* walls."

The negative reaction to *Turn-On* was swift and severe; the Denver affiliate pulled the plug mid-broadcast, informing viewers that "the remainder of this broadcast will not be seen." Other markets, including Baltimore and Little Rock, decided to pass on future episodes after the closing credits. When Bristol-Myers pulled their sponsorship, also within 24 hours of the first broadcast, ABC officially cancelled the series, though no formal announcement was made. The less said, they figured, the better.

24
WHEN CARROTS ATTACK

Lost in Space
CBS, FEBRUARY 28, 1968

Where were you on October 16, 1977? Chances are that, like most of the country, you were glued to CNN or one of the other news stations, to watch Alpha Control's launch of the Jupiter II. You know, the Jupiter II—the spacecraft that carried the Robinson family on their mission to reach Alpha Centurai? Come on, it was in all the papers!

Actually, the story of *Lost in Space* begins in 1964, when producer Irwin Allen adapted a comic book published by Walt Disney called *Space Family Robinson*, a science fiction take on the classic novel *Swiss Family Robinson*. Disney wouldn't let Allen use the title but he kept the family name and the basic scenario, changing only the title to *Lost in Space*.

Guy Williams and June Lockhart, two of TV's most reliable players, were cast as explorer/scientists John and Maureen Robinson. Newcomer Mark Goddard signed on as the Jupiter II's pilot, Major Don West, and the Robinson brood was comprised of sexy Judy (Marta Kristen), cute Penny (Angela Cartwright) and precocious Will (Billy Mumy). Also along for the ride were a bubble-headed, Slinky-armed robot and treacherous foreign agent Dr. Zachary Smith, delightfully played by Jonathan Harris.

Like the Robinsons themselves, *Lost in Space* started off on one trajectory and then veered off in another direction. The first season featured straightforward sci-fi adventures, with just enough of Smith and the robot for comic relief. "It began as a very serious drama and we were enthralled with it," recalled June Lockhart. "It was really quite wonderful."

But with its second season, the series was no longer in black and white, and the stories became colorful in more ways than one. Inspired by the success of ABC's tongue-in-cheek take on Batman, *Lost in Space* became Space-camp, a Mr. Toad's Wild Ride tour of day-glo planets and rubber-masked space creatures. Smith was the focal point of almost every show, and the only suspense left for the audience was in wondering whether the sets would fall apart before the episode ended. "There was nothing we could do, unless you wanted to leave, and that's not professional. You have to complete your contract," said Lockhart, who made the best of one crazy situation after another.

Still, even the most dedicated of the show's cast may have experienced second thoughts after receiving a script in the third season entitled "The Great Vegetable Rebellion," in which the Robinsons come under attack by intelligent plant life. "The shooting of it was beyond anything you could imagine. We could not keep it together," Lockhart recalls.

The story begins with Dr. Smith picking a flower for the robot's birthday—and that's not even the weird part. Suddenly, he is accosted by a giant talking carrot, who tells him he has killed the flower, and now "A life for a life!" Tybo (the carrot, played by embarrassed actor Stanley Adams) sentences Dr. Smith to be turned into a stalk of celery.

The Robinsons attempt to rescue their wayward companion. John, Maureen, Don, and Penny trek through a jungle, John cutting a path through the greenery with a machete. "Every time Guy swung the machete and hit a plant the dialogue director would go 'Ooh! Ouch!' cause that was the sound the plants were supposed to make," Lockhart remembers. "We started giggling in our single file with heads down, trying to stifle and hide our laughs as we shuffled on!"

The family is captured in a giant hemp cargo net, the hemp providing a possible clue as to how this episode was conceived. Actually, my own theory is that writer Peter Packer used to get teased by schoolmates about his name (Peter Packer picked a peck of pickled peppers, etc.) and finally snapped, exacting his revenge on the entire vegetable kingdom.

Next, the Robinsons are imprisoned in a greenhouse surrounded by a force field. "Angela is lying on the floor of the greenhouse, her body having already taken 'root.'

She is covered in vines, and I watch as she attempts to suppress her laughter," Lockhart recalls. "On the floor is a big trap door. The script calls for the two leading men to lift the door, which I will hold up until they have both climbed down, and I then lower the trap door to the floor. The camera is placed downstage so that all that is seen by the viewer is the full front side of the door as it is lifted from the floor to screen the actors descent. Why? Because the truth is that the door is lying flat on the sound stage floor—there are no steps, there is no cellar.

"Therefore, to indicate going down a stairway, Guy and Mark each have to bend their legs a little at a time, and pretend to be walking down a flight of stairs behind the door. In reality our two heroes, after waving

Tybo the angry carrot (Stanley Adams) plots to turn the Robinson family into cole slaw.

153

goodbye for the descent, have to crawl off stage on their hands and knees and finally off the set on all fours out of camera range. I must remain holding the door looking at the floor pretending to see straight down the nonexistent flight of steps, while out of the corner of my eye I can see Mark and Guy off stage on the floor, rolling around in hysterics!"

One might expect the actors' attempts to hide their laughter to be edited out, but they happened so frequently during this episode that they are still visible in several scenes. Mark Goddard might be the worst offender; more than once he turns away from the camera, with his lip quivering and his eyes tearing up from the effort to maintain control. "Mark and Angela and Guy and I giggled all the way through it because it was so preposterous. Irwin Allen disciplined Guy and me by writing us out of the next two episodes at full salary," Lockhart said. "Mark Goddard knew he should have been written out too, but they needed someone to drive the ship."

"The Great Vegetable Rebellion" was the second-to-last episode of the series, which makes sense in retrospect because once you've battled militant produce, there are precious few worlds left to conquer. *Lost in Space* was canceled in 1968, after three years and 81 adventures. Though it has not influenced our popular culture as profoundly as *Star Trek*, the series remains a fond memory for a generation of junior space travelers, for whom "Danger, Will Robinson!" has become as famous a catch phrase as "Beam me up, Scotty."

A postscript: *TV Guide* ranked "The Great Vegetable Rebellion" at #76 on its list of the 100 Greatest Episodes in TV History. Yes, 'Greatest.' Says June Lockhart, "I was very amused that they would include that because it is certainly one of the best 'worst' television shows ever broadcast."

23
BREAKFAST CRIME

FOX after Breakfast
FOX, AUGUST 12, 1996

Mixing original and syndicated series, movies, and sporting events, the FX network doesn't look much different from TNT, USA, or a dozen other cable outlets. But when the network debuted in September 1994, there was nothing on television like FX, or 'fX,' as it was known back then. "TV made fresh daily" was their motto, and home base was a 6,500 sqaure-foot New York City apartment, complete with living room, bedroom, bathroom and fully-functional kitchen.

The jewel in the fX crown was *Breakfast Time*, a live two-hour morning show that combined the traditional elements of AM television—news, weather, interviews— with a unique, irreverent approach that accentuated recreation over information.

While *Today* and *Good Morning America* tried to ease viewers into a new day with the mild stimulation of a first cup of coffee, *Breakfast Time* was the video equivalent of a Big Gulp filled with Jolt Cola.

The show was blessed with two fearless, quick-witted hosts in Tom Bergeron and Laurie Hibberd, who thrived in the anything-goes environment. They were joined in the apartment by visiting viewers, who ate breakfast in the kitchen while the show progressed, celebrity guests, and a smart-mouthed orange puppet named Bob voiced by Al Rosenberg, a veteran of both the Howard Stern and Don Imus radio shows.

While Bob made suggestive advances on the movie-plugging starlets, Bergeron hijacked the news segments with pop culture references; following a Hurricane Marilyn update, he wondered aloud if Marilyn "had taken any suggestive looks at Cape Kennedy." Hibberd, hired to be the voice of reason on the playground, turned out to be more of a co-conspirator to the chaos than a counterbalance, as evidenced by her frequent dances through the apartment to the theme from *Josie and the Pussycats.*

"We were allowed to be as free-flowing and creative as humanly possible within the confines of a live two-hour morning show," Hibberd recalled. "We used to call the final rundown 'the first draft,' because we were always able to throw it out in case something better came along. As a broadcaster it was the most challenging and liberating experience in my life."

Newsweek hailed *Breakfast Time* as "possibly the future of television," and every day the show produced at least one moment worthy of a highlight reel. Sadly, most of the country missed all of them, as the fX network was then available in only 27 million homes nationwide. Because of New York's crowded cable capacity, the show was never seen in the city from which it originated, though some Gothamites improvised. While *The Today Show* aired on NBC, several network employees routinely gathered around the television in their break room to watch tapes of *Breakfast Time.*

In March 1996, fX announced that a one-hour version of their morning show would debut on the FOX network in August. "We spent two years in cable oblivion, and we

A show so good it could only be destroyed by highly-paid network executives: Tom Bergeron, Laurie Hibberd, and Bob the Puppet of Breakfast Time.

thought finally the rest of the country was going to see what good work we do," said Hibberd. But the network had other ideas. "They looked at it, knew it was a great show, but for some reason when they moved it to network they felt they had to change everything. And they took away everything that made it special."

Originally, FOX expressed interest only in Tom Bergeron and the apartment setting. "The last day of *Breakfast Time* when we all said goodbye, none of us had a job except for Tom," Hibberd recalls. "It wasn't until *Good Morning America* offered me a job that I was rehired."

When the new show, *FOX after Breakfast*, debuted, Tom, Laurie, and Bob the Puppet were all back, but the magic that energized its predecessor had vanished. A gaggle of new producers micromanaged every aspect of the show, certain they knew what worked on the network better than the original cast and creative team. Inexplicably, one of the strongest proponents for change was Peter Faiman, who cocreated *Breakfast Time* but apparently forgot why the show had worked in the first place.

"They figured that Tom was the strength, and let's face it, he was. Tom was a genius. But he needed some propping up," Hibberd explained. "He was given all the interviews and all the segments, and I was supposed to throw it to commercial. It got very weird. They took away our director, they took away (announcer) Jim Kocot, who was the heart and soul, they took away some of the producers and gave them lesser roles. When this guy came in who I had never met and said he was going to help me write jokes for the host chat, I knew we were on our way into the skids."

Even in its bastardized form, *FOX AB* earned favorable reviews: "The best network weekday morning show on TV" (*Fresno Bee*); "An anti-talk show, avoiding standard interviews in favor of infectious frivolity" (*Orlando Sentinel*); "Makes everything else on the air in the morning look dead" (*Las Vegas Review-Journal*). The show was given 52 weeks to find an audience, and it's possible that within that time the hosts might have ultimately overcome the restrictive format and outside interference. "Had it been any other year, they probably would have stayed with it a little longer, but two months before we debuted Rosie O'Donnell came out of the box with huge national ratings," Hibberd said. "She set the bar higher, and when we came on everyone expected the same thing. When it didn't happen they went into a tailspin."

Hibberd was released from her contract three months into the run. The puppet followed her out the door soon after, and Bergeron was saddled with rotating guest cohosts, none of whom had the first clue on how to make the show work. "My worst fear was that they were right, and I was the problem," Hibberd admits. "The fact that the ratings went further down after I left made me happy (laughs). But it was sad because all my friends were back there, and morale was in the toilet."

FOX after Breakfast was finally put out of its misery in August 1997, by which time Bergeron was also gone, having been replaced by Vicki Lawrence. That decision made as much sense as any that were made from the moment *Breakfast Time* left its comfortable cable home on fX.

"I try not to think about it that much," says Hibberd. "It's like a lost love; you try not to think about them, you try to think about who you're dating now." Laurie's dating CBS now, where she's a regular contributor to *The Early Show*, as well as the host of her own series on HGTV. Tom Bergeron replaced Bob Saget on *America's Funniest Home Videos*, and won an Emmy as the host of *Hollywood Squares*. Both have the broadcasting chops to never be out of work, but it's doubtful that either will ever find another outlet better suited to their talents than *Breakfast Time*.

Hibberd reminisces, "When I interviewed Elijah Wood for *Lord of the Rings*, I forgot he was on *Breakfast Time*, but he came up to me and said, 'you guys were the greatest.' I haven't walked into a meeting in the last eight years where someone didn't say, 'I can't believe you were able to do that show.'"

22
VANNA SPEAKS: BAD IDEA

The Goddess of Love
NBC, NOVEMBER 20, 1988

"The critics are going to be waiting for me, aren't they?"
—VANNA WHITE

Vanna White's path to fame is among the more unique showbiz stories of our time, but it's not unprecedented. The *Wheel of Fortune* letter-turner wasn't the first game show hostess to enter the pop culture with no outward sign of talent. That distinction belongs to Dolores Rosedale, better known to *Beat the Clock* viewers in the 1950s as the lovely Roxanne.

Roxanne's job consisted of intoducing contestants to host Bud Collyer, and presenting them with a copy of the *Beat the Clock* home game. But public curiosity about the hostess inspired thousands of fan letters, cover stories in major magazines, a best-selling Roxanne doll for kids (and lonely bachelors), and the chance to make movies, including a costarring role in *The Seven Year Itch* with Marilyn Monroe. Roxanne left the game show in 1955, amidst unfounded rumors that Collyer had grown jealous of her celebrity. Actually, she departed after her request for a hefty pay raise was denied by producers Mark Goodson and Bill Todman.

Vanna wisely hasn't made the same mistake; she's been with *Wheel* since 1982, and has adopted a humble, "aw, shucks" attitude toward her celebrity status. But like Roxanne, she could not resist a go at acting. In 1987 she accepted an invitation from NBC to star in *The Goddess of Love*, a made-for-TV movie romance with Vanna cast as the Greek goddess Venus.

Technically it wasn't her first film credit; just before landing the *Wheel* gig, Vanna appeared as cheesecake background in the low-budget feature *Gypsy Angels*, which wasn't even released until she became a household name. But *Goddess of Love* would be the first time she would say anything on television besides "Bye bye! We love you!"

"When I read the script, I thought yeah, I could be a great Venus," she told *Life* magazine. "The character seemed to be a fun-loving person, and so am I." But her first screen test proved so disastrous that the project was delayed so she could take three months of acting classes. "And I thought *Wheel* was hard!" she said of the lessons.

The second test proved satisfactory enough to green-light the project, and director Jim Drake tried to talk up his leading lady as the airdate approached. "Yes, Vanna can act," he said. "I think she has the potential to become another Judy Holliday." Cowriter Phil Margo was less enthusiastic. "Working with her was a pleasure because she knew what she was supposed to do. She brought cookies, knew her lines and was never tardy. But watching the words in our script, the result of a year's sweat and blood, turn to lead and sink through the floor on the set each day was sheer torture for me. I couldn't wait until we finished the damn thing."

"I'm doing my best," was Vanna's assessment. "This movie was more difficult to do than it appears because I'm playing a person who is 3,000 years old. I say things like 'What a quaint abode' and 'Where does thou slumber?'"

As the story begins, Venus' father turns her to stone because three of her husbands have died under suspicious circumstances. For 3,000 years, Venus resides in a museum, sentenced to remain a statue until she discovers the meaning of true love. She finally gets that chance with the help of Ted Becker, a Los Angeles hairdresser played by David Naughton.

On the eve of his bachelor party, Ted rehearses for the

"Wouldst thou buyeth a vowel?" Vanna White plays Venus in Goddess of Love.

upcoming marriage ceremony by slipping his wedding ring on the Venus statue. The goddess of love is magically revived, and believing Ted has proposed tries to take him back to her home on Mt. Olympus. Ted tries to explain that he already has a fiancée in Cathy (played by *Married … with Children*'s Amanda Bearse), but one look at Venus and he has second thoughts about the nuptials. Now torn between two women, Ted must also deal with two frustrated thieves who steal the Venus statue from the museum.

Three days before the movie aired, Vanna told the *Los Angeles Times*, "I hope people aren't expecting Shakespeare." As if anyone would expect the Bard to write such immortal lines as "Silence, mortal, or I will crush you" and the unforgettable "I am not here for your cold roast chicken. I am here for your love!"

It's cruel, but accurate, to report that Vanna White's performance as a statue is more convincing than her work as an animate being. Her wooden line readings and blank facial expressions quenched any trace of whimsy that might have emerged with a more capable performance. Reviews couldn't have been more scathing, but *The Goddess of Love* was a no-lose proposition for NBC; if the film was good they had negotiated an option for a Venus series; if it was awful, the curiosity factor in seeing a toga-clad Vanna doing something other than clapping and turning letters practically guaranteed a good rating. *Goddess of Love* placed a respectable second behind ABC's blockbuster miniseries *War and Remembrance*.

As for Vanna, her acting career simultaneously peaked and plummeted in one evening. "I think for the first movie I've ever (starred in) I did an okay job. On a scale of 1 to 10 … hmmm, I was maybe a 3 or 4." Then she paused. "That sounds awful, doesn't it?" That's okay, Vanna, we still love you—just don't expect to take a seat opposite James Lipton at the New School anytime soon.

21
YOU CAN'T GO HOME AGAIN

Life with Lucy
ABC, September 20–November 15, 1986

Sometimes a TV programming failure can provoke humor, either at the hubris of its creators, the silliness of the idea or the incompetence of the execution. This is not one of those times. There's no getting round the fact that *Life with Lucy* didn't work, but for anyone who grew up laughing at the sitcom exploits of Lucille Ball, there can be no joy in its quick departure. The series was an admirable attempt to add another chapter to her legend, but the daffy redhead could not compete with her video legacy.

Lucy had no burning desire to return to television. At age 75 she had established her status as the greatest sitcom performer of all time, and was content to stay home and play backgammon, while mixing in the occasional *Password* appearance or talk show chat with Joan Rivers. But when Aaron Spelling approached Ball with an opportunity for a new series, she couldn't resist one more comeback to the art form she made famous. "I missed going to work," she told *Dramalogue* magazine.

Spelling offered a full-season commitment of 22 episodes, where most series received a 13-show tryout, with Lucy given full casting approval and artistic judgment on all scripts. Her first act was rounding up the old gang. Vivian Vance had passed away and Desi was in poor health, but Lucy coaxed 80-year-old Gale Gordon out of retirement to once again play her vituperative comic foil, and she brought back the original *I Love Lucy* writers, Madelyn Davis and Bob Carroll. Perhaps that was a mistake, as a more contemporary approach might have been preferable. But Lucy required a support system of people she could trust, and even Aaron Spelling, then the most successful producer in television, wasn't about to say no to the Queen of Comedy. "It was my fault, because she trusted me and I went along with what she wanted," he would later admit.

No concession was made to how much time had passed since the halcyon days of Lucy Ricardo, or to how much the world and television comedy had changed. *Life with Lucy* stuck to the formula that sustained more than 500 episodes of previous Lucy shows—a broad comic premise, easily summarized in ten words or less, that built to a large physical comedy set piece for Lucy to tackle in her inimitable style.

This time she was feisty grandma Lucy Barker, recently widowed and moved into the home of her daughter (Ann Dusenberry), son-in-law (Larry Anderson), and their two kids. Lucy also assumed half-ownership in the hardware store run by her son-in-law's father, Curtis (Gordon), providing the two veteran comics with a variety of convenient props. In the first episode, Lucy accidentally triggers a giant fire extinguisher, burying herself and Gordon up to their necks in bubbling foam.

Despite the new premise, it was impossible to see *Life with Lucy* as anything but a reunion show. The names didn't matter, and they never did. There are people who have watched *The Lucy Show* and *Here's Lucy* for decades in reruns, and still couldn't tell you how the characters got from Danfield to Los Angeles, why Mr. Mooney was Lucy's boss in both cities, and when Lucy Carmichael became Lucy Carter.

But as a reunion it was a little late in coming, missing the window when the show would bring back fond memories of beloved characters, and be diminished by them instead. Classic TV fans had grown accustomed to textbook comic timing from Ball and Gordon, and uproarious routines that found Lucy in physically demanding, even dangerous straits. Though remarkably spry at 75, Lucy was no longer at the top of her game. Her reliance on cue cards is obvious, and the awkward pauses in her dialogue cannot help but induce sadness.

Her supporting cast adds little to the mix, though Gale Gordon is in fine fettle, arguably better than Lucy and the material. But when Lucy Barker rides a rolling ladder down a row of high shelves and crashes into Curtis's nose, it's not so much a slapstick bit as a potential lawsuit for the AARP. It's impossible to generate laughs from an audience that is concerned for the well-being of an actor; there were as many gasps as guffaws when Lucy tried some physical schtick, even if it was a milder variation on the madcap moments of her glory days.

ABC hoped that Lucy would do for their network what Bill Cosby achieved for NBC: the welcome return of a comedy icon in a breakaway hit that would propel the rest of their lineup into contention. But *Life with Lucy* was pulled after eight episodes. Ironically, one of the reasons the show didn't last was how lovingly it was received by the studio audience, which created a false sense of success with substandard material. Who could blame the fans, thrilled to be watching Lucy make a new television show, which was like watching Picasso draw or Willie Mays field a fly ball. Pandemonium greeted Lucy's entrance into every scene, and Gale Gordon was likewise welcomed back with sustained ovations. Had the show been a play, with tickets sold rather than given away, it might have run for years.

What doesn't become a legend most—Lucille Ball in Life with Lucy.

"I don't think Lucy knew how bad these shows were," recalled production assistant Stuart Shostak in Geoffrey Fidelman's superbly-researched *The Lucy Book*. "And the studio audiences misled us. They laughed uproariously at everything Lucy did. If they had reacted to the comedy the way the folks did at home, everyone would have realized there was a big problem and perhaps it would have been fixed."

Lucy was reportedly devastated by the series' cancellation, but one of the nicer things about television is how in most cases the bad stuff disappears quickly and the good stuff lives forever. One hundred years from now, *I Love Lucy* will still be entertaining new legions of fans, while *Life with Lucy* will have disappeared into the same vault that houses *The Bradys* and *The New Andy Griffith Show*. We shall not speak of them again.

20
IT'S A BOMB, IT'S A DISASTER, IT'S … SUPERTRAIN

Supertrain
NBC, FEBRUARY 7–JULY 28, 1979

Born of desperation, rushed into production, and saddled with the expectation of rescuing NBC from the ratings basement, *Supertrain* has become synonymous with dreadful television. As with Edsel and New Coke, its ineptitude is legendary even among those who never experienced its failure first hand—and judging from the ratings, that would be just about everybody.

Let us journey back in time to 1978, when much of NBC's prime time schedule was trailing local farm reports in total viewership. The job of righting the ship fell to maverick programmer Fred Silverman, who had already worked similar miracles at both CBS and ABC. Impatient for success, Silverman searched for new shows that would capture the public's imagination. He heard a pitch he liked from programming head Paul Klein about a luxurious supersonic train that delivered passengers from New York to Los Angeles in 36 hours. Each episode's journey would feature different guest stars and stories of comedy, drama, and intrigue—*The Love Boat* meets *Murder on the Orient Express.*

Silverman loved the idea and recruited producer Dan Curtis to develop the new series. Curtis envisioned a train that was so large it had to run on two separate tracks simultaneously, and was home to a disco, a swimming pool and a ballroom (yes, a ballroom on a train). Curtis's concepts drove the cost of the proposed series to $1 million an episode, twice the going rate; but after three shows he left to produce *The Winds of War.* Silverman was so convinced that *Supertrain* was a breakout hit that he ordered a pilot as a midseason replacement, with midseason just four months away.

Meanwhile, NBC's Brandon Tartikoff wondered why wealthy people would travel coast to coast by train in two days when a plane would get them there in five hours. Apparently he was the only one still thinking at that point.

Supertrain fever swept through the Peacock network. Crews worked round the clock filling three soundstages with enormous sets, while special effects experts built an elaborate miniature train set to be used for exterior shots. When the model was first demonstrated for network executives it derailed and crashed, a harbinger of things to come.

With all the attention lavished on the train, not much was apparently left over for scripts and casting, judging by the results. The cast was led by Edward Andrews as befuddled conductor Harry Flood. "All aboard!" he'd announce as each episode begins. "Engine room—Supertrain is ready to depart." Most of the time that was pretty much all he did. There were a few parallels to *Love Boat* in the crew, especially Robert Alda as lothario doctor Dan Lewis and a social director played with Julie

McCoy-like perkiness by Ilene Graff, but limited interaction with the passengers usually rendered their presence superfluous.

The first episode featured guest stars Zsa Zsa Gabor and Lyle Waggoner, not exactly a stellar lineup even by Pacific Princess standards. Reviews were horrific, but nothing could deter Silverman's confidence that *Supertrain* was the real deal. He scheduled the new series on Wednesday nights opposite two established hits, ABC's *Eight is Enough* and *The Jeffersons* on CBS. *Supertrain* failed to make even a slight dent in either shows' popularity, and in its second week lost more than half of the modicum of viewers it attracted in its Wednesday debut. After four episodes, the Train was shut down for repairs.

For all the money spent on special effects and production design, not much of the investment showed up on screen. Shots of the train in motion are obvious miniatures, the station where passengers embark is a dim, sterile depot, filled with steam blowing off cold steel; guest quarters on the train appear cramped and dark—at least *The Love Boat* was smart enough to take dramatic liberties with a cruise ship's cabin sizes—and the crew's uniforms made them look like hotel bellmen. There's nothing that suggests the comfort or luxury that was intrinsic to the premise.

And yet, such visual deficiencies were the least of the show's problems. The scripts started out derivative and then took a turn for the eccentric after the show returned from its hiatus, when the tone shifted away from frothy escapism and toward serious drama. "The Queen and the Improbable Knight" starred Paul Sand as a journalist who falls in love with the heir to the throne of Montenegro (Mary Louise Weller); the story unfolds with such similarities to *The Lady Vanishes* that the Alfred Hitchcock estate might have had a legitimate lawsuit. Another episode, "And a Cup of Kindness, Too" borrowed liberally from Hitchcock's *Strangers on a Train* and *Suspicion.*

Nothing worked. One scene in which two vicious mobsters drag the corpse of their victim down the train corridor is accompanied by incidental music more appropriate to a *Tom and Jerry* cartoon. Sometimes, it seemed as if no one was paying attention, even those who were getting paid to keep the show on its rails.

In his book *The Last Great Ride*, Brandon Tartikoff relates the story of his suggesting a plot for the series, in which heirs to the Rockefeller and Vanderbilt fortunes are to be married on the train, until the would-be groom spots guest star Cybill Shepherd at the prenuptial dinner. Another derivative plot, this time from the Cybill Shepherd film *The Heartbreak Kid*. His idea was accepted, yet when Tartikoff checked on its progress a few weeks later, he was told that a few changes had been made. Nothing serious, but now the families were Basque winegrowers who had feuded for centuries, and Shepherd was the p.r. woman for one of the vineyards.

A schedule change to Saturdays at 10 PM, in the hopes that *Love Boat* viewers would switch over to NBC after the Princess docked for another adventure, proved to be wishful thinking on Silverman's part. *Supertrain* lasted five more episodes before the axe fell, leaving a track of red ink in its wake. Silverman was so traumatized by its failure that he refused to return to the conference room in which the idea was pitched until its mahogany paneling was stripped and the conference table replaced.

Of all the shows with which he's ever been associated, Tartikoff reflected, "the all-time classic Vietnam fiasco, the one that stands out like a beacon, is *Supertrain*." And yet, it was a tremendous hit in France. Really. Feel free to insert your own Jerry Lewis joke.

19
THREE MOVIES, NO WAITING

Amy Fisher: My Story
NBC, DECEMBER 28, 1992

The Amy Fisher Story
ABC, JANUARY 3, 1993

Casualties of Love: The Long Island Lolita Story
CBS, JANUARY 3, 1993

Ever see the movie *Rashomon?* Check it out next time you're at the video store and they're all out of *Happy Gilmore*. Set in feudal Japan, the story revolves around a violent crime, and the varying accounts of what actually happened. The bandit's version is different from the victim's, while a witness to the event offers yet another variation. The truth, one suspects, falls somewhere in between.

One gets the same impression after viewing the three made-for-TV docudramas about "Long Island Lolita" Amy Fisher. This is not to suggest that watching all or any of them is a good idea, but when ranking embarrassing moments in television one has no choice. The shameful spectacle of ABC, CBS, and NBC tripping over themselves to rush this lurid tale into prime time resulted in all three films being aired within the same week. And, proving once again that it's impossible to underestimate the viewing taste of the American public, all three movies ranked among the week's 15 highest-rated shows. Seriously, what is wrong with you people?

All three films cover the basics: once upon a time, 16-year-old high school student Amy Fisher met Joey Buttafuoco, a married, thirtysomething owner of a Long Island body shop. In August 1992, Amy shot Joey's wife Mary Jo in the head, a crime that may or may not have been instigated by Joey. Mary Jo survived and Amy went to jail. But as with *Rashomon*, each film reveals more about who's telling the tale than the tale itself.

Amy Fisher: My Story was based on Fisher's book, and naturally offers the most sympathetic portrayal of the pistol-packin' dropout. As played by Noelle Parker, Amy is just a wayward romantic who fell for a big galoot that turned out to be bad news.

She is seduced by the worldly Joey, who then forces Amy into a life of prostitution before coercing her to kill his wife.

Parker closely approximates the bruised beauty of the real Amy Fisher, and Ed Marinaro (*Hill Street Blues*) somehow manages to find some humanity in Joey Buttafuoco, despite his depiction as the devil incarnate. But this is the least interesting of the TV movie troika, with a ploddingly-paced story, slipshot technical credits, and a heroine that nearly qualifes for sainthood.

For an opposing viewpoint, exhibit 'B' is *Casualties Of Love: The Long Island Lolita Story*, which recounts events as told by the Buttafuoco family. Here, we have Joey as a loving family man who becomes the innocent victim of an unbalanced girl's obsession. Amy follows Joey all over Long Island and tells her friends they're sleeping together, but good citizen Joey wants nothing to do with the nubile, doe-eyed temptress. Scorned by her dreamboat, Amy shoots Mary Jo to eliminate the competition.

Alyssa Milano, perched beneath an 18-inch tower of Jersey hair, plays Amy as the kind of girl who was born snapping gum and wearing jeans two sizes too small. This was Milano's attempt to escape the wholesome image of her *Who's the Boss?* sitcom character, and to the extent that she makes great-looking jailbait, she succeeds. Jack Scalia, former male model and *Dallas* heartthrob, plays goomba Joey. Apparently Brad Pitt wasn't available.

The third rendering, based on the reportage of *New York Post* journalist Amy Pagnozzi, is the best of a weak field. *The Amy Fisher Story* finds little to admire in

Drew Barrymore (left) and Alyssa Milano both played the infamous Amy Fisher in separate made-for-TV movies. Neither film was sponsored by hair care products.

either Fisher or Buttafuoco, and spends nearly as much time lampooning the media circus that resulted from the story as it does on the crime that caused it. Freed from the responsibility of rescuing anybody's reputation, the ABC entry aims for the gutter and plays the trashy material for all it's worth.

The casting of Drew Barrymore as Amy was inspired, even if she never quite nails the Long Island accent. "She looks like a small, petite girl. But she's the devil," says Mary Jo, as Barrymore turns up the slut-o-meter in a series of sexual escapades that have nothing to do with Joey, but everything to do with keeping viewers from changing the channel. Anthony John Denison is the most nondescript Joey of the bunch, and practically disappears from the movie in the final half-hour.

The real Amy Fisher was released from prison in 1999, after serving seven years of a 5–15 sentence. She's now a freelance writer with a column in the *Long Island Press* newspaper. "I committed a terrible crime when I was only 16 years old," she wrote in one of her first articles. "Today I am 28, a mother and almost a stranger to that teenage girl who became known around the world as the 'Long Island Lolita'… I am the person I always should have been, except for a brief but total, unfathomable lapse of judgment in my youth."

The Buttafuocos have divorced, and Joey now lives in California, where he continues to chase his 15 minutes of infamy under any spotlight that will have him. In the last few years he's challenged a female wrestler to a boxing match on *The Howard Stern Show*, and appeared in Snoop Dogg's MTV series *Doggy Fizzle Televizzle*.

18

DATELINE BLOWS UP A TRUCK, THEN CLAIMS IT'S DEFECTIVE

Dateline NBC
NBC, NOVEMBER 17, 1992

Journalism, in its purest form, demands the objective communication of facts. Television, with its pragmatic reliance on ratings and advertising revenue, invites a thousand tiny compromises into the journalistic ideal. On balance, it's amazing the system works as well as it does.

The minor infractions are irritating but understandable. "*Star Trek* fans in mourning. The story at eleven." was a prime time tease for Gene Roddenberry's death on a number of local news broadcasts. In that same amount of time the anchor could have said "*Star Trek* fans mourn Gene Roddenberry's death"; that would have been communicating the story. But it was deemed more important to entice viewers who didn't know if a cast member had died or a series had been canceled into watching the news. Using a man's passing to sell a product is shameful, but such tactics have been in place for so long that they're hardly noticed anymore, much less condemned.

But every so often television news commits a huge, glaring, honking blunder that serves as a wakeup call to how easily the system can be jeopardized. The most infamous (not attributable to Geraldo Rivera) may be *Dateline* NBC's investigation into the safety of General Motors' line of full-size trucks, which alleged that the vehicles were dangerous because of the location of their "sidesaddle" gas tanks.

There was evidence to support the allegation. General Motors was already in court fighting lawsuits from families who had lost loved ones in accidents. *Dateline*'s report featured 14 minutes of interviews and debate, followed by 57 seconds of crash footage that demonstrated how the tanks could catch fire in a sideways collision. Obviously, the trucks didn't always explode when they were hit, or the highways of America would be littered with shrapnel. But pictures are everything in television, and a piece on exploding trucks would not be complete without a truck that explodes. So NBC made sure they had one.

The network hired the Indiana-based Institute of Safety Analysis to stage two crashes. To get the desired dramatic footage, model rocket igniters were strapped to the vehicles during the test, and set off by remote control seconds before the crash. Predictably, they sparked and blazed like Fourth of July firecrackers. The placement of the rockets was not mentioned in the segment.

Working from a tip, General Motors launched it's own investigation into NBC's report, and found evidence of the tampering. At a subsequent press conference, they revealed the use of the rockets, and proved with x-rays that the gas tanks on the trucks had not ruptured, as *Dateline* claimed. Further, they found that the trucks had been fitted with gas-tank caps made for different model vehicles.

At first, the network dismissed GM's charges. "NBC does not believe that any statements made in the November 17 broadcast were either false or misleading," NBC News President Michael Gartner said in a letter to GM, released by the network. He admitted that the accidents were created with rockets, but defended the testing method. Just 24 hours later, Gartner reversed his position. "The more I learned, the worse it got," he admitted. "Ultimately I was troubled by almost every aspect of the crash. I knew we had to apologize."

"An electronic Titanic", *Los Angeles Times* TV critic Howard Rosenberg called the story; "an unprecedented disaster in the annals of network news, and perhaps the biggest TV scam since the Quiz Scandals." Former NBC News president Reuven Frank called it "the worst black eye NBC News has suffered in my experience, which goes back to 1950."

Surprisingly, the Institute for Safety Analysis stuck by their story, even while NBC was backpedaling from their findings. "I saw that I had been too ready to believe our so-called experts, without trying to find out who they were. I realized we were just plain wrong," Gartner said. The apology came too late to save his job. Soon after, Gartner was followed out the door by *Dateline* executive producer Jeff Diamond, his second-in-command, David Rummel, and segment producer Robert Read.

General Motors sued NBC for defamation. They received an on-air apology and $2 million in damages. Within the same month, GM was hit with a $105.2 million jury verdict, awarded to an Atlanta couple whose son died when his GM truck exploded in a collision. There were no rockets on that one.

17
A LONG, STRANGE TRIP

1977 Science Fiction Film Awards
SYNDICATED, JANUARY 21, 1978

There are no words. There simply aren't. Some masterworks of art are so unique, so utterly unforgettable that common speech is inadequate to convey their impact. Such is Michelangelo's Pieta. Such is Beethoven's 9th Symphony. Such is William Shatner's performance of "Rocket Man."

The year was 1978, a time when Shatner's vocal stylings had not yet achieved their inevitable immortality. It wasn't until the release of Rhino's *Golden Throats* compilations, featuring cuts from Shatner's failed 1968 concept album *The Transformed Man*, that Shatner would achieve his place in the pantheon of peerless musical interpreters.

His legend was still ascending when he agreed to host the 1977 Science Fiction Awards; hardly an A-list affair, but with the release of *Star Wars* the previous year, sci-fi had reached new heights of pop culture prominence, prompting the decision to televise the awards for the first time. William Shatner, already among the giants of the genre for his work as *Star Trek's* Captain James T. Kirk, hosted the black-tie affair.

The winners and losers on that brisk night in Los Angeles have long since vanished from memory; the only moment worthy of recollection begins with Shatner on stage, garbed in a slightly rumpled black tuxedo, a world-weary expression on his face. After taking a long drag on a cigarette, he begins to "act" the lyrics of Elton John's "Rocket Man" to minimal musical accompaniment that is frequently drowned out by his emotional bombast.

"The idea had to come from Shatner himself," believes Robert Schnakenberg, author of the *Encyclopedia Shatnerica*, the definitive study of the actor's life and career. "Remember, he covered the Beatles and Bob Dylan back in the late '60s when they were at the height of their popularity. In the 1970s, Elton John ruled the pop charts, so he went with that. "Rocket Man" perfectly melded sci-fi with pop music, so it was a natural fit for him. I suppose he could have gone with David Bowie's "Space Oddity," but "Rocket Man" is sung in the first-person, which gratifies Shatner's enormous ego."

What separates Shatner from every other vocalist in the history of recorded music is his ability to emphasize individual words at random, while simultaneously delivering the lyric either faster or slower than his accompaniment. With every return to the chorus, Shatner utters the song's title differently ("Rocket, man", "Rock it man", "a rocket, man?", "A ROCK IT MAN"). "His singing is full of lunatic cadences, inappropriate emphases, and seemingly pointless stops and starts," Schnakenberg observes. "It sounds almost like he doesn't know the language and is pronouncing the words phonetically."

The five-minute performance reaches a feverish crescendo, as Shatner bellows the fadeout while the viewing audience at home sees video images of three Shatners on stage, singing in unison. "You can see that he is desperately trying to re-brand himself as a sci-fi hero/poet after a decade spent trying to get away from *Star Trek* and the typecasting it engendered," Schnakenberg says. "By the late 70s, after years of depressing game show appearances and failed attempts to conquer other TV genres, Shatner had finally come to accept that his fate—not to mention his fortune—was tied up in the Captain Kirk persona. The decision to mix 'spacy' rock music and macho sci-fi swagger was pure genius—and pure Shatner."

Though the Science Fiction Awards have never been released on video, bootleg tapes have been floating around for years, and Shatner himself has addressed the performance in several interviews. "'Rocket Man' was a joke—not a joke, but something they asked me to do in a small-show, nightclub atmosphere … so I did Frank Sinatra doing that song," he told the *Onion* AV Club.

Today, the genius of William Shatner, singer, has at last been recognized by such artists as Beck, who paid tribute to the "Rocket Man" performance in the "Where It's At" video. Shatner has also appeared as a guest vocalist with Ben Folds Five, the band that backed him in his singing commercials for Priceline.com in the 1990s. But these efforts are mere shadows when compared to the performance that is more beloved by fans than even the best episodes of *Star Trek*.

"In terms of TV moments, I put it near the top," said Schnakenberg on where "Rocket Man" ranks in Shatner lore. "On record, of course, *The Transformed Man* and the truly execrable *William Shatner Live!* are tough to beat, but 'Rocket Man' is Shatner at his out-of-control, lost-in-the-70s best."

16
THIS ENTRY BROUGHT TO YOU BY PIZZA HUT

The Corporate Sponsorship Invasion
1987–present

The Century 21 Home Run Derby; The Wendy's Race Schedule; The Gatorade Play of the Day; The Toyota Halftime Show; The Dominoes Pizza Two-Minute Warning; The Coors Light Kick-off; The Smirnoff Ice Extra Point; the Tostitos Fiesta Bowl. With the way television now presents sports programming, the four words fans have come to dread most are "brought to you by…"

We already have a place for television commercials, and that's between the programs, not during them. But that door cracked open back in 1987 and now there doesn't seem to be a moment in a sports presentation that isn't attached to a sponsor. The medium's influence has unleashed a plague of on-site banners, billboards, and company tie-ins. And in those grand old ballparks that have resisted corporate invasion, such as Chicago's Wrigley Field, advertisements are electronically superimposed on the red brick behind home plate. If they could get away with it, companies would tattoo their logos on the players themselves. Wait—boxers already do that courtesy of Golden Palace.com.

It wasn't always this way. Less than 20 years ago, The Kentucky Derby managed to get the race run without help from Visa, a baseball pitcher's earned-run average would be displayed on screen without an accompanying sales pitch, and golf tournaments were named after the celebrities who played in them. All that changed in 1987, when the Sugar Bowl became the first major sporting event to accept corporate sponsorship after signing an agreement with USF&G Financial Services. From 1987 to 1995, the event became the USF&G Sugar Bowl, until sponsorship was turned over to Nokia cellular telephones.

Purists were outraged but the floodgates had opened, and now such sponsorships are commonplace in college football. We've had the FedEx Orange Bowl, the Mobil Cotton Bowl, the Pacific Life Holiday Bowl, The Mazda Tangerine Bowl, The Diamond Walnut San Francisco Bowl, the Poulan Weedeater Independence Bowl, and the Chick-Fil-A Peach Bowl, which of course is part of Capital One Bowl Week. New Bowl games carry only a corporate name—the Blockbuster Bowl, the Carquest Bowl, the GMAC Bowl, the Outback Bowl, the Continental Tire Bowl. Only the Rose Bowl has thus far resisted selling out, though they toyed with a less intrusive form of sponsorship for a few years as "The Rose Bowl, presented by AT&T."

The trend spread to other sports, inspiring such marriages of advertising and athletics as The Pilot Pen Women's Tennis Open, presented by Michelob Ultra, "Chevy Moments" in the 2002 Winter Olympic Games, and the AFLAC post-Super Bowl show. Baseball telecasts present the Mastercard starting lineup, the Chevrolet Player of the Game, and overhead shots from the Bud blimp, reminding you that Budweiser is the official beer of Major League Baseball. Why does baseball need an official beer?

On the NASCAR circuit, where the cars and the drivers are already billboards in motion, there is no part of a race broadcast that won't be whored out to the highest bidder: "The Discover Card Pre-Race Countdown", "The Home Depot Race Summary", "The Bud Poll Award", "Lowe's Soozers", "Cingular call to the pit", "UPS lap leader board", "NAPA field summary", "The Autotrader.com move of the race".

Okay, time out. Memo to the sponsors: You had nothing to do with these games. You are not a part of their history and tradition. Writing a check should not entitle you to put your name ahead of theirs. The attempt to link your product with an event I want to see will in no way increase the likelihood that I will purchase what you're selling. In fact, if you become too aggressive with your pitches, I'll be certain to take my business elsewhere.

The backlash has already begun. Note what's happening with stadium naming rights. Chicago's Comiskey Park became U.S. Cellular Field in 2003, but many sportscasters continue to use the original name, which dates back to the early 20th century. And you'll still hear the San Francisco stadium referred to as Candlestick

Park on *Monday Night Football*, despite whatever company has the rights these days. The Chicago Bears organization didn't dare change the name of Soldier Field, a national monument dedicated to America's armed forces, so they sold advertising on the team itself. Bank One gave the Bears $30 million, and for the next 12 years we will watch "Bears football presented by Bank One." But as sportswriter Bill Hogan points out, "Do you think for a moment that John Madden is ever going to refer to Da Bears as 'Bears football presented by Bank One?' Not likely."

It seems the companies are the last to know that the money they're throwing around isn't doing much good. So while corporate sponsorship may never go away, viewers should channel their frustration into a perverse pleasure at how many advertising dollars are being flushed. At least until the sponsors wake up and move on to other endeavors. Coming soon: Visa presents Christmas.

15
JOHN LITHGOW AGAIN??!!

The Emmy Awards
ABC, CBS, FOX, NBC, 1948–PRESENT

On January 25, 1949, the first Emmy Awards honoring television excellence was held at the Hollywood Athletic Club. Just six statues were presented, before a live audience of 600. And on January 26, the first objections were raised over the selections, from people who were certain *Mabel's Fables* or *What's the Name of That Song?* deserved the Most Popular Television Program Award over the winner, *Pantomime Quiz*.

America's television fans have griped about the Emmys ever since, especially over the past two decades when there were too many blatant oversights to ignore. No award show is immune to poor choices from its voters and second-guessing among the masses, but the Emmys have produced more sour grapes than Ernest and Julio Gallo, and if this keeps up they risk a loss of credibility as television's most prestigious award.

Why do the same people win every year? Why do terrific shows like *Buffy the Vampire Slayer* and *Gilmore Girls* get no respect? How can we take the awards seriously when Michael Jeter from *Evening Shade* and Jonathan Winters from *Davis Rules* (don't ask) have won Best Supporting Actor in a Comedy Series, while Jason Alexander never took home the prize after nine years on *Seinfeld*? And why did John Lithgow win Best Actor for *Third Rock from the Sun* after the world had stopped watching and the show had been canceled?

Thomas O'Neil, author of *The Emmys* and an authority on the award's history, has heard these complaints before. On some points he's sympathetic, but O'Neil also defends the Academy of Television Arts & Sciences on some of its more controversial choices, or at least he has a good explanation for why they happened.

To simplify the interrogation, I've boiled down the complaints of a nation into four major categories:

1. The Nominating Process is Flawed.

Television shows should not be judged like movies, but that's essentially what happens every year, as eligible performers and TV shows submit one episode for the Academy's consideration. So it really doesn't matter what sort of creative journey an actor takes with his character over the course of 22 shows, because many voters will assess his performance from one 30- or 60-minute fragment.

"Theoretically they're supposed to vote based on the whole season, but the only guarantee we have is that they watched the episode submitted," O'Neil says. "In 2002, Tyne Daly (*Judging Amy*) had by far the best tape for Best Supporting Actress, and Alison Janney (*The West Wing*) had the weakest at just nine minutes, but she won. So clearly they were voting on the season that year."

Still, O'Neil says if your favorite actor or show deserved to win but didn't, chances are it's because of the episode they selected for review. "*NYPD Blue* held the record for the most nominations—26—and it was the coolest show on TV when it premiered, but it lost the Emmy to *Picket Fences*. People are still outraged by that, but I looked at the episodes that were screened and (*Fences* producer) David E. Kelley was just more shrewd with what he submitted. That's also why Susan Lucci kept losing 18 times, because she couldn't pick a sample of her best work to save her life, until she finally blundered into what the judges were looking for."

But that doesn't explain why a lot of great shows are never even nominated, which brings us to...

2. Many Popular, Critically-Acclaimed Shows are Ignored.

Friends and *Seinfeld* have won a few Emmys, but certainly not as many as they deserved. *The Gilmore Girls* has swept the Television Critics awards but hasn't received a nomination in any major category since its first season. Fans of *Buffy the Vampire Slayer* are convinced that the Emmys are a crock. Joss Whedon's canny mix of horror, humor, and adolescent angst was acclaimed not only by viewers but television critics and the mass media as one of the most innovative and outstanding series of the past decade. Episodes such as "Hush" and the musical "Once More with Feeling" exemplify network television at its absolute best.

"It's the geezer problem," says O'Neil. "People over 40 years old don't even know *Buffy* is on the air. They're clueless about what is happening on *Friends* and they don't care. And until *Seinfeld* was being shown on 22 channels in syndication they never stumbled on it because they were always watching *Law and Order* reruns or whatever's on HBO."

And these are the people most qualified to vote on television's best achievements?

3. The Same People Win Every Year.

Emmy victories tend to run in streaks, a trend that began in the 1960s when Don

Adams won three straight Best Actor trophies for *Get Smart*, and Don Knotts won five times for *The Andy Griffith Show*. In the 1970s the Academy seemed to spread the wealth a little more; *The Mary Tyler Moore Show*, *All in the Family*, and *M*A*S*H* received dozens of nominations, and most if not all of their featured performers earned at least one Emmy. But in the '80s streaks were back, as John Larroquette thanked the Academy four years in a row for honoring his work on *Night Court*, and the Best Actress in a Drama award always went to either Cagney (Sharon Gless) or Lacey (Tyne Daly). More recently, *Frasier*'s Kelsey Grammar and David Hyde-Pierce, and *NYPD Blue*'s Dennis Franz have owned their respective categories.

"I think this is a good thing," says O'Neil. "These are among the greatest actors in TV history, and I'm glad they're not being penalized for still doing good work five years after their show premiered."

4. Pay Cable Channels Have an Unfair Advantage.

When the first season of HBO's *The Sopranos* lost the Emmy to ABC's *The Practice*, the outcry was so dramatic that the Emmy organization actually changed its voting procedures. Why did this decision compel the Emmys to change their ways, when other stupid decisions they made over the last four decades did not? And why should cable series with their unrestricted violence, adult language and sexual content be nominated in the same categories as network series that don't have the same latitude?

"TV is TV. You can't say HBO should be in a different class of evaluation," O'Neil believes. "It's just that they're more adventurous, and they'll try new things on pay cable because they have to get attention, whereas broadcasters have to appeal to the broadest possible audience. So they take no chances and just reinvent the workplace comedy, the family-based comedy, the cop and lawyer shows."

Fair enough. But sometimes it seems that HBO could broadcast a bowel movement and it would get 12 nominations. The dominance of *The Sopranos*, *Sex and the City*, and *Six Feet Under* requires an explanation beyond their quality. In 2001, four of the five nominations for Best Writing went to episodes of *The Sopranos*. "The nominations are determined by popular vote, and that's a case where HBO is buying those votes," O'Neil reveals. "They're blitzing the trade papers with ads, ambushing the viewers at home with videotapes and inviting them to swank screenings." Since such practices are apparently legal, the nominating process is as equitable as the old Chicago mayoral elections.

Thomas O'Neil keeps his own list of personal Emmy outrages; "*Roseanne* never won Best Comedy Series because of a bias against blue collar shows; Jackie Gleason never won an Emmy; one of TV's most beloved women, Angela Lansbury, is one of the least loved by Emmy—16 nominations, 16 losses."

However, he is quick to defend the current system when it works. "The greatest legacy of the Emmy Award is that it saved the following shows from cancellation: *All in the Family*, *Cheers*, *Hill Street Blues*, *Cagney & Lacey*, *Mission: Impossible*. None of those shows would be remembered today if they hadn't won."

John Lithgow, though. Sheesh.

14

SHE'S SO OUTRAGEOUS

The Anna Nicole Show
E!, AUGUST 4, 2002–JUNE 1, 2003

Every few years, another show lowers the bar of what television classifies as entertainment, and is credited with accelerating the decline of Western Civilization. Since 2002 the reigning title-holder has been *The Anna Nicole Show*, starring a zaftig platinum blonde who has proven that in the current era of television personality, an actual personality is not required.

The series was inspired by *The Osbournes*, MTV's surprise hit reality show in which cameras follow the everyday life of Ozzy Osbourne, heavy metal's self-proclaimed Prince of Darkness. *The Osbournes* worked because Ozzy has been a controversial rock icon for three decades, and it's oddly fascinating to watch a guy with his madman reputation puttering around the kitchen, cleaning up after the dog and trying to find the History Channel in his cable listings. There was also a dysfunctional but loving family dynamic at work, as Ozzy's level-headed wife Sharon and kids Kelly and Jack also contributed to the series' watchability.

If you're going to build a reality series around somebody, it ought to be someone viewers already care about, but Anna Nicole Smith probably wasn't known to much of the country. She barely qualifies for celebrity status, having been a Playboy Playmate of the Year, a Guess Jeans model, and a hot tabloid topic after her marriage to 88-year-old billionaire J. Howard Marshall, now deceased. While Marshall's heirs protest the will that left billions to Anna, the ex-Texas stripper drifts through a directionless day-to-day existence, with cameras recording every moment of self-indulgent inactivity.

There's no supporting cast here, at least not anyone to provide Anna with competent help or a moral center. All of her companions are on her payroll, gladly catering to her spoiled whims and tolerating her tantrums, as long as the money keeps rolling in. She is joined on the show by her lawyer and head sycophant, Howard K. Stern, and her purple-haired assistant Kim, who has Anna's image tattooed on her arm and looks at her boss with the same glazed expression that St. Bernadette had at Lourdes. Anna's 13-year-old son, Daniel, may be the smartest of the bunch, and not just because he tries to stay off camera as much as possible. One can only imagine what his school and social life has become since Mom started sharing her life with America.

The first episode, "House Hunting," sets the tone for everything that follows. Anna, dressed in a low-cut pink top, her mop of blond hair unkempt, looks like Angelyne with a hangover as she tours prospective new homes. Her favorite test is to crawl into the homeowners' beds and simulate sex. During taped introductions of the remote segments, Anna seems chipper and rational, but in the non-rehearsed scenes she mutters, groans, and whimpers like a child. Her slurred speech sometimes requires the use of subtitles, and when she manages a coherent sentence it emerges without much thought behind it. "Why do they even have the news?" she asks Kim. "It's totally depressing."

Episode two introduces interior designer Bobby Trendy, who seems a normal enough guy when he first drops off fabric samples at Anna's home, but as the series continues he transforms himself into a cartoon character, who shamelessly plays to the camera as if auditioning for a revival of *La Cage aux Folles*. With his bizarre outfits and obviously put-on mincing and lisping, he embodies a more offensive caricature of a gay man than even the most ardent homophobe could imagine. The rest of the episode is devoted to Anna receiving half of her deceased husband's ashes (the other half went to his son). As she takes the box on a tour of her house, we're not sure whether to laugh or stare in disbelief.

In episode three, "The Eating Contest," Anna challenges Daniel, Howard, and Kim to see who can devour the most food at an Italian restaurant. At one point, Anna goes to the ladies room, and Howard lurks outside the door, wondering if she's throwing up to gain an advantage. Why would anyone find this interesting to watch?

For a former model, Anna shows no trace of vanity during the series, appearing in either too much makeup or none at all, and wearing stretch pants and too-tight t-shirts that expose her protruding belly. In scenes shot from a low angle to make her posterior look even wider, it's obvious there's an attempt on the part of somebody to present her in the most unflattering light possible, a task made easier by Anna's crude and obnoxious behavior.

Subsequent episodes are built around Anna's visit to the dentist, her passion for roller coasters at Magic Mountain, and her riotous trip to Las Vegas, where she cavorts with strippers and enjoys group lap dances. "We were staying at the Rio Hotel," she remarks, "which was named after … well, I'm not sure what it was named after." We meet a clairvoyant communicator who diagnoses separation anxiety in Anna's dog, Sugar Pie, and watch as Anna is reunited with her cousin Shelley, who looks as if she just stepped off the set of *Hee Haw*.

One of the more telling moments in the series emerges when Anna appears on a radio show, after the first episodes of *The Anna Nicole Show* have aired on the E! channel. The hosts ask the questions that were on most viewers' minds: "Are you on something? Painkillers?" "What happened between the time you were Playmate of the Year and now?" Offended, Anna storms out, even more petulant than usual, clearly not used to the events in her life being the subject of public scrutiny. Yet there's no trace of embarrassment, which may be the most troubling revelation of all.

Apparently, Anna Nicole Smith sees nothing wrong in the way she conducts herself, and certainly there are some advantages in its outward trappings. She travels by limosuine, stays in opulent hotel suites, and goes on shopping sprees without ever asking for a price. "I think you're great, but I think you're being exploited," one fan tells her. "I don't mind," she responds, "as long as I'm being paid for it."

The Anna Nicole Show won an Emmy for the design of its animated title sequence, and the award was actually deserved. To a theme song that encapsulates her life in 30 seconds, a cartoon Anna moves from poverty in Texas through her current merry widow status, her real life sounding like the premise to a wacky new sitcom starring Fran Drescher. "You're so outrageous!" chirps the song, but upon further review she's shallow, spoiled, and more than a little sad. Happily, since the show's cancellation in 2003, Anna has lost more than 40 pounds and looks better than she has in years; if she ever decides to lose a little more dead weight, Howard K. Stern may find himself looking for a new client.

13

GOD BLACKMAILS ORAL ROBERTS

Oral Roberts
SYNDICATED, JANUARY 4, 1987

The history of Christian television would make a fascinating book subject in itself. At their best, televised worship services bring a positive message to anyone seeking such guidance, and are a godsend to those who are unable to get to church. But regrettably, religion on television has come to be defined by its charlatans. The scandalous downfall of Jim Bakker and Jimmy Swaggart still casts a shadow over such admirable ministries as those of Robert Schuller and Joel Osteen.

Oral Roberts was one of the first televangelists to take his crusade to the airwaves, but the fiery Pentecostal preacher has also been a lightning rod for controversy, even among the Christian community. Claiming the ability to cure the sick with a healing touch has brought him both legions of converts and an equally determined number of detractors. At one of his first healing crusades in the 1940s, one critic expressed his outrage with a pistol, firing a shot that barely missed Roberts' head.

Love him or hate him, Roberts has heard it all and has stood firm in his message and his alleged gift of direct divine intervention. When you stutter as a child and your parents name you Oral, you get used to catching ridicule. After surviving a life-threatening battle with tuberculosis as a teenager, Roberts dedicated himself to his faith, claiming to have heard God say, "You are to take My healing power to your generation. You are to build Me a university and build it on My authority and the Holy Spirit."

Roberts made his TV debut in 1954, by which time he had already taken his ministry around the world, preaching before audiences in the tens of thousands. He fulfilled his heavenly pledge with the opening of Oral Roberts University (ORU) in Tulsa, Oklahoma in 1965. But then God gave Roberts a new mission in 1977, to build a hospital, and once again the preacher was equal to the task; despite concerns from the American Medical Association and the Oklahoma state government, The City of Faith Hospital opened in 1981.

But in 1986, the facility and the ministry's other medical missions had fallen into debt. He described the dilemma to his TV congregation, and donations poured in as they always had, but this time they weren't enough. So on January 4, 1987, Oral Roberts told his flock that he had received the following message from God: "I told you to raise $8 million to carry on My medical work. You have from January 1 to March 31 to get it done. If you don't, then your work is finished, and I am going to call you home."

The announcement generated front-page headlines ("Oral Roberts Says God is Going to Kill Him if He Doesn't Raise $8 Million!"), and the story was covered on the nightly news shows. Other prominent ministers denounced Roberts' claim, saying God doesn't deal in extortion, while comedians thanked their maker for the new material (Johnny Carson: "If tonight's monologue bombs, God is going to call me home").

Roberts retreated to his prayer tower, and vowed to stay there until the money was raised, or until he got the call. "At no time in all my years in the healing ministry had I felt Satan had loosed so many of his forces against me, nor had so many human leaders and opinion makers made me the topic of their conversations—and mostly in a mocking way," Roberts wrote in his autobiography, *Expect a Miracle*. His son Richard appeared on *Larry King Live* and *Good Morning America*, attempting to explain that being "called home" really wasn't such a bad thing and deep down God was a pretty nice guy, but he could not deflect the tide of criticism that Roberts' announcement had raised.

As the deadline approached, Roberts received daily updates from his chief financial officer on how much money had been collected. In March, he went on television and said he was still $1.3 million short. The next day, a dog track owner in Miami flew to Tulsa and presented Roberts a check in that amount. "Did God ask you to do this?," Roberts asked. "I don't know," said the man, "but I know it wasn't the devil."

When Roberts announced his triumph and the fact that he'd apparently be sticking around, he absorbed a new round of criticism for accepting money from a guy that owns dog tracks. The preacher responded by quoting a verse from Haggai 2:8: "The silver is mine, and the gold is mine, saith the Lord of hosts."

The incident left a bitter taste in the mouths of many believers, and just one year later Jim Bakker was caught with one hand in the collection plate and the other down the blouse of church secretary Jessica Hahn. Bakker went to prison, and televangelists suffered a setback from which they have yet to recover. The drop in donations affected ministries both virtuous and vice-ridden, and as a result Roberts closed the City of Faith hospital in 1989. God was not available for comment.

12

BABY YOU CAN DRIVE MY MOM

My Mother the Car
NBC, SEPTEMBER 14, 1965–SEPTEMBER 6, 1966

In 1964, Jerry Van Dyke turned down the role of first mate on an ill-fated ship in *Gilligan's Island*. The show was a hit, with audiences if not critics, so when Van Dyke was given a second chance at TV stardom, he eagerly signed on to play lawyer Dave Crabtree in *My Mother the Car*. The show was canceled after one season, and still earns votes as one of the worst television embarrassments of all time.

And yet, it's hard to fault Van Dyke's decision. The *Gilligan* script didn't read like something that would play for the next 40 years, and though *My Mother the Car* wasn't any better, its premise had potential given the number of successful sitcoms that had similarly fanciful themes (*Bewitched, Mr. Ed, I Dream of Jeannie*). With shows about witches and talking horses already on the air, the idea of a guy's mother being reincarnated as a 1928 Porter convertible doesn't seem as far-fetched.

The series had gifted people behind the wheel as well in Allan Burns and Chris Hayward, two of the twisted geniuses behind *The Adventures of Rocky and Bullwinkle*. Burns later won Emmys for his scripts on *The Mary Tyler Moore Show*; Hayward became a writer-producer on *Barney Miller*. So what went wrong?

There was nothing inherently amiss with the concept; in the pilot, Dave is shopping for a family station wagon, when he walks past a vintage roadster that has clearly seen better days. A door opens by itself, smacking him on the backside. "Hello, Davey, it's your mother," the car says through its radio speaker. He buys "Mom" and brings her home, much to the dismay of his family. Perhaps his wife Barbara (Maggie Pierce) and the two kids (Cindy Eilbacher, Randy Whipple) would understand if they knew the full story, but in true sitcom fashion, Mom will only speak when Dave's alone.

The show's other featured character was Captain Manzini, played by Avery Schreiber, a ruthless car collector determined to buy or steal the Porter by any means necessary. The voice of Mother was provided by 1940s movie actress Ann Sothern, previously of the series *Private Secretary*.

"*My Mother the Car* tried combining the U.S. fascination with cars, sex, and Mom." *Time* magazine wrote in a typical review, "But something happened in casting: Mother is an invisible Ann Sothern; and as for hero Jerry Van Dyke, he has finally answered the question, what is it that Jerry hasn't got that Brother Dick has?"

The show would probably not have lasted even one season had it not been up against two other series aimed at decidedly older audiences: *Rawhide* on CBS and *Combat* on ABC. For families with children, *My Mother the Car* was the only available option on Tuesday nights at 7:30, but judging from the ratings most of them probably watched a couple of episodes, then turned the TV off.

It's hard to pin the series' failure on one single determinant. But from the awful opening theme song to the last of the closing credits, *My Mother the Car* was a lemon. The scripts were horrifically unfunny, there was nothing memorable about any of the characters, and the gimmick of the talking car resulted in neither clever family reunion dialogue exchanges nor man-vs.-machine slapstick. Jerry Van Dyke and Avery Schreiber, two born second bananas thrust into lead roles, couldn't carry the show opposite an inanimate object. Suddenly, what David Hasselhoff did in *Knight Rider* looks a lot more impressive.

But the real compare-and-contrast opportunity here is with *Mr. Ed*, a series with practically the same concept. That show worked because the roles were clearly defined. Wilbur (Alan Young) was the straight man, and Ed delivered the punch lines. To compensate for the horse's limited facial expression, Ed was given the distinctive voice of former cowboy star Rocky Lane, who could draw laughs with even the simplest jokes.

My Mother the Car had a template to study but failed the exam. The selection of Ann Sothern is inexplicable since the producers also auditioned Jean Arthur and Eve Arden, two of the silver screen's great comediennes. Granted, the car was rarely given anything funny to say, and Mother wasn't really developed as a character beyond a basic Jewish mother stereotype, but it's hard to imagine Arthur or Arden not doing a better job.

At first, Sothern recorded her lines while she watched a tape of the episode, but later the producers decided that wasn't necessary and just let her read her script into a tape recorder. That may have worked for John Forsythe on *Charlie's Angels*, but comedy requires a rhythm beyond regular conversation, and Sothern's inability to react to Van Dyke's lines further sabotages material that needed all the help it could get.

There was also a missed opportunity in the Manzini character—why not have him be the only one besides Dave to know that the car talks? It would certainly have made his obsession with the Porter more fathomable, launched several potential get-rich-quick schemes that might have provided serviceable plots, and given both Schreiber and Sothern someone else to play off.

Mother's Day in the home of Dave Crabtree (Jerry Van Dyke) always means a trip to Jiffy Lube.

But as written and performed, *My Mother the Car* managed only one funny episode, in which Mother drags her son to a drive-in to see a movie marathon of her favorite actor, Sonny Tufts. This in itself is funny, for Tufts is legendary for his performances in such golden turkeys as *Cat Women on the Moon*. Though Dave wants to bolt, Mother refuses to go, and in the final scene Sonny Tufts himself appears to meet his biggest fan. "Sonny Tufts!" swoons Mother, who then pops her radiator cap. One good moment in 30 shows. Even *The Flying Nun* had a better track record.

11
PLEASE, STOP SINGING

The Brady Bunch Hour
ABC, January 23–May 5, 1977

Where to even begin?

If you've seen the Cirque du Soleil perform, you might think you've witnessed the ultimate in avant-garde spectacle. In shows such as "O" and "Mystere", the French-Canadian theatrical troupe has devised a surreal blend of colorfully-garbed oddities, baggy pants comedy and bizarre music, resulting in a new entertainment form that could only emerge from a whimsically warped view of reality. But it's got nothing on *The Brady Bunch Hour*. Even Cirque performers would look at this late-70s variety show and say, "OK, that's just weird."

How could America's most beloved television family get sucked into a Fellini-esque nightmare of sequinned tuxedos, disco music, synchronized swimmers, and Rip Taylor? All it took was a few lies and a few dollars, two of Satan's favorite traps.

Let's journey back to 1976; though *The Brady Bunch* had been off the air for two years, reruns played throughout the day across the country, and crushed whatever competition was scheduled against them. The series' success in syndication captured the attention of ... wait for it ... Fred Silverman, who thought the *Brady* cast would be a natural in the variety show format that was then pulling in big numbers for Donny and Marie Osmond. Three years later, Silverman would try again to emulate the Osmonds' success with *Pink Lady and Jeff*. And no one has ever pressed charges.

They got Barry Williams, who was trying to launch a music career, by promising that he'd be the star of the new show. As achievements go, this was the equivalent of being invited to take the window seat on the Hindenberg. Four of the remaining Brady six—Maureen McCormick, Susan Olsen, Christopher Knight, and Mike Lookinland—had found it difficult to separate themselves from the original series, and figured if everyone was going to think of them as Bradys they might as well get paid for it. Eve Plumb wisely chose to pass, and was replaced by Geri Reischl, forever immortalized as "Fake Jan." Florence Henderson was a musical theater veteran who figured she would be right at home, but Robert Reed should never have sacrificed his dignity to this disaster, though Williams revealed that he did so willingly.

"I really did want to do it," he told Barry in the book, *Growing Up Brady*. "I mean, I've studied voice and dancing. I'm terrible at both, and proved it to be true, but when (producers) Sid and Marty Krofft met with me, they described the whole thing in very positive terms, and I thought, 'What fun!'" I wonder if he still felt that way after taking a pratfall in a swimming pool, while wearing an orange and maroon tuxedo with a big bow tie that looked like it should light up and spin.

After the opening musical number of the first episode, the family gathered to discuss how to kick their musically-challenged father out of the act. At one point they try to hire Tony Randall as the new Mr. Brady, because Mike can't sing. Hey, memo to the kids: Broadway ain't ringin' your phone either.

Also in the first episode, we learn that the family, at Bobby's request, has given up their humdrum suburban life for a shot at show business. Trying to pretend these were still the same characters from *The Brady Bunch* was one of the more ridiculous aspects of the series, as none of them had the same personalities and no allowance had been made for the fact that all the kids were three years older. Instead, they had to act dumber than they ever did on the original show. The verbal sparring matches between Bobby and Cindy were especially foolish, and more appropriate for six-year-olds than for two young adults approaching voting age.

"I had absolutely nothing to do with it," said *Brady Bunch* creator Sherwood Schwartz. "Fred Silverman called the producers of *Donny & Marie* and asked them to do a similar show with the *Brady Bunch*. Those producers had only two alternatives; they could say 'Sure,' and get another show on the air. Or they could say, 'we're sorry, we don't have the rights to do *The Brady Bunch*.' They chose to say 'sure' and went ahead with the show, failing to notify me or even to notify Paramount, which owns *The Brady Bunch*. I hated the idea of that variety show, and so did Paramount, but Paramount had a problem. They did a lot of business with NBC and didn't want to antagonize Fred Silverman."

"*The Brady Bunch Hour* was perhaps the single worst television program in the history of the medium," Barry Williams admits, and there is really no explanation for television this bad. It's impossible to single out individual moments, as it all runs together now into a blur of ghastly images: the performance of "Car Wash" as characters from The Wizard of Oz; the Brady kids saying "we want to sing the music of our generation!" and then opening the show with "Baby Face", a chart-topper from the 1920s; The Water Follies Swimmers and the Kroffette Dancers; Greg in a white Elvis jumpsuit doing The Hustle; a 1950s roller rink scene, in which the three Brady brothers try to pick up their sisters; a family singalong on Donna Summer's orgasmic "Love to Love You Baby."

It is something of a mystery as to how Donny & Marie got away with doing essentially the same type of corny program, which was a hit then and is still remembered fondly by fans. What did they have that the Bradys didn't? Well, musical talent, sure. But Florence, Barry, and Maureen could sing, and even Fake Jan doesn't embar-

The Brady family patiently await their five o'clock feeding.

rass herself in a solo cover of Elton John's "Your Song." Maybe the Bradys needed an ice rink instead of a pool.

At the very least, you'd think by now the nostalgia bug would have kicked in, and the show's mix of *Brady Bunch* and disco and other 1970s TV stars might be considered a camp classic. But even that is not possible with a show this dreadful. The writing, the music, the performances and the costumes (my God, the costumes) all came together to create something too horrific for even guilty pleasure status. But the memory lingers on, as evidenced by the series being spoofed on both *The Simpsons* ("The Simpson's Smile-Time Variety Hour") and *That '70s Show* ("The Forman Bunch Variety Hour"). There was also a DVD release of two episodes. No one knows why.

10
THE HEIDI BOWL

OAKLAND RAIDERS VS. NEW YORK JETS
NBC, NOVEMBER 17, 1968

Baseball still claims the mantle of national pastime but, for as long as anyone can remember, America's most passionate sports obsession has been football.

Sundays during the NFL season are Leave-Me-Alone days for much of the male populace, *Monday Night Football* has been a weekly tradition for more than 30 years, and Super Bowl Sunday has practically become a national holiday.

Televised games often run longer than their assigned time slot, but the network always stays with the action until the final whistle. And every time you get to watch the last three minutes of the fourth quarter instead of a *Full House* rerun, say a silent thank you to a man named Dick Cline, who changed NFL broadcast policy after a game that has come to be known as the Heidi Bowl. NFL Films ranked it tenth among the most memorable football games of the 20th century, though most of the country never saw its thrilling conclusion.

On November 17, 1968, The New York Jets traveled to the Oakland Coliseum to play the Raiders in a pivotal AFL showdown. Both teams were 7-2 and considered Super Bowl contenders. Previous Jets-Raiders contests were gridiron wars that left both teams bloody and beaten, and this one was no exception. Though Jets quarterback Joe Namath and Raiders QB Daryle Lamonica combined for nearly 700 yards passing, resulting in seven touchdowns and five lead changes, there were also 19 penalties for a total of more than 230 yards.

The penalties were in part responsible for the game running longer than its time slot; at 7 PM Eastern time, the Jets were leading 32-29 with 50 seconds left. NBC went to a commercial after the Jim Turner field goal that gave the Jets the lead, but rather than return to the game the network began its broadcast of *Heidi*, a new made-for-TV movie based on the classic children's book, starring Jennifer Edwards as the pigtailed Swiss miss.

While viewers in the Eastern and Central time zones watched Heidi yodel her way through the Alps, Daryle Lamonica threw a 43-yard touchdown pass to halfback Charlie Smith, giving Oakland a 36-32 lead. During the ensuing kickoff, Earl Christy of the Jets fumbled on his own 10-yard line; Raiders fullback Preston Ridlehuber picked up the loose ball and scored the Raiders' second touchdown in 42 seconds. The Raiders went on to win, 43-32.

The switch from the football game to *Heidi* was made by Dick Cline, NBC's supervisor of broadcast operation control (BOC). "I was saved by the set of conditions [distributed to network executives each week]," he said in an interview with NFL Films. "I had it in print. In fact, the vice president of my division told me that if I had taken it on my own and stayed with the game, I would have been fired."

Network policy necessitated the switch, as NBC had already sold the *Heidi* advertising time to the Timex watch company. But NBC president Julian Goodman happened to be watching the game, and actually tried to override the agreement. His attempt to reach Cline was unsuccessful because thousands of calls from angry football fans had already crashed the network's phone exchange at Manhattan's Rockefeller Plaza. By the time Goodman's orders reached Cline, it was too late to carry them out. The game's final score was revealed on a crawl at the bottom of the screen, as Heidi herded goats with her grandfather. No one was more surprised than the wife of Jets coach Weeb Ewbank, who had already called to congratulate her husband on the victory.

Goodman apologized for the switch 90 minutes after the game ended, and issued a formal apology the next day. The *New York Times* ran a derisive front-page news story, with the headline "Jets 32, Raiders 29, Heidi 14." In his nightly news broadcast, David Brinkley blamed football fans' frustrations on a "faceless button pusher in the bowels of NBC." But the much-maligned Cline didn't lose his job over the incident; in fact, he was promoted by the network one week later, and now works as a director on CBS's NFL coverage.

Daryle Lamonica still remembers the game as the most memorable in which he played. Two months later, the Jets came back to beat the Raiders in the AFL championship game, setting up their improbable victory in Super Bowl III, still remembered for Joe Namath's pre-game guarantee of victory over the heavily-favored Baltimore Colts.

As a result of the Heidi Bowl, NBC changed its policy regarding the broadcast of NFL games, and other networks followed suit. The network also installed a special phone in the broadcast operation control room, wired to a separate exchange, to make certain that decisions affecting programming are hastily conveyed. It is still referred to as the Heidi Phone.

The term "Heidi Bowl" has entered the sports lexicon, and is trotted out whenever a sporting event of any kind is not broadcast to its rightful conclusion. Every football season, if the Raiders play the Jets, some broadcaster will invariably remind viewers to stay tuned no matter what the score, cause you-know-what might happen. But the most lasting impact of the Heidi Bowl is a guarantee to football viewers that the game will stay on, even if one team appears on the verge of defeat, which is great news for fans of the Arizona Cardinals.

9
WITH THIS RING, I THEE SHED

Who Wants to Marry a Multimillionaire?
FOX, FEBRUARY 15, 2000

"I'll be your friend, your lover, and your partner."
—DARVA CONGER *to Rick Rockwell*

When history recalls our current television era, from some point in the future when it can be properly put into perspective, one of its most prominent figures will be Mike Darnell, the FOX Network executive who developed reality programming from low-cost filler to a mainstream genre. You don't know his name but you've certainly seen his handiwork: *When Animals Attack*, *Temptation Island*, *Joe Millionaire*, *Celebrity Boxing*, and *Who Wants to Marry a Multimillionaire?*

This is not to say that he belongs on a list with the medium's other pioneer/innovators; William S. Paley, Norman Lear, Roone Arledge, Steven Bochco, all of whom made the playground a better place to play. Darnell's contributions to television are equivalent to what a canary contributes to the newspaper at the bottom of his cage.

The debacle that put Darnell on the map began after the producer noticed ABC's success with the game show *Who Wants to Be a Millionaire?* "It struck me that part of the reason it was so successful was wish fulfillment," he said. "I thought, 'what else do people wish for?' They wish for a relationship. They want to get married. And I thought, 'how could I combine the two?'"

Once FOX was aboard with the idea, a nationwide search was launched for a millionaire seeking a wife, and a bevy of potential brides. Thousands of women applied, which is rather disturbing in itself. For its mystery man of megabucks, Darnell selected Rick Rockwell, a 44-year-old failed standup comic whose most significant showbiz achievement was a role in the sequel to *Attack of the Killer Tomatoes*. Rockwell, born Richard Balkey, adapted his comedy routines into motivational speaker conferences, aimed at teaching humorless corporate types how to create an entertaining presentation. From this and a few shrewd real estate investments, he supposedly built a fortune sufficient to qualify as FOX's groom-to-be.

The two-hour broadcast aired on the day after Valentine's Day from Las Vegas, a city hardly famous for lasting romantic commitment. In the showroom of the Las Vegas Hilton, host Jay Thomas introduced 50 contestants, ranging in age from 19 to 45. With Rockwell sequestered in a darkened booth, each contestant offered a brief reason why she should be selected.

The field was narrowed to ten semifinalists, who appeared in both evening gown and swimwear exhibitions, and made suggestive overtures to the hidden groom. A former cheerleader promised she was "really good at 'sit and spin'"; emergency room nurse Darva Conger promised, "I'll be your friend, your lover, and your partner. You will never be bored."

Contestants answered questions designed to assess their moral rectitude, some of which were based on how Rockwell had described his perfect mate to producers. Samples: "What do you consider an ideal Friday night?" and "What would you do if you found a woman's name and phone number in your new husband's pocket?" The unseen Rockwell occasionally responded to something he liked with a thumbs-up gesture.

The field of ten was narrowed to five, all of whom reappeared garbed in wedding gowns. Each was asked what qualities would bring out the best and worst in them, and whether they considered children important. Rockwell consulted his mother, who was in attendance, and his friends, then emerged from the shadows and selected Conger, 34, a Gulf War veteran from Santa Monica, California.

"I know exactly what I'm looking for in love and in life and it's here tonight," Rockwell said, before making the proposal official. A judge was summoned to the showroom to perform the wedding ceremony. Before an audience of 23 million, Rockwell embraced his bride-to-be and planted a long, passionate liplock on the trembling Conger, whose frozen smile and stiff shoulders suggested that Rockwell might not be her idea of Prince Charming. Actually, when the guy finally appeared on camera, with his square head and an intense gaze commonly associated with dangerous drifters, many of the rejected brides breathed a sigh of relief.

But alas, "happily ever after" was not to be for our prime time lovebirds. Though the pair honeymooned in Barbados, the marriage was never consummated, and afterwards they parted company as soon as the plane landed. Two weeks after the show aired, Conger filed for an annulment. "Neither the contestants nor the show's producers seriously contemplated creating a proper marriage," Conger said in the filing. "The marriage was a mutual mistake of fact and was entered into solely for an entertainment purpose." She did, however, keep the $100,000 in prizes and Isuzu Trooper awarded for being Rockwell's choice.

After basking in the glow of a huge rating, the joy at the FOX network proved equally passing, as allegations surfaced against both Rockwell and Conger that scuttled the network's plans to rerun the special, and make the show an annual Valentine's Day event.

Apparently, FOX's "thorough" background check failed to reveal that Rockwell had a restraining order filed against him in Los Angeles by a former girlfriend, who had accused him of assault. His financial status was also called into question, as most multimillionaires don't live in a 1,200-square-foot tract house with two broken toilets in the backyard. Several companies for whom Rockwell claimed to work as a motivational speaker said they had

The exact moment when television sank into the abyss: Rick and Darva tie the knot on Who Wants to Marry a Multimillionaire?

never hired him, and his claim to have opened for Jay Leno in Lake Tahoe? Never happened, said Leno's representatives.

Meanwhile, Conger's Gulf War status was challenged, seeing as how the closest she got to the Middle East was a falafel joint near Illinois's Scott Air Force Base. When asked about her record on *Inside Edition*, Conger said, "I am a Gulf War veteran. I was on active duty in the Air Force at the time of the Gulf War. Anyone on active duty at the time of that war is considered a Gulf War veteran." After railing against the intense public exposure she received from the special, Conger posed nude for *Playboy* in August 2000.

Perhaps these two actually deserved each other after all.

One year later, there was still enough interest in the dysfunctional couple to inspire a reunion on CNN's *Larry King Live*. "I've been worried sick about you," said Rockwell to his runaway bride. Conger, now remarried, apologized for the situation. "I never should have been there," she lamented. "This was never a relationship. This was a bad TV show."

8

A GANGSTER'S LAST LAUGH

The Mystery of Al Capone's Vault
SYNDICATED, APRIL 27, 1986

The hucksters who work the carnival circuit live by one essential objective—get the rubes inside the tent, by any means necessary. Promise them amazing miracles, exotic wonders, horrifying spectacles, and if the unicorn turns out to be a goat with a waffle cone glued to its forehead, then that's their fault for being so gullible; what matters is you've got their money.

At his worst, Geraldo Rivera has brought this same philosophy to broadcast journalism. At his best, the lawyer turned reporter is quite nearly the maverick crusader he believes himself to be. His 1970s' exposé of shocking abuses in New York City's mental hospitals was an exceptional example of investigative journalism. But somewhere along the way, Rivera fell into the tabloid trap, elevating himself into a bigger story than the subjects on which he reported.

Geraldo's descent from hard-hitting reporter to sideshow attraction began when he learned that Chicago's Lexington Hotel was scheduled for demolition. The once grand dame of downtown society had also been the headquarters of mobster Al Capone, but had since fallen into a pitiful state of disrepair. When what appeared to be a sealed vault was discovered in the basement, Geraldo jumped to the dubious-at-best conclusion that the vault might have been used by the infamous gangster. So he announced his intention to open the vault live on the air in a two-hour syndicated television special.

For weeks leading up to the broadcast, promos speculated on the possibilities of what might be found—money? Guns? Private papers? Bullet-riddled corpses in tattered pinstripe suits?

Get the rubes inside the tent, by any means necessary.

"A massive concrete chamber has been discovered," Rivera announced in ominous tones as *The Mystery of Al Capone's Vault* began. "This is an adventure you and I are going to be taking together. Tonight, the mystery will be solved!"

The first tease comes just five minutes into the show, when we get our first glimpse of the vault's exterior. Geraldo describes the preparations to pull down the outer wall with a bulldozer, before consulting an architectural expert with Chicago's Historic Landmark Society. "What might we find?" the intrepid journalist asks. "I don't know," the expert replies. After that startling revelation, we are taken on a tour of what's left of the Lexington, a ruined shell of a building, now subjected to one last indignity before a wrecking ball can put it out of its misery.

While the show has apparently forgotten about the wall being pulled down, viewers are treated to newsreel footage of Chicago in the roaring '20s, accompanied by Geraldo's overheated narration on Capone's rise to power, and the fact that more than $20 million of his ill-gotten gains were never found. "It's a longshot, but maybe those missing millions are what we'll find in here," he hints. "Or maybe we'll find the bones of his criminal rivals or documents or weapons or bootleg booze."

Just in case they hit the jackpot, Geraldo introduced Internal Revenue Service agent Dennis Sansone, who reminds the folks at home that it was a tax evasion charge that brought the mobster down, and declared that the IRS is still trying to collect $800,000 in unpaid taxes from a guy who's been dead since 1947. So whatever may be in that vault, he's there to make sure the government gets its cut.

At last, the scene shifts back to the subterranean cavern. Geraldo cautions his audience that it's a deep vault, "so don't expect to see gold bars out front right away." But when the wall is finally pulled down, there's still more dirt and debris to dig out. So as the excavation begins, it's time for another history lesson on Prohibition and organized crime.

While the jackhammers rattle, viewers are subjected to one filler piece after another; Geraldo talks to the current head of the Women's Christian Temperance Union, shows a film clip of Rod Steiger in the 1959 film *Al Capone*; explores the history of the tommy gun, fires one of the vintage weapons into a row of bottles, then interviews a journalist who covered the Capone era.

By now, the first hour of the show has elapsed, and more than a half-hour has passed without any mention of the vault. At this point, you know you're being jerked around, but having gone this far you can't resist staying tuned to see how it comes out. You're in the tent.

Another batch of commercials. Geraldo explains that they've hit an obstacle, yet another wall, and this one's made of thick limestone. But they're prepared to blast so just be patient. And alert viewers are starting to think maybe there shouldn't be this many walls in a "massive concrete chamber." While explosives experts line the wall with dynamite, viewers watch a taped bio of Eliot Ness and a clip of Robert Stack in *The Untouchables*.

The impediment is destroyed. "We're getting there," Geraldo reassures us. But first, let's look at a history of the tunnel system beneath Chicago, and talk to actor Buddy Rogers, who recalls having dinner with Capone. To be fair, the Rogers piece is the only interesting non-vault-related segment in the telecast. Back to live action, but Geraldo says "nothing new or exciting to report yet," so instead we take a tour of Capone's Miami residence, and learn all about the St. Valentine's Day Massacre.

"The digging continues" Geraldo assures us with just 20 minutes left in the show, and it's time for one last documentary piece on Capone's arrest, imprisonment, release, declining health, and death at age 48. But now it's put up or shut up time. "I don't know how to tell you this ... at eight minutes to the hour we've found another wall in here." Uh-oh.

In the show's final segment Geraldo, now cognizant that he has come up empty, is no longer the exhilarated witness to history he was two hours earlier. All he has to show for his efforts is one 60-year-old whiskey bottle. "It seems we struck out with the vault. I'm disappointed about that, I'm sure you are too." At least the IRS got screwed, though there's no word on whether Dennis Sansone confiscated the bottle and tried to collect the deposit.

"I hope you enjoyed the adventure of the chase," Rivera cajoles, with visions of his career passing before his eyes. "But our sonic or seismic tests must have been slightly awry; we didn't find the hollow spaces that we were led to believe were in there." And there you have the most amazing revelation of the incident, surprisingly overlooked by much of the derisive post-mortem coverage: on a show entitled *The Mystery of Al Capone's Vault*, Geraldo Rivera didn't even find a vault.

"What can I say, I'm sorry. Good night. I'm sorry," says our host as the final credits roll, before walking off into the darkness, leaving the crew of hardhat excavators and other laborers standing in the shot wondering if they can go home now. Al Capone may have been a crook, but it was Geraldo who just stole two hours from your life.

The Mystery of Al Capone's Vault earned a 57 rating, the highest ever recorded for a syndicated special. By comparison, the "Who shot J.R.?" episode of *Dallas* scored a 53, and the Beatles on Ed Sullivan only managed a 45. More than half the televisions in use on April 27, 1986, were tuned to Geraldo Rivera digging through an empty hotel basement. "My career was not over, I knew, but had just begun," Geraldo wrote of the show in his autobiography, *Exposing Myself*. "And all because of a silly, high-concept stunt that failed to deliver on its titillating promise."

More recently, as a foreign correspondent for the Fox News channel, Geraldo has been peeking in caves looking for Osama Bin Laden, and still coming up empty.

7

SCRAPPY CRAPPY DOO

The Scooby and Scrappy-Doo Show
The Scooby and Scrappy-Doo Puppy Hour
The 13 Ghosts of Scooby-Doo
ABC, September 22, 1979–September 6, 1986

It is one of the few universal truths left in our capricious, inconstant world: every-body hates Scrappy-Doo. Most Saturday morning cartoon buffs would rather be strapped to a chair and force-fed a 24-hour marathon of *Davey and Goliath* and *The Snorks* rather than endure one *Scooby-Doo* episode featuring his obnoxious nephew. You could charter a plane to Nepal, scale the most forbidding peak in the Himalayas, find a hidden cavern inhabited by holy men who have lived lives of quiet contem-plation for generations; mention Scrappy Doo, and these men of peace will slowly raise their eyes from their meditation and reply, "That little bastard ruined the show forever. Puppy power, my ass."

Attempt a web search for Scrappy-Doo and you'll see page after page of sites rip-ping the character from ears to tail. The Cartoon Network website, a celebration of all things animated, once offered a "Slime Scrappy" game. In their marvelous book *Saturday Morning Fever*, a study of Saturday morning TV from the 1960s to the 1990s, authors Timothy and Kevin Burke wrote "In all of our research and discus-sions, we have yet to discover a more universally loathed character than Scrappy-Doo."

Americans, as a rule, tend to like puppies. Most of us love them. So it's aston-ishing that a cartoon puppy could arouse such venomous emotions in an otherwise sympathetic populace. But Scrappy-Doo deserves every insult heaped upon his over-sized head. From his first appearance, in the 1979 episode "The Scarab Lives," he shattered the group dynamic among the Scooby gang that sustained every earlier Scooby-Doo incarnation through good shows and bad.

Based on their enduring popularity and four decades of adventures, it's arguable that Saturday morning TV never introduced a more beloved cast of characters than Fred, Daphne, Velma, Shaggy, and Scooby. Debuting in 1969, *Scooby-Doo, Where Are You?* ran two seasons and remains the gold standard among hardcore Mystery, Inc. fans. But *The New Scooby-Doo Mysteries* and *The New Scooby-Doo Movies* also have their admirers, and have rarely been off television since their first run.

No one would argue that *Scooby-Doo* before Scrappy was Peabody Award mate-rial. The mysteries were hardly worthy of Agatha Christie, or even Nancy Drew. But we liked it the way it was. We enjoyed the familiar clichés, the obvious misdirection of the first new character being a suspect but never the guilty party; the unmasking of the ghost/monster at the end, prompting the oft-quoted tag line "I'd have gotten away with it, if it hadn't been for you meddling kids."

Never a rolled-up newspaper around when you need one: the infamous Scrappy-Doo.

We liked the roles each character played; team leader Fred and clumsy but cute Daphne, brainy Velma, always first to discover the important clues; and Shaggy and Scooby, inveterate cowards and inseparable best pals. We enjoyed the speculation about what these characters were up to that couldn't be shown on a kid's show. Were Fred and Daphne gettin' it on in the back of the Mystery Machine? Was Velma a lesbian? Did Shaggy have the munchies from too much Maui Wowie?

But all the fun stopped when Hanna-Barbera developed a cute sidekick fetish, and added unnecessary characters to many of its most popular shows. The Flintstones discovered the Great Gazoo, the Jetsons were saddled with Orbitty, and the Scooby gang met Scrappy. The plucky pup, son of Scooby's sister, Ruby Doo, officially joined the gang in the first episode of *The Scooby and Scrappy-Doo Show.* He remained with the series for more than 160 episodes.

Some of these latter incarnations, particularly *The Thirteen Ghosts of Scooby-Doo,* had some interesting twists that might have been worth exploring, if it weren't for Scrappy's constant interference. Whenever there was danger, he'd dash into the fray with a bold threat, usually "Let me at 'em!" or "I'll splat 'em!" His most frequent battle cry was the inane "Puppy power!" bellowed in an irritating, high-pitched voice supplied first by Len Weinrib, formerly of the Krofft TV bomb *Magic Mongo,* and later by Don Messick, one of Hanna-Barbera's MVPs.

Like Adric on *Doctor Who* and Wesley Crusher on *Star Trek: The Next Generation,* Scrappy-Doo was the cocky know-it-all punk kid who always thought he was smarter than the rest of the gang, who had been solving mysteries for years without his help, thank you very much. Once viewers realized that Scrappy was the new de facto leader of the gang, television sets across America clicked off, and a generation of bleary-eyed kids, still high from the rush of their sugar-coated breakfast cereal, staggered out of the house on Saturday morning for the first time, leaving the last happy memories of their childhood behind.

What is most astonishing is that the only people unaware of public opinion on Scrappy worked at Hanna-Barbera. They brought him back for six seasons and in the series of direct-to-video adventures launched in 1998 with *Scooby-Doo on Zombie*

Island. Scrappy has appeared in *Scooby-Doo and the Ghoul School, Scooby-Doo and the Reluctant Werewolf,* and *Scooby-Doo Meets the Boo Brothers.*

After more than two decades, hating Scrappy Doo has become a cliché. A "Scrappy sucks" tirade used to identify you as a discerning connoisseur of Saturday morning kidvid, now it's like stand-up comics who still think airplane food is funny. That's why portraying Scrappy as the villain in the 2002 live-action *Scooby-Doo* film felt like beating a dead issue, rather than the clever in-joke the writers intended. Far better to just forget him altogether, the way the rest of us wish we could. That's the only appropriate fate for a character with few peers in the role of buzzkill for a beloved franchise. There's Shemp, there's Jar Jar Binks, and there's Scrappy Doo, and the worst of these is Scrappy.

6
THE QUIZ SHOW SCANDALS

Dotto
NBC

The $64,000 Challenge
CBS

Twenty-One
NBC, 1956–1959

For anyone under the age of 40, the fixing of a few television game shows in the 1950s doesn't seem like the type of milestone that would constitute a turning point in the history of the medium. But that perception is a result of having grown up in a media culture already shaped by the scandal, and its impact on the relationship between the television industry and the viewers at home. "1959 was the year of the original sin," said Robert Thompson, Director of Syracuse University's Center for the Study of Popular Television. "It's the fall from grace of American television."

It's a story about more than greedy sponsors, desperate producers, and average-Joe contestants who were tempted by overnight fame and the kind of money that changes lives in exchange for a compromise of integrity that, they were told, no one need discover. The timing of the revelations, just as television emerged from its formative years into a promising adolescence, forever changed how Americans looked at that new electronic piece of furniture in the family room.

"Before that, there was still an idea that this medium might actually be a powerfully good social influence, and that wonderful things would come from it," said Thompson. "The quiz show scandals put everybody in the same boat of looking at television as a lying, moneymaking, money-hungry, profit-oriented medium, and we've kept that attitude ever since."

As if that wasn't severe enough, the movie *Quiz Show* (1994) raised the stakes, interpreting the scandal as a morality play with America as tragic hero. What began as a newfound disillusionment with television now symbolized a nation's loss of innocence, as the feel-good Fifties gave way to the wake-up calls of the cynical 1960s.

The first game shows aired on radio in the 1940s, simple question-and-answer contests with prize money that rarely topped a hundred bucks. But when television adapted the format, producers discovered that higher prizes attracted more viewers. In 1955, *The $64,000 Question* ranked among the highest-rated shows in the medium's young history. A host of quiz shows were launched, hoping to attract the same following, and that's where the trouble began.

"It was a slippery slope. It was never one of those moments when anybody said in a conspiratorial way, 'We're gonna fix these things,'" Thompson explained. "It was a series of compromises. You start in ways you can justify, then you're doing things you can't justify but it's too late."

Some of the new shows were dull. The game play was repetitious, the contestants uninteresting, and the sponsor who sank his advertising budget into the game demanded a better result. "The producers came to the conclusion that the only way to make the game work was to guarantee that there would be some kind of excitement," Thompson said. "The only way to control the quality of the drama was to give it a boost."

In August 1958, a former contestant on the game show *Dotto* walked into the Complaint Bureau of the New York District Attorney's office, claiming that the game was fixed. The contestant, Edward Hilgemeier, produced a notebook page from a contestant who had won on the show, which listed answers to questions before they had been asked. The investigation widened after prosecutor Joseph Stone was contacted by Herbert Stempel, a City College student whose battles with Columbia University English Professor Charles Van Doren on the game show *Twenty-One* had been watched by an audience of 50 million. Stempel claimed he only lost to Van Doren because he was ordered to do so.

21 *host Jack Barry (center) cautions Charles Van Doren (left) not to answer the questions until he's asked them. After losing to Van Doren, Herbie Stempel (right) exposed the fixed quiz show.*

Stempel had defeated several contestants before being matched against Van Doren, and producers knew they had a classic confrontation in the making. "Van Doren was presented as the fair-haired boy, the world's most eligible bachelor, and Stempel was this nerdy braniac. When they started tying over and over, the show became hugely successful," Thompson said.

In *Twenty-One*, the money at stake doubled every time there was a tie, and when Stempel and Van Doren squared off for the last time, the stakes had risen from $500 a point to $2,500 a point. A round of questions concerning the fates of King Henry VIII's six wives brought Van Doren the victory and $129,000 in winnings. He appeared on the cover of *Time* magazine, and parlayed his fame into a correspondent's position on NBC's *Today Show*. Similar offers to the less photogenic Stempel were not forthcoming, and after unsuccessful attempts to further cash in on his fading celebrity, he told Joseph Stone about the cover-up.

"I feel guilty to have been part of the entire situation," Stempel told the *Daily Mirror* in 1957. "I think I was morally wrong—but I was blinded by the glitter and glamor of show business. But 99 out of 100 people would have done the same thing."

A New York grand jury investigation unearthed details of how the contestants were coached before their appearances, and how they were taught to act as if they were struggling to find the answers that had already been provided. Popular players were invited back for repeat appearances, and when public interest waned they would take a dive. Network executives denied the allegations, as did most of the contestants subpoenaed to testify. "Nothing in my experience prepared me for the mass perjury that took place on the part of scores of well-educated people who had no trouble understanding what was at stake", said prosecutor Stone.

"What they counted on was that the contestants who became part of this would not want to talk about it," Thompson said. "It was a different culture back then. There was a sense of shame, not like now where people go on *Jerry Springer* and air their dirty laundry. Contestants would much rather go home and be the person who won the game, rather than the person who had the answers slipped to them."

The case was taken up by the House of Representatives, where standing-room only hearings culminated in the testimony of Charles Van Doren, who confessed his participation in the cover-up. "I was involved, deeply involved, in a deception," he told a House Committee.

As a result of the quiz show scandals, Congress made rigging a television game show a federal crime. Networks abandoned the practice of single sponsorship of its shows, which gave those sponsors undue influence on the content of programming. "The networks took control of all nonfiction programming, and new rules were put in," said Thompson.

Almost fifty years have passed, but the lessons learned are still put into practice on today's game shows. "They were incredibly paranoid on *Who Wants to Be a Millionaire?*," Thompson reveals. "They had interns assigned to accompany contestants, even to the bathroom. The people who wrote the questions were segregated behind security doors in an entirely different building than the production people.

All of these safeguards were put in place to make sure nobody could suspect them of anything."

The chances of another cover-up are unlikely anyway, Thompson admits, given the public appetite for scandal. "It would be almost impossible to pull this off today, because too many people would have to know about it. With tabloids and three 24-hour news networks, there are so many venues to spill the beans."

5

CNN SALUTES "SEXY" PAULA ZAHN

CNN
JANUARY 5–6, 2002

In television as in life, there are unwritten rules. In the field of news, one of those rules is that broadcast journalists are evaluated only on their professional credentials and job performance. It's okay to think an anchorman is attractive, it's okay to choose one newscast over another because of a beautiful female reporter, but it's never okay to acknowledge their looks publicly. The times it has happened—Arthur Kent being dubbed the "Scud Stud" during the first war with Iraq, "Money Honey" Maria Baritromo making stock prices sound seductive—have brought swift and severe reaction from the objectified journalist; the news is not a beauty contest, and we went to college and everything, so just keep those comments to yourself.

So how could CNN, the cable network that redefined television's role in news gathering and reporting, forget this most rigid of unwritten rules in 2002, in their promotion of a morning show hosted by Paula Zahn? It's one thing if you or I break the code and fantasize about a romantic weekend with Rudi Bakhtiar, but the network is not supposed to lead the wolf whistles. CNN's "check out the babe" campaign was immediately condemned as an astonishing lapse in judgment, and the 15-second spots were pulled after just ten airings over one wild weekend.

Paula Zahn arrived at CNN after a stint with FOX News, though she was still best remembered for her ten years on CBS where she cohosted *CBS This Morning*. The deal, worth $2 million a year, placed Zahn as the host of *American Morning with Paula Zahn*, a new series that the network hoped would revive its daybreak ratings. Changing viewer habits in the morning hours can be a difficult task, and CNN was apparently determined to get the word out by any means necessary.

The infamous promo opens with pictures of the blond Zahn talking like a serious journalist, while in voiceover a male voice asks "Where can you find a morning news anchor who's provocative ... super-smart ... oh yeah, and just a little sexy?" As the word "sexy" flashed across the screen in red letters, a quick shot of Zahn's lips is accompanied by the sound of a rapidly descending zipper. My, oh my.

Red-faced CNN officials blamed the spot on a lack of oversight, claiming that the promo had never been seen or approved by Zahn or anyone outside the promotions department. "It was a major blunder," said CNN chief Walter Isaacson. "I am outraged and so is Paula, who has spent more than 20 years proving her credibility day in and day out on the air. The proper procedures were not followed."

The spots produced a variety or reactions, all negative but with varying degrees of amusement. CNN's 24-hour news rivals at FOX had a blast with the story, calling the promo "a sign of desperation". "It makes you wonder who's running the place over there," Kevin Magee, Fox News vice president of programming, told Reuters. "It's

Gentlemen, start your zippers, it's CNN's Paula Zahn.

undignified. It diminishes a first-rate woman journalist to label her as sexy." said Don Hewitt, producer of *60 Minutes* since dinosaurs roamed the earth. "Why doesn't CNN say that Wolf Blitzer is sexy? He must be sexy to somebody."

As for Zahn herself, she issued an initial statement declaring herself offended ("CNN management has apologized to me and assured me that a mistake like this will not happen again") but softened her stance a few days later; "How come they say I'm 'just a little sexy'? I'm very sexy."

Once the uproar began to subside, media observers wondered if the ad hadn't achieved what CNN intended all along, to get everybody talking about their new morning show and its $2 million host. Having the promo department fall on its sword maintained plausible deniability among the actual journalists at the network, and the promo's near-instant retraction suggested a dedication to protecting Paula Zahn's professional reputation. But if the goal of a promotional campaign is to increase public awareness, the "sexy" ads were a resounding success. Viewers who never saw the spots probably read the coverage of them, where they learned that Paula Zahn is hosting a new morning show on CNN, and some people think she's a little sexy. Mission accomplished.

The risk of manufacturing a scandal is in whether the benefits of exposure are outweighed by ridicule from late night TV comics and such Internet humor sites as *The*

Onion and The Borowitz Report. Under the headline "Morning Anchor Loses Hottie Status in Latest Clarification", Borowitz reported that within days of the promo, CNN "issued a clarification indicating that, in its view, Ms. Zahn was 'not sexy at all.'"

"After taking a closer look at that promo, and at Ms. Zahn herself, we feel compelled to clarify our position further," the faux CNN statement goes on. For the next 24 hours, executives said, the crawl at the bottom of the screen on CNN will feature items like, "Seen Paula Zahn Lately? Yuck!!!"

American Morning with Paula Zahn did boost CNN's ratings, but the show still trailed *Fox & Friends* on FOX News. Undaunted, CNN promoted Zahn to anchoring its prime time coverage, in a new series called—wait for it—*American Evening with Paula Zahn*. That show replaced *Connie Chung Tonight*, which was cancelled after just nine months despite its kinda sexy host.

4

AN APOLOGY WORTH 1,000 WORDS

You're in the Picture
CBS, JANUARY 20, 1961

Bad TV shows come and go all the time, but the circumstances surrounding the spectacular flameout of *You're in the Picture* are unique in television history, and should be studied by future generations as an all too rare example of honesty and full disclosure in a medium that thrives on unfulfilled promise.

The show aired only once, before falling victim to disastrous reviews and the dashed expectations of its creators. But it's what happened after that initial broadcast that makes *You're in the Picture* exceptional; for the first and only time, the time slot in which the show's next episode would have aired was devoted to apologizing to the nation for developing and airing such a terrible program. Television has made countless mistakes since 1961, but this may be the last one they've publicly acknowledged.

You're in the Picture was a game show in the classic golden age style. Following the model of *What's My Line* and *I've Got a Secret*, the host moderated a guessing game played by a panel of four celebrities. After nearly a decade of success with *The Honeymooners* and his own variety series, Jackie Gleason was one of America's most beloved personalities, and his popularity and quick wit made him a natural choice as moderator for the new show.

"It's sensational, really sensational. I think it'll be one of the best panel shows," Gleason told the *Los Angeles Times*. So confident was the rotund comic that he laughed off concerns that the debut of *You're in the Picture* would be overshadowed by another event that January day—the inauguration of President John F. Kennedy. "Oh, yeah, that fella from Hyannisport," said Gleason. "Well, good luck to him."

There were high hopes that a new series with Gleason at the helm would draw an all-star panel; the host suggested Raymond Massey, Bea Lillie, Jonathan Winters, and Lauren Bacall. But when the first episode aired on January 20, 1961, it was with the less stellar quartet of Pat Harrington, Jr., Jan Sterling, Pat Carroll, and Arthur Treacher. And that was the least of its problems.

The game itself was relatively simple. A crudely-drawn cartoon picture, rendered on a wall-sized piece of plywood, is wheeled onto the stage. At Gleason's command, "Will the panel kindly step in," the four celebrities would insert their heads through porthole-shaped openings in the picture, at which time they assume the identity of a person or creature in the scene. They are unable to see the painting, and their assignment is to figure out what picture they're in by asking questions that can be answered 'yes' or 'no.'

The first game featured a painting of Pocahontas rescuing John Smith from being beheaded, as two other Indians look on. Gleason offered one clue, saying the picture depicted "A slice of life." Harrington and company asked questions such as "Am I a character in history?" and "Am I in modern dress?" which Gleason would answer, often with a humorous ad lib. Other puzzles depicted the song "Itsy Bitsy Teeny Weenie Yellow Polka Dot Bikini" and the Metropolitan Museum of Art.

The show's biggest mistake was not having contestants. If the panel guessed the picture, 100 care packages were donated in their name; if they failed, the packages were donated in Gleason's name. Since there were no winners or losers, there was no suspense created in the playing of each game, and viewers had no rooting interest into whether the puzzles were solved. Gleason gamely tried to fill the many awkward silences through the first show, but the studio audience remained unenthusiastic for much of the broadcast.

The members of the panel weren't having fun either, especially when their heads were protruding through the plywood holes (during a rehearsal, Pat Carroll's head got stuck in one of the pictures); sometimes they had trouble hearing Gleason's answers. By telecast's end, the perturbed host couldn't resist asking, "What am I doing here?"

The reviews were scathing. "A draggy, stodgy, unfunny concoction," said the *Chicago Tribune*. "In his other shows, Gleason has been a man of action, of many changes, and of great versatility. In this one, he was just a fat man chained to a chair, saying nothing funny."

One week later, viewers willing to brave another dose of *You're in the Picture* were surprised to see a bare stage with one chair in the center, and no celebrity panel. Announcer Johnny Olsen welcomed viewers to "what will probably be a very unusual program." Gleason entered, sat in the chair, and got down to business. This program, he said, is "the first of its kind." "We have a creed tonight," he explained, "Honesty is the best policy."

"Last week we did a show called *You're in the Picture* that laid, without a doubt, the biggest bomb in the history of television. I've seen bombs in my day, but this made the H-bomb look like a two-inch salute." The audience, relieved to realize they were no longer alone in hating the show, laughed and applauded as Gleason continued to deprecate his own series. He explained how the show was conceived, read excerpts from the bad reviews, recalled other flops in his career, and attempted to explain why anyone originally thought *You're in the Picture* was a good idea.

The result was one of the most fascinating and hilarious half-hours in television. Critics loved Gleason's *mea culpa* as much as they hated the series that inspired it; "one of the funniest shows in television history," wrote one Hollywood paper. *Time* magazine called it "an inspired post-mortem." *Variety* compared the broadcast to Orson Welles' radio drama *War of the Worlds* in the extent to which it startled the audience, and hailed the apology as "the year's lustiest one man show."

Sadly, the practice of TV personalities publicly apologizing for their poor decisions did not catch on. Imagine if Jason Alexander had to admit his regret over starring in *Bob Patterson*, or NBC president Warren Littlefield said "Sorry about that," after calling *Inside Schwartz* "must-see TV."

You're in the Picture is not available on video, but both the debut episode and the apology are archived at the Museum of Television and Radio in both New York and Los Angeles, and it's worth a visit to view this fascinating failure.

3
DEPRAVITY ON PARADE

The Jerry Springer Show
SYNDICATED, SEPTEMBER 30, 1991–PRESENT

"Never miss a chance to have sex or appear on television."
—GORE VIDAL

In one sense, *The Jerry Springer Show* stands here for the troublesome number of talk shows over the past two decades that celebrate aberrant human behavior. I cannot think of a television trend that has been more unpleasant to witness, nor calls into question more clearly the future of the republic.

Though Springer's show is the most extreme, one could argue there are worse offenders; for all the one-time Cincinnati mayor and hooker picker-upper has done to lower standards of human decency, at least he's honest about it. Unlike talk show hosts who try to pass off their exercises in seedy voyeurism as philanthropy (Sally Jesse Raphael, Maury Povich), Jerry knows he's shoveling manure and doesn't pretend he's doing so as a public service.

There was a time when taboo subjects such as incest and domestic violence had a place in the talk show format—that was when Phil Donahue covered them in the late 1960s and early 70s. Back then, frank discussions of private behavior were a revelation on television, and by bringing such issues into the light Donahue let viewers facing the same circumstances know that they weren't alone, and they could find help.

But once that door is opened, it stays open, and after the 500th show about incest, there's no vestige of enlightenment left in the topic. In 2004, where information is available through 100 channels of television and millions of websites, is there anyone who still doesn't know that some people lead very twisted lives?

So when Springer presents shows titled "I Stole My 12-Year-Old's Boyfriend!", "I Want to be a Teen Stripper!", "Our Brother is a Pimp!"; "My Boyfriend is a Girl!", "I Want to Join a Suicide Cult!", and "I'm Proud to be a Racist!", the only objective is exploitation and entertainment. And though Springer may be the ringmaster of this shameful circus, the real head cases are the guests who appear on the show, and the audience who cheers every humiliation and every fight.

It's repugnant to take pleasure in human suffering. But in every one of Springer's myriad shows dealing with infidelity, a weeping woman who has learned her husband has been sleeping with her sister will also be the recipient of a gleeful "Big fat whore! Big fat whore!" chant from the Springer faithful.

When exactly did the moral compass of our society stop working? And by "moral compass" I don't mean in the Bill Bennett/Jerry Falwell sense, where anything that doesn't pay strict adherence to a JudeoChristian ethic is condemned; but surely there must be a line beyond which everyone can agree we need not tread without sacrificing a piece of our soul. On *The Jerry Springer Show*, audiences have watched a man profess his romantic love for a horse, and french kiss the beast on the air; a nun discussed pimping out her parish; a man proudly explained his fetish for sleeping with homeless women; a father proposed marriage to his daughter—this is O.K. now?

There is no justification for television this base, but Tim Kasser, a psychiatrist and associate professor of psychology at Illinois's Knox College, offers an explanation for its success. "There's this thing in psychology called 'downward comparison'; we're always comparing ourselves with others, and we can compare upward, to someone who's smarter or better-looking. But generally, upward comparisons make us feel lousy, because we're shown that we're not as good as we might be, while downward comparisons make us feel good because we're at least better than that loser. *The Jerry Springer Show* is a great place for downward comparison. My life may not be great, people think, but at least my daughter doesn't want to be a stripper."

That might account for some private sense of satisfaction in a home viewer, but it doesn't account for the frenzied responses of the live audience. "Freud said that people are motivated by two basic drives, sex and aggression, and if you take a look at the *The Jerry Springer Show*, that pretty much captures it," Kasser explains. "The problem is if we all ran around expressing our sexual and aggressive desires, we'd be in trouble. What we've had to do as individuals and as a society is repress those kinds of desires, but we still want that stuff. *Springer* is a place where we can take those feelings and they get whipped up and it feels good. It allows expression of that part of ourselves in a relatively safe environment."

So is there no cause for concern? Is the show a harmless outlet for behavior that wouldn't be acceptable in another forum? "At some level, (a show like this) validates a way to live one's life. Clearly that's not what's best for society or people's happiness," Kasser believes. "The show does nothing but lower the standards of what is acceptable, reasonable behavior. Downward comparison may be fun, but there are healthier ways to feel better about yourself."

And what of Springer's guests, for whom the concept of shame is clearly as unfamiliar as the concept of good grooming, who reveal the most intimate details of their lives for public consumption? "We live in a culture that celebrates celebrity, so we get this idea in our head that one of the ways we can show we're a success or a worthwhile person is to become a celebrity," Kasser explains. "Even if it was about something very intimate or embarrassing or violent, (Springer's guests) feel that in a way they were in the same league as Michael Jordan or Britney Spears. And given that our culture over and over pounds into our head that that's something important in life, people who are unlikely to become celebrities otherwise see this as a chance to do it."

It has been alleged that Springer's guests are 'plants', and certainly their intelligence level rivals that of a Boston fern. But in this case 'plant' refers to an actor who plays the role of a guest, resulting in a scene not unlike professional wrestling, where fights both verbal and physical are staged to generate an enthusiastic audience response. Who knows if we can add dishonesty to Springer's list of decency violations, but if Kasser is correct than he need not hire people to debase themselves, since enough willing candidates are ready to volunteer.

Jerry Springer has a law degree from Northwestern University. He served as one of Senator Robert F. Kennedy's presidential campaign aides, and at the age of 33 was elected Mayor of Cincinnati with the largest plurality in the city's history. After leaving office he became anchor and managing editor of Cincinnati's highest-rated newscast, and received seven Emmy Awards for his nightly commentaries. He's an accomplished man who, like his guests, traded dignity for celebrity. "Be good to each other," he says at the close of each episode, but if people took that advice there wouldn't be a *Jerry*

Jerry Springer sometimes gets so caught up in the bizarre antics of his guests that he forgets his name.

Springer Show. As long as the fans scream "Jer-ry! Jer-ry!" one suspects he really wants people to be as bad to each other as humanly possible.

2
IT WAS ALL A DREAM

Dallas
CBS, SEPTEMBER 26, 1986

> *"Bobby is gone and can never come back. I appreciate my*
> *public and would never fool them."*   —PATRICK DUFFY

On a brisk spring day, in a nondescript studio on a Hollywood side street, Patrick Duffy stood in a shower stall in the center of a soundstage. When the shower door opened, Duffy turned toward the camera, smiled, and said, "Good morning." The crew was told they were shooting an Irish Spring soap commercial. In truth, they were co-conspirators in the greatest cop-out in the history of dramatic television.

For this wasn't really Patrick Duffy, but Bobby Ewing, the saintly younger brother of J.R., husband of Pam, son of Miss Ellie, who was killed in a murderous hit and run in the final episode of *Dallas*'s eighth season. But how could it be Bobby, when 300 million viewers in 98 countries saw him get mowed down by jealous headcase Rebecca Wentworth? The solution, revealed to the world in the series' ninth season debut, was that the accident never happened.

With one shower, Duffy wiped out 30 episodes of continuity on television's most popular show; Pam's marriage to Mark Graison? Gone. Ray and Donna's adoption of a hearing-impaired child? Forgotten. The bomb planted in Jamie Ewing's car by Angelica Nero? Never exploded. Turns out, viewers had devoted seven months of their lives to a story that unfolded only in the dreams of Pamela Ewing (Victoria Principal).

The plot twist was a drastic solution to a sobering problem. With the departure of Duffy and producer Leonard Katzman, *Dallas* lost four million viewers and dropped from first to seventh in the ratings. Stories of international intrigue took the series far from its Western roots, and shifted the focus away from the Ewing family. "I wasn't happy with that year," recalls Larry Hagman, who played the scheming J.R. Ewing. "They put a lot of glitz in, trying to be like *Dynasty*, I guess, and it just wasn't *Dallas*. Leonard had also left, and we had another producer (Phil Capice) who I couldn't stand. He was undermining the morale of the company. So I made a stand, and we got rid of him."

"*Dallas* had become a women's show," said Katzman upon his return. He fired everyone associated with Capice and brought back most of the original production team. But that wouldn't be enough without also restoring the Cain & Abel-esque conflict between J.R. and Bobby, which was at the heart of the series' best stories. "When Patrick left the show, I didn't have anybody to play with," Hagman said.

For his part, Duffy had wanted to depart *Dallas* after five seasons, but stayed two more years to fulfill his contract. He was granted his request for a heroic departure—Bobby was killed while saving Pam's life—and a deathbed scene that allowed the character to say his goodbyes to the family. It was powerful, emotional, and had an air of finality to it, unlike most soap deaths where a body is never recovered.

On February 27th, 1986, Larry Hagman called Duffy and asked him to come back. Duffy declined, but Katzman kept after him, with sweeter deals and higher pay-checks, until the actor finally re-upped for three more years, at a salary of $75,000 per episode, almost double the $40,000 he had made before Bobby bought the farm.

With one problem solved, the real challenge began. How in the world could Bobby Ewing return? "I didn't have any idea. I usually stayed out of that kind of stuff," said Hagman. "They thought of everything, even a twin brother. Everybody was racking their brains to figure out how to get him back." Said costar Charlene Tilton (Lucy): "Everyone criticized the shower scene, but I never heard anyone come up with a better idea."

Actually, there were two other options under consideration. The first had a criti-cally-injured Bobby revived at the last moment by an intern, after the family left his bedside. Unable to walk or speak, he recuperated in a private hospital for a year before making his miraculous return. Another possibility was having Duffy come back as an evil lookalike, created by plastic surgery, who would infiltrate the family with nefarious results.

The dream solution made the most sense, as it quickly solved the dilemma and allowed the show to return to business as usual without any troublesome plot threads from the previous year. But it also carried the greatest risk of offending viewers by testing the boundary of what they would accept. The idea was first proposed by Duffy's wife, Caryn. According to *People* magazine, Duffy laughed and told her it was outrageous but that he admired her imagination. A week later, he met with Katzman, who had come up with the same solution.

In the final episode of season eight, Pam awakened in her bedroom, surprised to hear the sound of water running in the shower. She walked hesitantly toward the bathroom, and opened the shower door, to see Bobby, alive and smiling. A summer of speculation as to what would happen next was resolved when *Dallas* opened its ninth season. Like Dorothy returning from Oz, Pamela recounted all the strange events that she had imagined. "It was only a dream," Bobby told her, while millions of fans yelled "Oh, come on!"

"When it came on the air everyone said, 'Give me a break.' I was flabbergasted myself," Hagman admits. "I know we lost some viewers, but we also stayed on another four years. And those were my big money years. I was making $250,000 a show, which was pretty good back then. So I was very happy to have him back."

1
THE WORST TWO HOURS OF TELEVISION EVER

The Star Wars Holiday Special
CBS, NOVEMBER 17, 1978

"This is the great secret of Star Wars, *the three-eyed cousin who lives in the barn attic, humping sheep and eating spiders. This is the thing that doesn't get mentioned at American Film Institute dinners. This is the thing even Peter Mayhew can't be paid to talk about at conventions."*
—*Oh, the Humanity website*

"George Lucas, the man behind the Star Wars *phenomenon, refused to acknowledge the existence of the special. When it was brought up, he would suddenly become aloof and pissy, sort of like whenever anyone mentions* Forever Monaco *to Jean-Claude Van Damme."*
—KEITH ALLISON, Teleport City Movie Reviews

"Aroooo ... errrrragghhh ... Arrrrrrrrrr."
—LUMPY, *son of Chewbacca*

For 20 years, *The Star Wars Holiday Special* was an urban legend, like the story of Mikey from the Life Cereal commercials exploding from a combination of Pop Rocks and Coca Cola. Was there really a television show featuring the entire cast of *Star Wars*, in character, singing and cavorting with celebrity guests like Art Carney and Bea Arthur?

It seemed too bizarre to be true. And if there was such a show, why wasn't it available for purchase? Certainly George Lucas, who authorized enough action figures and related merchandise to fill the warehouse at the end of *Raiders of the Lost Ark*, is always eager to open another revenue stream into Skywalker Ranch.

But there are no secrets left in the age of the Internet, where the Jedi faithful gather to share their passions on newsgroups, and tape exchange websites offer viewers the chance to rediscover the television of their youth. And somebody, somewhere, had *The Star Wars Holiday Special*. Within a few months, if not weeks, copies circled the globe, and thousands of fans finally had the opportunity to see this legendary missing chapter in a story set a long time ago, in a galaxy far, far away.

And then the realization hit; yes, we had seen this before. We had just blocked the memory for two decades through intense denial. But now the evil had returned, and woe to anyone that fell into its clutches.

The real nightmare began when non-fans watched the show, and gained a laser cannon full of anti-geek ammunition. "Tell me," they'd scoff, "how exactly does Harvey Korman fit into the Empire's plans to crush the Rebel forces?" And there was no possible comeback, because even the most devoted fan had to acknowledge that the *Holiday Special* was the worst atrocity ever committed to their fantasy universe. Worse than Jar Jar. Worse than Carrie Fisher's English accent in *A New Hope*. Worse even than Lucas's Special Editions in which Greedo shoots first.

The misfortune begins aboard the Millennium Falcon, where Han Solo (yes, Harrison Ford) hopes to get his buddy Chewbacca (Peter Mayhew) home in time to celebrate Life Day, an important event on the Wookiee calendar. Back at the Chewbacca household, we meet his family—apron-clad wife Mala, his father, Itchy, and his son, Lumpy, who proceeds to bark, roar, and grunt at each other for ten minutes, with no subtitles provided. There's a brief respite while Lumpy amuses himself with a musical hologram, that resembles a community theater production of Cirque du Soleil, but then it's more grunts and groans, and the realization hits that Wookiees are best taken in small doses. This will be the first time you hit the mute button. The second will be when Princess Leia sings.

Wookiees live in primitive treehouses but have mastered many sophisticated devices, including the combination big-screen TV and interplanetary communicator, which Mala uses to contact Luke Skywalker (Mark Hamill). The young Jedi in training, who for some reason wears more eye makeup here than Elizabeth Taylor in *Cleopatra*, assures Mala that Chewbacca will be home in time, then he and R2D2 return to their work on a malfunctioning droid. Mala then changes the channel, and finds a cooking show hosted by Harvey Korman in drag, who teaches her the recipe for a dish called Wookiee Ookies.

While Mala cooks in the kitchen, old man Itchy works up a head of steam with some virtual reality goggles tuned to what can only be described as Wookiee porn. Diahann Carroll appears as Itchy's fantasy girl, writhing in a slinky silver number and singing such lyrics as "I am your pleasure. Enjoy me." Meanwhile, Mala's had enough of Harvey and tunes in Leia (Carrie Fisher) and C3P0, who offer their best wishes for a happy Life Day.

The story takes a dramatic turn when the treehouse is invaded by Imperial Stormtroopers. Viewers at home shouted "Shoot Lumpy first!" but alas, the white-armored drones are as inept here as they are in the movies, and content themselves with messing up Lumpy's room and watching a Jefferson Starship video. No, really. Classic rock fans will be relieved that Grace Slick somehow avoided this embarrassment, but Paul Kantner, who frequently criticized later Starship incarnations for recording corporate rock drivel like "We Built This City," was apparently not above dressing like a member of Kaptain Kool and the Kongs, and performing a song that makes "Nothing's Gonna Stop Us Now" sound like "Stairway to Heaven."

And that's just the first half.

The second hour opens with an animated interlude that introduces the bounty hunter Boba Fett, before his first live-action appearance in *The Empire Strikes Back*. It's an inglorious debut for one of the most celebrated figures in the *Star Wars* universe.

When the story continues we're on Tattooine and inside the cantina at Mos Eisley space port, which apparently is now owned by Bea Arthur. Harvey Korman returns, this time as a lonely traveler who puts the moves on her until the bar is closed by the Empire, prompting Bea to sing a farewell to her patrons. This is the only watchable segment of the special; Arthur is a musical theater veteran who does everything she can to create a poignant moment while surrounded by rubber-faced aliens.

Finally, Han delivers Chewie home, and the Life Day celebration begins. Chewbacca's family don red robes and carry candles in the official procession, while all of his *Star Wars* friends arrive to share in their joy. As Luke, Leia, Han, C3P0, and R2D2 observe the ceremony, Leia is inspired to sing a Life Day carol. Carrie Fisher, who appears to have arrived straight from a three-day bender on planet Happy Dust, warbles a painfully off-key tune that may be based on the *Star Wars* theme; it's hard to know for sure, given that she couldn't find the melody with a star chart.

"Even as a high-schooler, I thought this was a clumsy way to cash in on the popularity of a great movie," says Kevin J. Anderson, author of several *Star Wars*-related bestsellers. "It had none of the charm and energy of the original film." Ah, but is it canon, as sci-fi fans say? All the characters are there, and it contains the introduction of Boba Fett—how can the events depicted in the special not be considered part of the *Star Wars* universe?

"It's not canon. Period." Anderson argues. "I was specifically told that by LucasFilm, and told to ignore it when I wrote *The Essential Star Wars Chronology* with Dan Wallace."

But while the debate continues, the cast, the hardcore Jedi fans and the residents of Skywalker Ranch just wish the whole subject would go away. "When I was researching *The Illustrated Star Wars Universe*, we found a bunch of the production paintings of the Wookiee tree houses by Ralph McQuarrie," Anderson recalls. "McQuarrie is a great artist, and the paintings were fine. I wanted to use them, but George refused because he didn't want anything from the *Holiday Special* in any "official" Lucas-sanctioned publication. In fact, one of his assistants said, 'If we could track down every bootleg copy and burn it, we would.'"

Either that's Bea Arthur in the Mos Eisley space port, or the 'Maude Lookalike Contest' attracted some strange hopefuls.

APPENDIX
OUR DISTINGUISHED RUNNERS-UP

Here, in no particular order, are 25 more moments that should not have happened on television.

1. The 1980–1981 cast of *Saturday Night Live*: If you're a collector of the compilation tapes, don't expect "The Best of Denny Dillon" anytime soon.

2. *Boohbah* (2003): From the folks who brought you the trippy Teletubbies, here's another PBS kids show that will encourage your two-year-old to utter his first words—"What the hell?"

3. *Are You Hot?* (2003): Seeped in the fungus-ridden shallow end of the reality TV pool is this putrid mess, in which celebrity judges such as "International heart-throb" Lorenzo Lamas pass judgment on the physical attributes of strangers. Docked additional points for stealing a Howard Stern bit that Stern did better.

4. *The Tortellis* (1987): Here's an idea—let's take the most obnoxious character to ever appear on *Cheers*, Dan Hedaya's Nick Tortelli, and give him his own show! What's next, a spinoff for the prissy shrink? Hey, wait a minute...

5. Batgirl Needs Rescuing Again (1967): I was delighted when sexy Yvonne Craig donned a skintight batsuit and joined the fight against crime in Gotham City on *Batman*. But what was the point when the character became a perpetual hostage, easily bested even by such lightweight guest villains as Milton Berle's Louie the Lilac? Holy useless!

6. *The Dean Martin Roasts* salute Peter Marshall (1979): After a series of now legendary Vegas roasts honoring show business icons such as Frank Sinatra, James Stewart, and John Wayne, you knew these specials had run out of steam when the Man of the Hour was the host of *Hollywood Squares*.

7. Santo Gold infomercial (1986): It's amazing how many people remember this surreal mix of junk jewelry, Mexican wrestling, and film clips from the cannibal slasher movie *Blood Circus*. The brainchild of Santo Rigatuso, who appears in the spot and sings the theme song ("I got bracelets for your arms! Santo Gold Santo Gold!") this may be the most inexplicable half-hour of television ever. Rigatuso later served time in prison for mail fraud, after failing to convince a judge he was mentally incompetent. Had the judge seen this infomercial, the verdict might have been different.

8. *Jabber Jaw* (1976–1978): The most derivative cartoon ever made. A Scooby-Doo inspired cast of Hanna-Barbera teenagers sing Josie & the Pussycats' rejects, while their buddy Jabber, an oversized shark, babbles like Curly from the Three Stooges, and steals "I get no respect" from Rodney Dangerfield.

9. *The Morton Downey Jr. Show* (1987–1989): The granddaddy of every decibel-shattering talk show featuring an obnoxious host yelling at obnoxious guests.

10. *Revenge of the Nerds III* (1992) and *IV* (1994) and *Problem Child III* (1995): As if television didn't manufacture enough crap on its own, it sometimes gets drafted as a dumping ground for film series that should have ended after one installment.

11. *Playing It Straight* (2003): Three episodes of homophobic hijinks were enough to convince even the morals-challenged FOX network that this show overstepped the bounds of reality TV smarm.

12. *It's About Time* (1966–1967): Deservedly forgotten Sherwood Schwartz sitcom about the exploits of Gronk and Shad (Joe E. Lewis and Imogene Coca), a grunting prehistoric cave-couple transplanted to modern-day Los Angeles. Catchy theme song, though.

13. *Rudolph's Shiny New Year* (1976): After producing a holiday classic in *Rudolph the Red-Nosed Reindeer* (1964), Rankin-Bass went back to the stop-motion well once too often for this dreadful follow-up, which belongs on the Island of Misfit Television.

14. The Video Vortex: First there was MTV, a network devoted to music videos. Then Music Television morphed into Drunk-Naked-Teenagers Television, and the videos went to MTV2. But now MTV2 has also been co-opted by loud dumb shows about too-rich rock stars and too-stupid singles on the prowl. Maybe by MTV17 they'll get it right.

15. *The New Leave it To Beaver* (1985–1986): Proving you can't go home again, the further adventures of Wally and the Beav are chronicled in this depressing series that portrays a thirty-something Theodore as an unemployed, divorced, distant father.

16. God Will Get You for That, CBS (2004): Censorship clung to Janet Jackson in her post-Super Bowl TV appearances, including *Late Night With David Letterman*. At one point, Jackson expressed her exasperation with Letterman's boob-related questions by saying "Jesus." The word was bleeped by CBS.

17. *USA Today—The Television Show* (1988–1990): Because the one thing that's been missing from television for too long is colorful pie charts.

18. Admiral James Stockdale in the 1996 Vice-Presidential Debate: It was a sad moment when a proud American hero was turned into a punchline by the unblinking stare of live television. By the halfway point, even viewers who would never have supported the Ross Perot ticket were praying for Stockdale to complete a coherent sentence.

19. Frank Zappa Hosts *Saturday Night Live* (1978): Producer Lorne Michaels never allowed this disastrous episode to be rebroadcast. Zappa couldn't remember a single line, and resorted to obvious cue card reading and snide remarks to the audience in the midst of sketches.

20. *The Love Boat Follies* (1982): Finally surrendering to the sacks of viewer mail demanding to see Captain Stubing tapdance in a shiny silver suit, *The Love Boat* invited musical greats Carol Channing, Della Reese, Van Johnson, Ethel Merman, and Cab Calloway aboard for a special two-hour cruise featuring a shipboard revue that sent passengers fleeing for the lifeboats.

21. *Playboy's 50th Anniversary Celebration* (2003): Any doubts that the glory days of *Playboy* are long gone vanished after viewing this bleak spectacle. The highlight was watching Pamela Anderson's increasingly frustrated attempts to keep Hugh Hefner's hand from drifting too far up her miniskirt.

22. *Baywatch Nights* (1995–1997): Tired of all the attention paid to the slow motion running of *Baywatch* babes Pam Anderson, Yasmine Bleeth, Gena Lee Nolin, and Traci Bingham, David Hasselhoff launched this hilarious spinoff, in which the lifeguard turned supernatural private detective investigates lady vampires, strange sea creatures, and cannibal demons.

23. *She's the Sheriff* (1987–1989): Awful, awful show designed as a comeback vehicle for Suzanne Somers, in which she plays a single mother and sheriff of a California border town opposite a deputy that hates her and a colorful array of smalltime crooks. Hilarity did not ensue.

24. *AfterMASH* (1983–1984): So apparently all that "Goodbye, Farewell and Amen" stuff in the final episode of *M*A*S*H* was just a cruel jest. Was anyone really that curious about what happened to Klinger after he finally got out of the army?

25. *The Lingerie Bowl* (2004): This gridiron battle between scantily-clad models was supposed to lure nudity-seeking viewers away from the Super Bowl halftime show featuring Janet Jackson. Gotta love irony.